Professor Boris Bigalke, MD
Eating Immortally

Professor Boris Bigalke, MD, MBA (Oxford, UK), LL.M. works as an attending and head of the DGK CardioMRI Qualification Center at the German Heart Center of the Charité (DHZC), Campus Benjamin Franklin, Clinic for Cardiology, Angiology and Intensive Care Medicine. He also practices complementary medicine with Traditional Chinese Medicine (TCM), Traditional Tibetan Medicine (TTM) and yoga movement theory as a sideline. Professor Bigalke is a specialist in internal medicine and holds specializations and additional qualifications in cardiology, acupuncture, nutritional medicine DAEM/DGEM® and magnetic resonance imaging.

After studying medicine at the Free University of Berlin, he continued his scientific and clinical career at the Eberhard-Karls-University of Tübingen.

Further training led him to surgery at the LIJ Medical Center, Albert Einstein College of Medicine, New York, USA, to TCM at the WHO Collaborating Center, Beijing, China and to TTM at the Qusar Tibetan Healing Centre, Dharamsala, Himachal Pradesh, India.

During a long-term research stay, he also worked at King's College London, Division of College London, Division of Imaging Sciences and Biomedical Engineering London as an Assistant Professor/Honorary Lecturer.

He also completed a Master of Business Administration (MBA) Healthcare Management at Magna Carta College, Oxford, UK, and a Master of Laws (LL.M.) with a focus on medical law at the Dresden International University.

He is Associate Editor in the journal "ESC Heart Failure" and reviewer in various medical journals and author of more than 130 scientific peer-reviewed publications. Professor Bigalke has been elected as one of Germany's top physicians in FOCUS-Gesundheit 2021 in the category of cardiological sports medicine, and in 2023 and 2024 in the categories of hypertension and nutritional medicine.

Professor Boris Bigalke, MD

Eating immortally:

Groundbreaking insights for eternal youth, explosive energy and a life at full throttle!

Disclaimer:
The content of this book has been presented to the best of our knowledge and conscientiously and corresponds to the current state of scientific knowledge. The content presented here is intended solely for neutral information and general education. It does not constitute a recommendation or promotion of the diagnostic methods, treatments or medicines described or mentioned. The instructions, exercises and tips provided may not help every reader and are based solely on personal opinion. The content of the book does not claim to be complete, nor can the timeliness, accuracy and balance of the information provided be guaranteed. The content of this book is in no way a substitute for professional advice from a medical doctor, pharmacist, physiotherapist and/or licensed fitness trainer, and it should not be used as a basis for independent diagnosis and starting, changing or stopping treatment of illnesses. Always consult a medical doctor you trust if you have any health questions or complaints! The author accepts no liability for any inconvenience or damage resulting from the use of the information presented here.
For better readability, gender-neutral wording has been omitted. All masculine spellings refer equally to all genders.

Address of Correspondence:
Professor Boris Bigalke, MD, MBA (Oxford, UK), LL.M.
Klinik für Kardiologie, DHZC – Charité Campus Benjamin Franklin
Hindenburgdamm 30, D-12203 Berlin, Germany

Bibliographic information of the German National Library:
The German National Library lists this
publication in the German National Bibliography;
Detailed bibliographic data is available on the Internet
can be accessed via http://dnb.dnb.de

The automated analysis of the work in order to obtain
information in particular on patterns, trends and correlations
correlations in accordance with §44b UrhG ("text and data mining")
is prohibited.

This book was translated by Professor Boris Bigalke, MD, from the original German edition titled:"Unsterblich essen: Bahnbrechende Erkenntnisse für ewige Jugend, explosive Energie und ein Leben in Vollgas!"

Production and Publishing:
BoD – Books on Demand, Norderstedt

ISBN: 978-3-7578-9030-8

For Ulla and for everyone who wants to live a long and healthy life!

Contents

Chapter 3: Changing nutritional medicine 56

Chapter 4: Lifestyle supplements and superfoods for longevity   85

Chapter 5: Elimination of noxious substances

Chapter 6: Recipes 220

Introduction

Biological vs. chronological age: a consideration of the differentiation between age and health

The concept of age is complex and multidimensional. While chronological age simply measures the number of years since a person's birth, biological age reflects the physiological state and functioning of the body.[1] This distinction between biological and chronological age is critical to a comprehensive understanding of ageing and its impact on health and well-being.

Chronological age is the most commonly used method to determine a person's age. It is a simple number based on the calendar that indicates the time since an individual was born. It is undeniable that **chronological age** plays an important role in life, as it influences **legal status, social norms and personal expectations**. However, chronological age often neglects individual differences in physical condition and health. In contrast, **biological age** refers to the **actual condition** of the body and its organ systems. It takes into account the functioning of organs, the presence of disease, genetic factors, lifestyle and environmental factors that influence health. On the one hand, a person may be **chronologically 50 years old**, but has a **biological age of 40 years due to a healthy lifestyle and good genetic predisposition**. On the other hand, someone could have a biological age that is older than their chronological age due to illness, poor nutrition and other risk factors.

The difference between biological and chronological age has far-reaching implications for health and ageing. **Individuals with a younger biological age** often have **better physical function,**

greater resistance to disease and a longer life expectancy. They can also maintain a higher level of activity and independence. However, people with a biological age above their chronological age are more susceptible to disease, physical limitations and a shortened lifespan.

The distinction between biological and chronological age is important for health care, public health policy and individual lifestyle choices. It emphasizes the importance of preventive measures aimed at slowing down biological ageing and maintaining health throughout life. By adopting a healthy lifestyle, exercising regularly, eating a balanced diet, avoiding tobacco and managing stress appropriately, people can **help to reduce their biological age and improve their quality of life**. Of course, an increased age should not be at the expense of quality of life. Quality of life would be assessed quite differently from person to person, including physical health, psychological well-being, social relationships, material wealth, education, environmental quality and personal safety.

Aims

The aim of this book is to inspire interested people to beat chronological age by subjecting their body, mind and soul to a radical rejuvenation cure so that biological age progresses less rapidly.

How this can be achieved is described in detail in the following chapters; thus, this involves an overall concept of physical activity, sleep and rest phases, nutrition, lifestyle supplements, avoidance of harmful influences (noxious substances) and cooking recipe suggestions.

Chapter 1: Physical activity

Physical activity is an essential part of a healthy lifestyle and plays a key role in maintaining health and reducing the risk of a wide range of diseases and health problems. It is important to integrate regular exercise into everyday life and maintain an active lifestyle in order to promote long-term health and well-being.

What is the right amount of exercise?

The goal of walking 10,000 steps per day is a widely accepted recommendation for physical activity and health. This figure was not chosen at random, but is based on research results and guidelines from various health organizations. There are now an increasing number of studies that even consider **8,000 steps per day to be a sufficient** measure.[2] And a meta-analysis, i.e. a study of studies, showed that there is no longer a significant survival benefit to be seen with more than 8,000 steps per day.[3] In a further meta-analysis of eight prospective observational studies with more than 20,000 participants, it was found that older people (>60 years of age) with 6000-9000 steps per day have a 40-50% reduced cardiovascular risk compared to people of the same age with 2000 steps per day.[4] In addition to cardiovascular diseases, physical activity apparently also helps to prevent the development of various types of cancer, even if the exact biological mechanisms of action are not yet understood in detail.[5]

For those who are sedentary, however, there is good news from a British study (Vitality Habit Index 2024) from the working group of **Professor Joan Costa-Font** from the **London School of Econom-**

ics over an observation period of ten years that just **5,000 steps per day** can significantly increase life expectancy.[6]

However, it is important to note that the number of steps is not the only measure of physical activity. The intensity, duration and variety of activities are also important. It is therefore advisable not to focus exclusively on the number of steps, but also to integrate other forms of exercise such as strength training, stretching and aerobic exercises into one's daily routine. Healthy middle-aged and older people, as well as patients with cancer or cardiovascular disease, benefit from a longer life expectancy if they exercise regularly, regardless of previous physical activity.[7]

The American College of Sports Medicine (ACSM) recommends performing **about 150 minutes of moderate, "aerobic" physical activity** three to five days a week and **"muscle-strengthening activities" two to three times a week.**[8]

Endurance sports or weight training?

Whether endurance sports or weight training is better depends on a person's individual goals, preferences and health. Both forms of training offer different benefits.

Endurance sports

Improves cardiovascular health: Endurance sports such as running, cycling or swimming can promote heart health and reduce the risk of cardiovascular disease.

Increases endurance: Regular endurance training improves one's physical stamina, which means one can stay active for longer without getting tired.

Promotes fat burning: Endurance exercise may help to reduce excess body fat and control weight.

It is well known that a quick feeling of satiety and calorie restriction contribute to body weight reduction. A study has found that endurance sport in particular leads to a faster satiety effect due to the increased formation of N-lactoyl-phenylalanine, a molecule consisting of lactate (lactic acid) and the amino acid phenylalanine.[9]

Weight training

Increases muscle strength and mass: Resistance-based strength training helps build muscle strength and mass, which can improve physical performance.

Improves body composition: By building muscle mass, strength training can help reduce body fat and improve body composition.

Strengthens bones: Strength training can increase bone density and reduce the risk of osteoporosis and fractures.

A combination of endurance and strength training is often best, as both are important components of a comprehensive fitness program. However, **aerobic and muscle-strengthening activities should be done at least three hours apart**, as strength gains are weakened in the same session.[10] The type and intensity of training should be adapted to individual goals and needs, taking into account health and possible limitations.

The role of health promotion for so-called "weekend warriors", i.e. people who are very busy at work and only manage to exercise at the weekend, is the subject of much controversy. In principle, this compact sports schedule, even if the physical activity is less frequent and intensive than regular, daily training, still seems to be beneficial for health and prevent sudden cardiac death.[11] A retrospective analysis from a British bio-database also showed that sport focused on one or two days has a comparably favorable prognosis compared to training evenly distributed over the week due to the significantly reduced cardiovascular risk in both groups.[12]

In order to avoid excuses regarding bad weather conditions, costs or the effort involved in purchasing strength equipment and weights or going to the gym on a regular basis, the following section presents sports that make it possible to do something for physical and mental health and longevity with little time and cost.

Calisthenics

The term calisthenics comes from Greek language and literally means "beautiful strength". It is a form of physical training that aims to develop strength, endurance, flexibility, coordination and body control **using one's own body weight**, i.e. a gym, swimming pool, weight machines or weights are not necessary for this sporting activity. Exercises include pull-ups, press-ups, dips (lowering and lifting between parallel bars), squats, lunges.

Intervention studies emphasize the benefits of calisthenics training due to the low time, cost and equipment requirements, which can also be incorporated into the daily routine of untrained people in almost any location with the aim of promoting health and preventing illness.[13]

Pull-ups

Pull-ups are an exercise that strengthens the muscles in the upper back, biceps, shoulders and core. They can be used to build muscle as well as to improve functional strength and bodyweight training. There are different hand positions used for pull-ups. The choice of hand position influences the muscles that are used more during the exercise.

Variants

Wide grip (overhand grip wider than shoulder width): The palms are facing outwards. This position targets the outer parts of the latissimus dorsi and also puts more strain on the shoulders and upper back. However, a wide grip can put excessive strain on the shoulders (rotator cuff). For this reason, people with shoulder problems should take a more cautious approach or consider alternative grip positions.

Narrow grip (overhand grip at shoulder width or closer): As with the wide grip, the palms are facing outwards. The narrow grip focuses more on the middle of the back (latissimus dorsi) and the biceps muscles. The trapezius and rhomboids are involved in pulling the shoulder blades together.

Reverse grip (underhand grip or comb grip): In this position, the palms are facing inwards. A reverse grip emphasizes the biceps muscles and the lower part of the latissimus dorsi. The brachialis, which lies under the biceps, is also used more intensively.

Parallel grip (hammer grip): These are pull-ups on a parallel bar with the palms facing each other. This position also works the biceps and middle back muscles. The shoulder muscles, especially the deltoids, are also activated to support the movement.

Muscle groups

Latissimus dorsi (broad back muscle): The latissimus dorsi is the main muscle used in pull-ups. This exercise is particularly effective for developing the outer part of the latissimus dorsi.

Biceps brachii: The biceps, located on the front of the upper arm, are strongly activated to bend the elbows and pull the body upwards.

Back muscles: In addition to the latissimus dorsi, other muscles in the upper back, such as the trapezius muscle and the rhomboid muscle, are also activated to pull the shoulder blades together and stabilize the back muscles.

Brachialis: This muscle lies under the biceps and also supports the flexion of the elbow.

Lower trapezius: The lower part of the trapezius muscle, which covers the upper back, is activated during the downward movement to stabilize the shoulder blades.

Brachioradialis: The brachioradialis is a muscle in the forearm that is also active during pull-ups.

Abdominal muscles: The abdominal muscles are used to stabilize the torso while the body is pulled upwards.

Push-ups

Push-ups are a versatile exercise that strengthens the triceps, chest muscles, shoulders, back and core. Push-ups are often part of fitness routines, military training and general training programs.

Variants

Wide push-ups: With the hands wider than shoulder-width apart to work the chest muscles more.

Close push-ups: With the hands closer together to activate the triceps more.

Diamond push-ups: The hands are positioned so that the fingers and thumbs form a triangle, which puts the focus on the triceps.

One-armed push-ups: With one hand on the back to increase intensity.

Muscle groups

Pectoral muscles (pectoralis major): By using different hand positions, for example a wider or narrower grip, the chest muscles can be used to varying degrees.

Anterior deltoid muscle (deltoideus anterior): The shoulder muscles are activated during push-ups, especially the front part of the deltoid muscle.

Triceps: The back of the upper arms, the triceps, is activated during the extension of the elbows.

Serratus anterior: This muscle, which covers the lateral parts of the chest and the upper ribs, is used to stabilize the shoulder blades and support the movement.

Abdominal muscles (rectus abdominis et obliques): To keep the body stable during push-ups, the abdominal muscles are also activated.

Back muscles: The muscles in the upper back are also used to stabilize the shoulder girdle.

Gluteal muscles (gluteus maximus): The gluteal muscles are used to keep the hips stable and the body in a straight line.

Dips

Dips (bar support) are a bodyweight exercise that works several muscle groups in the upper body and arms. The exercise is usually performed on parallel bars (dip bars). A larger, more complex piece of gymnastics equipment is the parallel bars, as known from school lessons.

Muscle groups

Triceps brachii: The main work during dips is done by the triceps. This muscle on the back of the upper arm is responsible for extending the elbow joint.

Pectoral muscles (pectoralis major): Dips also target the chest muscles, especially when the upper body is tilted forward. This effect is enhanced if the dips are performed with a wide grip.

Anterior deltoid muscle (deltoideus anterior): The anterior shoulder muscles are activated to support the forward movement of the arms.

Rhomboid muscle (rhomboids): The rhomboid muscle, which lies between the shoulder blades, is activated during dips to ensure stability of the shoulder girdle.

Gluteal muscles (gluteus maximus): The gluteal muscles are used to keep the hips stable and the body upright.

Lower trapezius muscle: The lower part of the trapezius muscle, which covers the upper back, is also involved.

Abdominal muscles (rectus abdominis et obliques): The abdominal muscles are activated to keep the torso stable.

Squats

Squats are an excellent exercise in calisthenics, a form of training that focuses on bodyweight-based exercises without additional equipment. Squats strengthen the leg muscles, especially the thighs (quadriceps), glutes (gluteal muscles), and the muscles of the hips.

Variants

Basic squat technique: The basic technique for squats in calisthenics is to stand upright, place the feet shoulder-width apart and bend the knees while pushing the hips back. The back should be kept straight and the body lowered as if sitting on an invisible chair. One should also ensure that one breathes evenly during the movement. A common mistake is to hold one's breath. One should inhale when lowering into the squat and exhale when coming up from the squat.

Deep squats: This involves trying to go as deep as possible while maintaining correct form. This helps to activate the muscles through a greater range of motion and promotes flexibility.

Pistol squats: This is an advanced variation of the squat where the entire body weight is balanced on one leg while the other leg is extended. This form is therefore more recommended for well-trained athletes.

Explosive squats: This is an advanced form of squat, also known as jump squats or **plyometric squats**. When coming up from the deep squat, one jumps into the air. This exercise integrates strength, speed and coordination and is an effective way to strengthen leg muscles and improve jumping power. This type of exercise is particularly popular in sports such as basketball, volleyball and sprinting.

Muscle groups

Quadriceps (front thigh muscle): For the extension of the knees.

Hamstrings (rear thigh muscles): For hip flexion and extension of the knees.

Gluteal muscles (gluteus maximus): For hip extension.

Adductors and abductors: For stabilizing the legs.

Trunk muscles: For the stability of the trunk during movement.

Lunges

Lunges are an exercise that works the muscles in the legs, buttocks and core. It is a functional exercise that promotes strength and stability in the lower extremities.

Variants

Stationary lunges: The classic variation in which the back leg does not move after the lunge.

Lunges with a step backwards: Here, a step is taken backwards instead of forwards.

Running lunges: Here, lunges are performed in a continuous, dynamic movement.

Muscle groups

Quadriceps (front thigh muscle): Activated during flexion of the front knee.

Gluteal muscles (gluteus maximus): Activated when standing up from a lowered position.

Ischiocrural muscles (posterior thigh muscles): Helps stabilize and flex the posterior knee.

Adductors and abductors: Work together to stabilize the legs.

Core muscles: Activated to stabilize the upper body during the exercise.

Jumping rope

Although jumping rope is not directly a calisthenics exercise, it can still be used as a supplement to a calisthenics workout. It is an effective way to burn calories, promote cardiovascular health and improve speed. Jumping rope requires timing and coordination between the eyes, hands and feet, which can improve motor skills.

The exercises can be performed both indoors and outdoors and only require a skipping rope, of which there are now skipping rope systems with plastic-coated metal wires and weights on handles to enable faster movements in addition to simple hemp ropes. Different muscle groups are activated while jumping rope, including the legs, torso, arms and shoulders. It is therefore a full body workout.

Cardiovascular training

Jumping rope is an excellent way to strengthen the cardiovascular system. It increases the heart rate, improves endurance and promotes overall heart health. According to the **Harvard Step Test, approximately 10 minutes of jumping rope is equivalent to 30 minutes of jogging** for cardiovascular endurance.[14]

Burning calories

Jumping rope is an effective method of burning calories and can therefore be integrated into a fitness program for weight loss.[15] In addition to the duration and intensity of the physical activity, calorie consumption also depends on age, gender, body size and physical condition. Even if studies determine an apparently exact calorie consumption, the following calorie figures are more of a rough estimate.[16,17]

Light rope jumping: Approx. 200-300 calories per half hour.
This estimate is based on a body weight of around 70 kg.
Moderate rope skipping: Approx. 300-400 calories per half hour.

This is a slightly more intense workout with higher speed and possibly variations in technique.

Intense rope skipping or High-Intensity Interval Training (HIIT): Up to 500 calories or more per half hour. High-intensity jumping rope, especially in the form of interval training, can further increase calorie consumption.

Variants

Basic rope skipping: The basic form of rope skipping, which involves simply jumping over the rope as it swings continuously across the floor. This can be done **with forward movement or remaining** in place **with either one hop** or **two hops per revolution**.

One-leg rope skipping: This involves jumping on one leg only to improve balance and strengthen the muscles on one side.

Criss-cross jumping: Criss-cross rope jumping involves moving the arms crosswise in front of the body while the rope swings over the head and under the feet.

Backward rope skipping: The movement is backwards, which increases coordination and backward vision requirements.

Interval rope skipping: There is an alternation between intense and moderate jumping intervals to increase the intensity of the workout.

High-knee rope jumping: When jumping, the knees are alternately lifted up to activate the abdominal muscles.

Double Unders: In this advanced variation, the rope is passed under the feet twice per jump. This requires more speed, higher jumps and precision.

Muscle groups

Calf muscles (gastrocnemius and soleus): The calf muscles are used in each jump to push the feet off the ground.

Quadriceps (anterior thigh muscle): The quadriceps help to bend the knees when pushing off the ground

Hamstrings (posterior thigh muscles): The hamstrings work with the quadriceps to flex and extend the knees.

Gluteal muscles (gluteus maximus): The gluteus maximus is activated when pushing off the ground.

Abdominal muscles (rectus abdominis et obliques): The abdominal muscles are engaged to keep the torso stable and support an upright posture while jumping rope.

Shoulder muscles (deltoids): The shoulder muscles are used to swing the arms and turn the rope.

Back muscles: The back muscles help to maintain an upright posture and support the shoulders when moving the arms.

Arm muscles (biceps and triceps): The arm muscles are involved in swinging the rope and coordinating the movements of the arms.

Muscles in the hip area: The muscles in the hip area, such as the iliopsoas and sartorius, are also activated to lift the legs during jumping.

Yoga

Yoga is a traditional movement theory that has its origins in **the Buddhist-Hindu cultural area**. The word "yoga" originally comes from the **Sanskrit योग** meaning "union" or "integration".

Yoga is closely linked to the principles of **Ayurvedic medicine**. Yoga aims to bring body, mind and soul into harmony.

There are various forms and styles of yoga, but most include postures **(asanas)**, breath control **(pranayama)** and **meditation**. The main focus is on developing body awareness, flexibility, strength and inner peace.

Yoga has been shown to help **manage stress, relieve anxiety, lower high blood pressure, improve sleep quality and cognitive performance and alleviate depression.**[18,19,20,21,22,23] According to the Buddhist-Hindu tradition, there are **7 chakras (energy centers)** in the body.[24]

Yoga aims to promote physical and mental well-being by improving the flow of energy in the body and increasing overall balance and flexibility. It consists of a series of movements and postures that can be adapted to different fitness levels and is often used for both physical exercise and therapeutic purposes.

It is important to note that yoga is not limited to any particular religion, although it is often associated with **Hindu, Buddhist or philosophical traditions**. In many cultures, yoga is valued as a holistic practice for well-being and self-development.

Ten simple movement and holding positions from yoga that can be performed while standing were adapted here based on established references.[25,26,27] All exercises should focus on inhaling and exhaling. The individual movement and holding positions should each be repeated three to five times, so that a total of just **10 minutes** should be invested in the ten exercises **each day**.

1. Cloud Hand
2. Low Mudra (symbolic hand movement/position)
3. High Mudra (symbolic hand movement/position)
4. Right and Left Sideways Movement
5. Forward and Back Bend
6. Right and Left One-Leg Stand
7. Clockwise Spinning Top
8. Deep Hip Jump with Liberating Pull-up of the Arms
9. Standing Balance
10. Windmill

In the cloud hand, the hands are positioned on the lower abdomen with the palms facing upwards. As if drawing water, one moves one's hands up to the solar plexus (breastbone level) and stretch out the arms with the palms facing outwards, as if a cloud is being pushed aside and with it worries, stress and problems. It is important to breathe out as one extends the arms.

Fig. 1: Cloud Hand

The low mudra is intended for the sacral chakra. The interlaced palms point downwards at the level of the solar plexus (in front of the breastbone) and move downwards. Then the palms turn upwards and return upwards to the starting position in the solar plexus area.

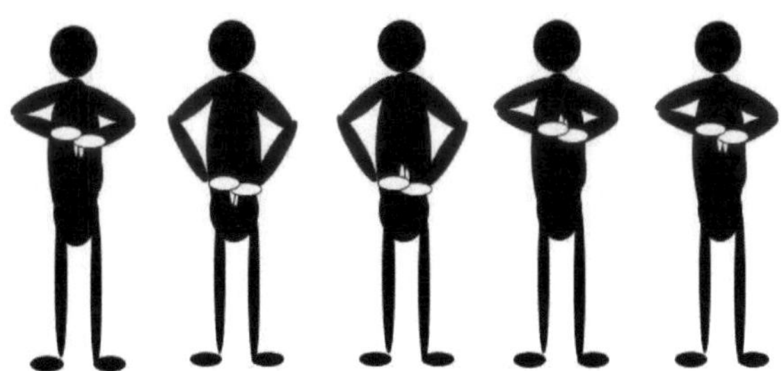

Fig. 2: Low Mudra (symbolic hand movement/position)

The high mudra is focused on the throat and crown chakras. The hands are clenched into fists in front of the neck and are placed in a semi-circle above the head. There the fists open, the palms turn from the inside to the outside and draw energy from below, which is then brought back up to the body. In addition to the cloud hand, this exercise is well suited to relieving stress.

Fig. 3: High Mudra (symbolic hand movement/position)

In the right and left side movement, arms are first stretched
upwards and then aligned parallel to the respective
upper body side movement. These are simple movements that
are particularly useful after long periods of sitting.

Fig. 4: Right and Left Sideways Movement

In the forward and backward bend, the hands are first supported on
the thighs in front as in a kowtow or prayer, then the upper body

straightens up and the arms are stretched upwards and then over-stretched backwards almost as if sun worship were taking place.

Abb. 5: Forward and Back Bend

The right and left one-leg stand involves standing on one leg for around 10 seconds while the other leg is bent at the standing leg. This exercise is important for coordination and inner balance. If one is unsure about one's stability and center of gravity, one can spread one's arms out for support.

Fig. 6: Forward and Left One-Leg Stand

In the clockwise spinning top, the arms are spread out with the palms facing outwards and then rotated around their own axis in a clockwise direction. As with the one-leg stand, this exercise is also used for inner balance. For better focus, the exercise can also be performed with eyes closed at an advanced stage. As with all exercises, attention should be paid to breathing in and out.

Fig. 7: Clockwise Spinning Top

When performing a deep hip jump with a liberating pull-up of the arms, the jumping movement from the squat should be performed from the hips and not from the knees. This exercise also helps to release tension.

Fig. 8: Deep Hip Jump Liberating Pull-Up of the Arms

The standing balance involves standing on one leg while the other leg is extended backwards in a horizontal position. The torso tilts forward accordingly and both arms are extended forward in parallel. Then switch to the other leg. Again, the aim is to achieve inner balance.

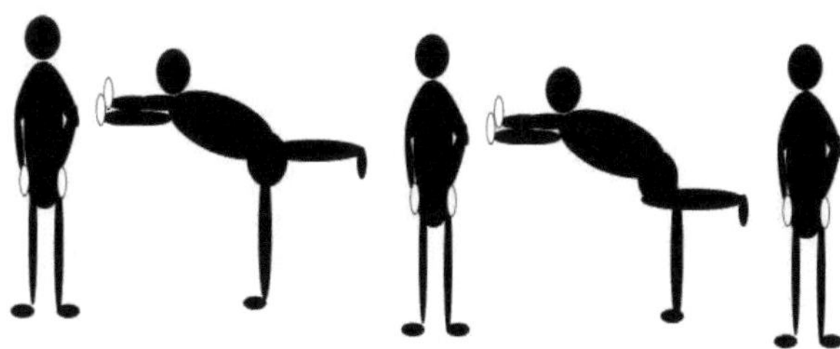

Fig. 9: Standing Balance

The windmill works several muscle groups in the arms, shoulders, neck and back to relieve tension. Arms are stretched out sideways in the neutral position, then the left arm is lifted upwards and the right arm is positioned diagonally downwards. The legs and lower torso remain unchanged throughout the exercise. The left arm leads backwards with the upper body turned to the left and the right arm follows in a horizontal position with the upper body turned to the left. The right arm then takes the lead and is stretched upwards, with the left arm now pointing diagonally downwards. The upper body turns back to the zero position from the beginning. Then the left arm is lifted upwards again, now guiding the upper body with a twist to the right. The right arm is diagonally down again and is then brought into a horizontal position together with the left arm while the upper body is rotated backwards to the right. The right arm now takes the initiative and stretches upwards with the left arm coming diagonally downwards. The right arm guides the upper body back to the zero position from the beginning. At the beginning, the windmill should be performed slowly and with pauses. Once one has internalized the movement sequence, one can then also perform fast scooping movements.

Fig. 10: Windmill

Conclusions

- A small dose of sport is an effective "medicine pill".
  Just do it!

- Only 10 minutes of exercise a day helps to prevent health
  problems, manage stress and improve quality of life

- Regardless of the weather, money and time can be saved:
  calisthenics, jumping rope and yoga can be done practically
  anywhere at any time without a gym, equipment or weights

Chapter 2: Sleep, rest, music: under-estimated pillars of health

In the fast-moving modern world, which is characterized by constant activity and an excessive striving for productivity, many people tend to underestimate the importance of sufficient sleep, relaxation and soothing music. Yet sleep, relaxation and music are not just pleasant aspects of daily life, but fundamental pillars of health.

Sleep

As a biological process, sleep plays a crucial role in the regeneration of the body. During sleep, not only are energy reserves replenished, but repair mechanisms are also activated. Cells regenerate, the immune system strengthens and hormone production is regulated. A lack of adequate sleep can lead to a variety of health problems, including a weakened immune system, increased risk of cardiovascular disease, diabetes mellitus and mental illness.

In addition, sleep has a significant impact on cognitive function and emotional stability. A well-rested person shows a better ability to concentrate, faster reaction times and improved problem-solving skills. The link between sleep deprivation and cognitive impairment is well documented and should serve as a warning signal of the importance of getting a regular and sufficient amount of sleep.

Duration, quality and depth of sleep play a crucial role in health.

Sleep duration

A three-hour reduction in sleep duration disrupts the function of T cells, which are responsible for the body's defense against infection.[28] In a study of more than 116,000 people from 21 countries, which also took regional and cultural differences into account, it was shown that an average sleep duration of 6-8 hours per day best protects against hard primary prognostic endpoints such as cardiovascular events and death.[29] Both **too long** and **too short, either way of this sleep duration is unhealthy**. One review found that outside of the optimal sleep window, **sleep deprivation** by one hour results in up to 11% risk of death, **coronary heart disease, stroke and type 2 diabetes mellitus**, whereas **sleep excess** by one hour results in an even higher risk (up to 17%) of **stroke, coronary heart disease and type 2 diabetes mellitus**.[30]

Sleep deprivation as therapy

Sleep deprivation is controversially discussed as a therapeutic measure for depression in psychiatry. There has been some research since the 1970s suggesting that sleep deprivation can have a short-term antidepressant effect, particularly in people with depression.[31] The exact mechanisms underlying this short-term improvement are not fully understood, but it is thought that changes in circadian rhythms **("internal clock")** and neurotransmitter systems may play a role. The antidepressant effect of sleep deprivation usually appears to be temporary, and most people experience a return of depression symptoms when they resume normal sleep. A recent review and meta-analysis finds no evidence and therefore no justifying indication for guideline-based sleep deprivation treatment for depression.[31]

Power Nap

A power nap, a short nap of around 10 to 30 minutes, can offer many health benefits if used correctly.[32] A short nap can help to reduce stress levels and improve alertness, concentration and cognitive performance, especially after intense physical activity or strenuous work. In addition, a power nap can help combat fatigue during the day and shorten reaction times. Studies have shown that a short midday nap can support memory performance and learning, improve retention of new information and improve long-term memory.[33] Ideally, a power nap should be taken in the early afternoon (a kind of **"siesta"**) to take advantage of the natural drop in energy levels during the day without disturbing night-time sleep. People who power nap too late in the day (e.g. late afternoon), nap for more than 30 minutes during the day or have already slept more than six hours the night before are at increased risk of cardiovascular disease and death.[32,29]

Sleep quality

Studies have shown that most people with sleep disorders have problems falling asleep, followed by problems sleeping through the night or waking up early.[34] Problems sleeping through the night provoke **vascular calcification (atherosclerosis)** through the increased release of inflammatory cells, which are associated with the **develop-**

ment of heart attacks and strokes.[35] According to a review, sleep disorders lead to an increased risk of stroke (up to 55% higher), cardiovascular death (up to 33% higher), coronary heart disease (up to 28% higher), high blood pressure (up to 27% higher), dementia (up to 50% higher) and cancer in the hormone-active organ thyroid (up to 24% higher).[36]

Depth of sleep

The stages of sleep are often divided into five phases: four stages of non-REM sleep (NREM) and the Rapid Eye Movement (REM) phase.[37] The REM phase is a stage of sleep characterized by rapid eye movements, increased neuronal activity and vivid dreams involving the processing of emotions. Memorization or consolidation of memory content occurs mainly during NREM sleep, especially during deep sleep (N3) and middle sleep (N2).[38] Assessment of sleep depth can be done using a variety of methods, including **polysomnography** (a sleep study that measures brain waves, muscle activity and other parameters), **actigraphy** (measurement of movements during sleep) and **subjective self-reports of sleep quality**.[39] Adequate sleep depth is important for regeneration, recovery and overall well-being.

Circadian rhythm

The circadian rhythm **("internal clock")** is a biological process that repeats in a roughly 24-hour cycle and controls numerous physiological and behavioral changes in the body. These rhythmic fluctuations influence many aspects of our lives, including the sleep-wake cycle, body temperature, hormone production, metabolic activity and memory performance. The circadian clock is mainly influenced by light. The alternation between day and night helps to synchronize the circadian clock and maintain the circadian rhythm. Results from cave experiments have shown that the human circadian rhythm persists even in the absence of external timers such as light.[40] This has particular significance for shift workers, miners or business travelers and airline personnel on transcontinental flights, as it has been shown that external disruptions to the circadian rhythm can affect physical and mental health.[41]

Hormones

Melatonin and cortisol are two important hormones that play a key role in the regulation of the sleep-wake cycle. Both endogenous hormones interact to control the sleep-wake cycle and influence sleep quality.[42]

Melatonin helps to initiate and maintain sleep by signaling sleep readiness, while cortisol promotes a more active state and wakes the body. A balanced release of melatonin and cortisol in the circadian rhythm is important for healthy sleep and well-being during the day.[43] Disruptions in this balance can lead to sleep disorders and other health problems.

Taking artificially produced melatonin has become quite popular, especially when traveling across multiple time zones (jet lag) or working shifts. However, it is not suitable for everyone and can also cause side effects such as headaches, dizziness, nausea and drowsiness.

Therefore, melatonin should always be taken under **medical supervision**, especially by children, pregnant or breastfeeding women and people with other health conditions or taking medication. In addition, melatonin should not be considered a substitute for healthy sleep hygiene and lifestyle changes, such as creating a relaxing sleep environment, limiting screen time before bedtime and maintaining a regular sleep-wake cycle.

Natural extracts

In addition to melatonin, natural extracts of **saffron** (Crocus sativus) or **valerian** (Valeriana officinalis) are in great demand for the treatment of sleep disorders. Both have potentially calming and sleep-promoting properties. The sedative effect of saffron extract is thought to be due to its interaction with neurotransmitters such as **serotonin** and **GABA (γ-aminobutyric acid)**.[42] Valerian contains compounds known as valeric acids, which may have a sedative effect by increasing the activity of the neurotransmitter GABA in the brain and also have a stimulant effect at the serotonin receptor.[44] The effectiveness of extracts of saffron and valerian in the treatment of sleep disorders can vary widely.

Benzodiazepines

Benzodiazepines are a class of drugs that are given to treat anxiety and epilepsy, but are also commonly used to treat sleep disorders. Although they can be effective in promoting sleep, they are not without risks and can have a variety of side effects.

Although benzodiazepines can be effective in treating anxiety, sleep disorders and other conditions, they also have potential for side effects such as a **hangover** with daytime sleepiness, memory and concentration problems, slowed reaction time, breathing problems, **paradoxical reactions** (agitation, aggression, hallucination) and **dependence**, especially with prolonged use or at higher doses.[45]

As a general rule, people with sleep disorders should speak to a medical doctor before using sleeping pills. In addition, lifestyle changes for good sleep hygiene should be considered, which are explained in detail below.[46]

Sleep hygiene

Regular sleep-wake cycle: One should try to go to bed and get up at the same time every day, even at weekends. A regular sleep-wake cycle helps to regulate the body's internal clock and improve sleep.

Sleep environment: Create a comfortable sleeping environment that is cool, quiet and dark; if necessary, use earplugs or a sleep mask to minimize disturbing noises or light sources.

Avoid caffeine and stimulants: Consumption of caffeine (coffee, tea), theobromine (chocolate, cocoa) and other stimulants such as nicotine and alcohol, especially in the hours before bedtime should be limited. These can disrupt sleep and prolong the time it takes to fall asleep.

Relaxation techniques: Relaxation techniques such as autogenic training, yoga, meditation, progressive muscle relaxation or breathing exercises can help to reduce stress and prepare the body for sleep.

Limit screen time before going to bed: Using electronic devices such as cell phones, tablets and computers just before bedtime should be avoided, as the blue light emitted from screens can interfere with the body's production of melatonin can be impaired.

Regular physical activity: Regular exercise can help to improve sleep quality, but intense physical activity just before bedtime should be avoided as this can interfere with falling asleep due to the adrenaline rush.

Food intake time: Heavy meals and large amounts of liquids just before bedtime should be avoided.

Avoiding naps: If taking naps during the day, limit their duration and avoid long naps late in the day as this can disrupt nighttime sleep.

Develop a sleep routine: Create a relaxing sleep routine that helps prepare for sleep, e.g. by reading, taking a warm bath or listening to soothing music.

Relaxation

In nowadays fast-moving world, with the pressure to be productive and constantly available, many people tend to view rest as secondary or even superfluous. However, the exact opposite is true: in addition to the aforementioned sleep, rest is an essential pillar of health and well-being that should not be neglected.

First of all, rest plays a crucial role in the regeneration of the body. During periods of rest, the body has the opportunity to regenerate and repair itself. Tissues are renewed, muscles are repaired and the immune system is strengthened. Without sufficient rest, these regeneration processes can slow down or be disrupted, which can lead to health problems in the long term.

In addition, recovery is important for mental health. In a world that is often characterized by stress, hectic and excessive demands, relaxation offers the opportunity to calm the mind and reduce stress. **Relaxation techniques such as meditation, yoga and breathing exercises can help** to calm the mind and promote mental relief. This in turn helps **to prevent anxiety, depression and burnout.**

Rest is also important for maintaining performance and productivity. Regular periods of rest can improve cognitive function and concentration. Taking time for rest can increase performance and improve the quality of work.

Furthermore, rest plays a central role in promoting relationships and social bonds. Shared leisure activities can strengthen friendships, deepen family bonds and improve general well-being. Recreation offers the opportunity to interact with others, laugh together and share positive experiences.

"Always-on" lifestyle: poisonous for one's health

Rest is important to maintain balance in life. In a society that is often characterized by an "always-on" lifestyle, it is easy to get lost in work and neglect the needs of one's body and mind. The increase in intensive screen use (now mainly via smartphones) has a negative impact on physical and mental health.[47]

Consequences for health

Stress and overload: Constant access to digital devices and constant availability can lead to a feeling of constant excitement and excessive demands. The pressure to always be available and respond immediately to messages can cause stress and anxiety.

Sleep disorders: Constant use of screens before bedtime can affect the quality of sleep. As mentioned above in the section on sleep, the blue wavelength light from screens can inhibit the production of melatonin, the sleep hormone, which can lead to sleep disturbances and sleep deprivation.

Physical inactivity: Excessive use of digital devices can lead to people spending less time outdoors and being less physically active. This can lead to a sedentary lifestyle, which is associated with an increased risk of obesity, heart disease and other health problems.

Social isolation: Although digital technologies can facilitate communication, they can also lead to social isolation. Excessive use of online media can lead to people spending less time with face-to-face social interactions, which can lead to loneliness and isolation.

Digital distractions: The constant availability of entertainment and information online can cause people to spend their time and attention unproductively. This can affect productivity and lead to important tasks being neglected.

Digital fatigue: Constant use of digital devices can lead to eye strain, headaches and other symptoms of digital fatigue. This can affect quality of life and increase the risk of long-term eye and health problems.

Important steps for recovery

Recovery offers the opportunity to regenerate, reflect and reprioritize. By consciously taking time for rest and self-care, one can lead a balanced and fulfilling life.

Sleep: Sleep is one of the most important forms of recovery. As detailed above, during sleep the body has the opportunity to regenerate, repair tissue, balance hormones and consolidate memories. Adequate sleep duration and quality are crucial for health and well-being.

Relaxation techniques: Relaxation techniques such as meditation, breathing exercises, progressive muscle relaxation and yoga can help to relieve stress, reduce muscle tension and calm the mind.[48] These practices promote relaxation and recovery on a physical and mental level.

Leisure activities: Leisure activities that are fun and relaxing are important components of recovery. These include hobbies, artistic activities, nature excursions, reading, listening to music and social activities with friends and family. Such activities offer a welcome break from everyday life and contribute to mental relief.

Exercise and sport: While physical activity is an important part of a healthy lifestyle, it is also important to allow sufficient time for rest and relaxation. Alternating between periods of activity and rest allows the body to recover and regenerate, which ultimately improves performance and prevents injuries.

Healthy diet: A balanced and nutritious diet supports recovery by providing the body with the necessary nutrients and energy to regenerate. Adequate fluid consumption is also important to keep the body hydrated and support the metabolism.

Self-care: Self-care practices such as massages, baths, sauna visits and spa treatments can help to reduce tension, loosen muscles and improve overall well-being.

Mindfulness and self-reflection: Scheduling time for mindfulness practices and self-reflection can help to calm the mind, reduce stress and promote a positive attitude. This can be done through meditation, journaling, nature observation or other intentional activities.[49]

Time limits on the use of digital devices: When screen time, especially smartphone use, is reduced, combined with an increase in physical activity, it can efficiently and cost-effectively promote mental health.[50]

In summary, relaxation is an essential pillar of health that encompasses a holistic view of well-being. By making time for relaxation, one can strengthen one's physical and mental health, increase one's performance and lead a fulfilling life. It is important to make rest a priority and integrate it as an important component of a healthy lifestyle.

The healing power of music: making music for health care

In modern civilized society, people are constantly exposed to stress, hectic lifestyles and a flood of stimuli, leading to a search for ways to maintain health and well-being. An often overlooked but extremely effective method of promoting health is making music. Music has always had a profound effect on the human mind, body and spirit, and numerous studies have shown that active music-making offers a multitude of health benefits that go far beyond mere aesthetic pleasure. Below are some of the reasons why making music is an important preventative health activity.

Stress relief and emotional well-being: Music has a unique ability to influence our emotions and put us in a relaxed state.[51] Making music allows us to focus on the moment, let go of everyday stresses and achieve a state of calm and serenity. Creative self-expression while making music can also be an outlet for emotions, which helps to reduce negative feelings and increase emotional well-being.[52]

Cognitive function and brain health: Making music requires complex brain functions, including attention, memory, coordination and problem solving. Regular music-making can improve and maintain these cognitive abilities, especially in older people.[51,53] In addition, music-making has been found to reduce the risk of neurodegenerative diseases such as dementia and Alzheimer's disease.[54]

Studies have shown that musicians often exhibit higher brain performance in areas such as language processing, memory and spatial thinking. These positive effects have also been described when listening to music, for example a piano sonata by Wolfgang Amadeus Mozart, and are often referred to as the **"Mozart effect"**.[55] Making music can already have a positive effect on a child's mental health perinatally, i.e. around birth.[56]

Social interaction and community: Music is a universal language that connects people from different cultures and backgrounds.[52] Making music in groups promotes social interaction, teamwork and a sense of belonging. By sharing musical experiences, relationships can be strengthened and the social network expanded, which in turn improves mental well-being and quality of life.

Physical health: Making music trains various physical skills such as fine motor skills, coordination and breath control. **Instrumental playing** often requires good posture and muscle control, which helps to strengthen the back, spine and other muscle groups. In addition, **singing** can **improve breathing** and **increase lung capacity**, which has a positive effect on overall physical fitness.[57]

Cardiovascular system: In addition to religious and entertainment reasons, music appears to be an additional non-drug option to improve health prognosis, especially in cardiovascular disease.[58] The **MANTRA study** has seen that patients with cardiovascular disease after cardiac catheterization do better in therapy from **noetic** ("consciousness expanding") **measures**, i.e. soothing music, healing prayers and biofield therapy (laying on of hands such as **Reiki**).[59] However, the **MANTRA II follow-up study** at nine different centers in the USA did not find any survival benefits, as the "vibrations" of music, voice or proximity to the therapist have very different effects on individuals and are apparently not measurable.[60]

If music is perceived as pleasant, it can certainly have a positive effect on blood pressure and heart rate.[61] The beating of the heart and the regulation of blood pressure cannot be controlled voluntarily, as they are supplied by the autonomic nervous system ("vegetative nervous system"). It therefore depends on the style of music (genre) and the volume whether the autonomic nervous system is stimulated or inhibited.[58] The active practice of relaxation music can favorably change gene expression in patients with coronary heart disease and is therefore a better health measure than "quietly reading" a book.[62]

Stress reduction and immune system: It has been found that making music lowers **cortisol levels** in the body, a hormone associated with stress.[63] Low cortisol levels can strengthen the immune system and improve the body's defense against disease. However, not only active music-making, but even just listening to music has been shown to help lower cortisol levels and cope with stress in everyday life.[64] In addition, the release of endorphins during music-making can lead to a feeling of well-being and relaxation, which in turn strengthens the immune system. One immune response noted in the "Mozart effect" was an "increase in natural killer cells, lymphocytes and interferon-γ", which could be of interest in the treatment of cancer, among other things.[55]

In summary, research shows that making music is far more than just an artistic activity - it is an effective form of healthcare for body, mind and soul. By regularly engaging in music-making, we can not only maintain our physical and mental health, but also connect more deeply with ourselves and others. At a time when the importance of prevention and holistic well-being is increasingly recognized, we should consider the transformative power of music as an essential pillar of our health practice.

Conclusions

- Medication and dietary supplements support sleep, but also have side effects that should not be overlooked

- Simple measures help with sleep hygiene

- Listening to and playing music can promote health

Chapter 3: Changing Nutritional Medicine

Over time, nutritional medicine has developed into a crucial area of healthcare. From the treatment of malnutrition to the prevention of chronic diseases, the importance of nutrition to the health of individuals and society has increased. However, nutritional medicine is in a constant state of flux, driven by scientific discoveries, technological advances and societal changes. Changes in nutritional medicine offer new opportunities to improve the health and quality of life of people around the world.

Are eggs healthy or dangerous?

It used to be accepted wisdom that foods rich in cholesterol, such as egg yolk (approx. 270 mg cholesterol), butter and shrimp, should be avoided to reduce the risk of cardiovascular disease.

Especially with regard to egg consumption, there has been an extremely controversial discussion in nutritional medicine for many years due to the sometimes contradictory study results, so that the previously incontrovertible doctrine is now wavering.

There are persistent studies and meta-analyses that show a connection between increased cardiovascular risk and cholesterol intake.[65,66] The consumption of **100 mg of cholesterol** is said to increase serum **cholesterol levels by 2 mg/dl**.[67] However, there are now numerous studies and meta-analyses that find no connection between dietary cholesterol and the development of cardiovascular disease and cardiovascular death, even in a 50-country comparison.[68,69]

Important ingredients of eggs: choline and lutein

Eggs could even have a cardioprotective effect due to their choline content from lecithin, because choline can lower homocysteine levels, as the amino acid homocysteine is said to increase the risk of cardiovascular disease.[70] Choline appears to prevent the excretion of cholesterol from the liver and also has an anti-inflammatory effect (reduction of pro-inflammatory interleukin-6).[71,72] In addition to choline, egg yolks also contain the antioxidant lutein, which is better absorbed by eating eggs than in the form of a dietary supplement.[73] This is another argument in favor of eggs! According to studies of the **"Blue Zones"**, the five regions in the world where most **centennials**, i.e. 100-year-old people, are found, the secret of longevity does not seem to lie in dietary or serum cholesterol, but in a diet with antioxidants that have an anti-inflammatory effect.[74]

Controversial guidelines

However, the current guidelines of the European Society of Cardiology (ESC) continue to dogmatically adhere to the recommendation of no more than 300 mg of dietary cholesterol per day.[75]

In contrast, the US cardiology societies (AHA/ACC) and the Dietary Guidelines Advisory Committee (DGAC), a body of scientists and experts appointed by the US Department of Agriculture (USDA) and the US Department of Health and Human Services (HHS), no longer see this link between the risk of cholesterol intake and the occurrence of cardiovascular disease, so that the original recommendation to limit dietary cholesterol to 300 mg per day has been abandoned.[76,69]

Guidelines ≠ medical standard

According to the Patients' Rights Act of 2013, an article in the German Civil Code (§ 630a BGB), medical doctors are obliged to comply with medical standards. Even if doctors would like to see guidelines from specialist societies as a kind of medical law for the correct treatment of patients, it is clear that treatment in line with guidelines does not necessarily protect against medical liability. After all, which guideline from which specialist society should be followed - the US, the European, the German, the cardiologists', the diabetologists', the nephrologists'? Their recommendations are not always the same and sometimes contradictory, sometimes even outdated with reference to certain sources. For this reason, the **German Federal Court of Justice (BGH)** ruled in 2008 that **guidelines cannot reflect the medical standard** and in 2014 that they **must not**.[77,78]

Dietary guidelines from the US now emphasize the importance of an **overall healthy diet and lifestyle** rather **than focusing solely on reducing cholesterol intake.** This includes recommendations to eat more vegetables, fruits, whole grains, **fats from avocados, nuts and olive oil** along the lines of the **Mediterranean diet**, while **limiting** the **consumption of saturated and trans fats**.

Mediterranean diet

The Mediterranean diet is a way of eating inspired by the traditional eating habits of people in regions around the Mediterranean. This diet is often considered one of the healthiest in the world. Two of the above-mentioned **Blue Zones** with the highest proportion of 100-year-olds in the population are located in the Mediterranean: **Sardinia in Italy** and **Ikaria in Greece**.

Main characteristics

Rich in fruit and vegetables: The Mediterranean diet emphasizes the consumption of fresh fruit and vegetables. These foods provide important vitamins, minerals, antioxidants and fiber. A **significant reduction in cholesterol levels** has been demonstrated with the daily consumption of ½ to 1 ½ avocados.[79]

Olive oil as the main source of fat: Olive oil is used as the main source of fat in the Mediterranean diet. It is rich in monounsaturated fatty acids and antioxidants, which can promote heart health. However, this effect has only been proven with the consumption of 1 liter of olive oil per week.[76]

Moderate consumption of fish and seafood: The Mediterranean diet includes regular consumption of fish and seafood, which are rich in omega-3 fatty acids and can help reduce the risk of heart disease.

Moderate consumption of poultry, eggs and dairy products: These protein sources are also consumed in moderate amounts in the Mediterranean Diet.

Reduced consumption of red meat: Red meat such as beef, pork and lamb is consumed less frequently in the Mediterranean diet and is replaced by other protein sources such as fish, poultry, pulses and nuts.

Frequent consumption of pulses, nuts and seeds: Legumes such as beans, lentils and chickpeas as well as nuts and seeds are important components of the Mediterranean Diet and provide protein, fiber and fats. In particular, eating 30 g of nuts per day can significantly reduce the cardiovascular risk.[80] The type of nut plays less of a role in **lowering cholesterol levels** than the quantity consumed (particularly strong effects can be seen from 60 g of nuts per day).[81] Despite the larger quantity of nuts consumed, there is a significant reduction in body weight.[82]

Moderate consumption of wine: Moderate consumption of **red wine** is also recommended as part of the Mediterranean diet, as it is considered to be beneficial to health due to its antioxidant and polyphenol content. The **positive effect of red wine** became known with the **"French paradox",** a phenomenon that, in contrast to the **white wine region of Alsace**, the French population has a **lower rate of heart attacks and coronary heart disease** despite the traditionally preferred consumption of cheese, butter and other foods.

The **positive effect of red wine** became known with the **"French paradox",** a phenomenon that, in contrast to the **white wine region of Alsace**, the French population has a **lower rate of heart attacks and coronary heart disease** despite the traditionally preferred consumption of cheese, butter and other foods with saturated fats.[83]

Better butter or margarine?

In addition to the recommendation to eat eggs vs. not eating eggs, there is another dualism in nutritional medicine when it comes to butter vs. margarine. Is cholesterol-rich butter or cholesterol-limiting margarine healthier? The current ESC guidelines and a statement by a panel of German nutrition experts continue to recommend the consumption of margarine rather than butter.[75,84]

However, as with the discussion on eggs, the question now arises as to whether the moderate use of butter should not be preferred to margarine.[85] For example, the so-called **portfolio diet** focuses on strict avoidance of eggs and butter and recommends increased consumption of plant sterols for long-term protection against cardiovascular disease.[86]

It should be borne in mind that **margarine** contains **plant sterols**, which actually help to lower cholesterol levels, but in higher doses have an atherogenic effect themselves (cause vascular calcification), and **also** contains **glycidyl fatty acid esters,** which even have a potentially carcinogenic effect, i.e. can be carcinogenic.[87,88]

Excessive intake of processed foods, including margarine, therefore does not necessarily appear to be healthy. A balanced diet rich in natural, unprocessed foods is generally considered a healthier choice. If there are **concerns about the ingredients in margarine**, alternative sources of fat should be considered instead, such as **olive oil, nuts or avocado**.

Is it justified to call fat a demon?

Adipose tissue plays an important role in regulating blood sugar levels in the body. It is not only a passive storage site for excess energy in the form of fat, but also produces various hormones and signaling substances. In addition, **fat cells can** also **produce pro-inflammatory substances such as cytokines** and fatty acids, which can impair insulin sensitivity.

Overall, **adipose tissue** is an **active endocrine organ** that influences blood sugar regulation and metabolism in the body through the production of various hormones and signaling substances. Healthy regulation of these hormones and appropriate adipose tissue function are therefore important for maintaining stable blood sugar levels and preventing metabolic disorders such as diabetes mellitus. For example, **Yale scientists** implanted new adipose tissue into insulin-resistant mice, which were then able to store excess glucose.[89]

As early as 2008, an intervention study showed that a **low-fat diet** had the **greatest yo-yo effect** on body weight after 2 years **compared to the Mediterranean diet and the hypocaloric diet**, i.e. practically nothing was achieved in terms of the desired weight loss, as the initial level was reached again.[90]

In 2011, a **Harvard study** conducted by **Professor Dariush Mozaffarian**'s working group on over 120,000 Americans over a period of four years found that the people studied who consumed high-fat dairy products had lost body weight, whereas those who consumed low-fat dairy products had gained weight, **which firstly appeared to be a paradox**.[91]

The following points can be identified as possible explanations:

1. Low-fat dairy products do not have the same satiating effect as high-fat products.
2. People may tend to consume double the amount of semi-fat products.
3. Semi-fat products often have a higher sugar/carbohydrate content than low-fat products.
4. High-fat products contain more calcium, which has a positive effect on the function of adipocytes during fat absorption via the hormones parathyroid hormone and calcitriol.

In Denmark, a **fat tax** was introduced in 2011 to make high-fat foods more expensive, but this was abolished after just 15 months.[92] Even though it may have been politically well-intentioned to encourage the country's citizens to eat a supposedly healthier diet, it turned out that people tended to switch to even unhealthier things such as particularly sugary foods or to shopping in nearby countries.

Some studies have found a link between a high **consumption of dairy products**, especially whole milk, and an **increased risk of prostate cancer**, while **other studies** show **no link** or even protection against breast cancer, colon cancer, type 2 diabetes mellitus, cardiovascular disease and osteoporosis through milk consumption.[93,94]

The diabolization of fat and the dualism of eggs vs. no eggs or butter vs. margarine should not ignore explosive revelations.

Explosive revelations of conflicts of interest

The following statements by **Harvard scientists** in the New England Journal of Medicine **in 1967** laid the foundation for the direction of cardiovascular research for more than half a century and probably beyond:[95]

"There can be no doubt that levels of serum cholesterol can be substantially modified by manipulation of the fat and cholesterol of the diet."

"...the practical significance of difference in dietary carbohydrate is minimal in comparison to those related to dietary fat and cholesterol."

A **revelation** published in the prestigious medical journal JAMA Internal Medicine **in 2016** revealed that the authors had **conflicts of interest with the sugar industry**.[96]

It is also worth noting that the **ESC** published **a risk score card in 2016,** a card to classify the risk of cardiac death.[97] The following factors are listed to determine the individual risk: age, gender, smoker/non-smoker, blood pressure values, cholesterol values.

What has been forgotten?

That's right: **sugar!**

Is it mere coincidence that a guideline commission simply forgets a classic cardiovascular risk factor such as **diabetes mellitus**?

After looking at the current study situation and taking into account the explosive conflicts of interest that have historically had an enormous impact on scientific research over the last 60 years, not everything seems to be clear-cut. It is also possible that research results have been steered in a desired direction, because who would want to present study results against an apodictic prevailing opinion? It therefore remains to be hoped that most of the scientific research was nevertheless conducted impartially. In principle, however, the seemingly clear knowledge about the supposedly healthy diet should be much more differentiated.

Calorie restriction

In addition to a Mediterranean diet, calorie restriction can also help to bring about the desired weight loss.[98] Reducing calorie intake without sacrificing nutrients has been linked to a longer lifespan and a reduction in age-related diseases. Calorie restriction is thought to slow metabolism and promote the activation of genes associated with longevity and health.[99]

The **ketogenic diet, low-carb diet and Atkins diet** are three different approaches to reducing carbohydrate intake that can benefit athletes in particular:

1. through improved performance due to more efficient use of fat as fuel,
2. through more stable blood sugar levels,
3. by shortened recovery time after training due to a reduced tendency to inflammation.

Ketogenic diet

The main aim of the ketogenic diet is to bring the body into a state of ketosis, in which fat is burned and ketones, which are by-products of fat metabolism in the liver, are used as an energy source.

The **proportion of carbohydrates** in a ketogenic diet is very low, usually limited to less than **5-10%** of the daily calorie intake. This usually corresponds to less than 50 grams of carbohydrates per day.

The **main source of energy** in a ketogenic diet is **fats**, which make up **about 70-80%** of the daily calorie intake.

Proteins make up the remaining **20-25%** of the daily calorie intake.

However, a ketogenic diet can lead to an increase in uric acid levels, as the body breaks down more fats and produces ketones, which can increase the risk of gout attacks.[100]

Low-carb diet

In a low-carb diet, the focus is more on reducing carbohydrate intake to keep blood sugar levels more stable and improve insulin sensitivity without necessarily putting the body into a ketogenic state. The carbohydrate content in a low carb diet is generally higher than in a ketogenic diet, but still significantly lower than in a typical Western diet.

Carbohydrate intake can vary depending on individual needs, but typically **carbohydrates make up around 15-20%** of daily calorie intake.

Fat intake is lower than a ketogenic diet at **around 60%**, but can vary depending on preferences and goals.

Protein, at **around 30%**, is in the moderate range at a higher level of daily calorie intake than a ketogenic diet.

Although a low-carb diet appears to be beneficial to health overall, the diet should be considered in more detail: **Quality and nutrient sources** in low-carb diets have a significant impact on survival, because a low-carb diet combined with animal fats and proteins has a poor prognosis, while a low-carb diet with vegetable fats and proteins has a better outcome.[101]

Atkins diet

The Atkins diet is a variant of the low-carb diet developed by the American cardiologist **Dr. Robert Atkins** and became popular worldwide in the 1970s.[102] The main principle of the Atkins diet is to drastically reduce carbohydrate intake while increasing the consumption of protein and fats.

As with the low-carb diet, the **carbohydrate intake is around 15-20%**.

The **fat content** is lower than in the ketogenic or low-carb diet, at around **40-45%**.

The **protein content** is relatively high at **around 40%**, so that the Atkins diet is often referred to as a high-protein diet.

The Atkins diet emphasizes protein-rich foods such as meat, fish, eggs and cheese, so a high content of cellular animal protein (excluding cheese and dairy products) can lead to an increase in uric acid levels in the blood.[103] Moreover, **it may appear to be a paradox** that an **increase in cardiovascular disease** has been attributed to the Atkins diet, which could be explained by a reduced consumption of fruit, vegetables and whole grain products and by the easy access to protein with industrially processed meat products.[104]

mTOR signaling pathway - key to longevity

The low-calorie diet offers promising benefits for health and longevity by influencing the mTOR (mechanistic Target of Rapamycin) signaling pathway, which plays a **key role in the regulation of cell growth, protein biosynthesis and glucose metabolism.**[105] The immunosuppressant **rapamycin**, which inhibits the mTOR signaling pathyway, was originally obtained from soil samples of bacteria from **Easter Island** (Polynesian "Rapa Nui") and named after it. The mTOR signaling pathway responds to a variety of environmental and cellular signals such as nutrients, growth factors, cell energy status and stress. A disrupted mTOR signaling pathway can lead to a variety of diseases such as cancers, metabolic disorders and neurodegenerative diseases.[106] Thus, research into this signaling pathway is the novel approach of medicine to develop new therapies for longevity. In addition to calorie restriction, the dietary supplements **curcumin, resveratrol** and the diabetes drug **metformin**, for example, interfere **with the mTOR signaling pathway**.

Caution:

Ketoacidosis is a serious complication that may occur in diabetic people. It occurs when the body does not produce enough insulin to regulate blood glucose levels and instead burns fats for energy, leading to an increase in ketones in the blood. Symptoms of ketoacidosis can include: excessive thirst, frequent urination, nausea, vomiting, abdominal pain, weakness, confusion, difficulty breathing and a sweet smell to the breath reminiscent of nail polish remover.

People who follow a ketogenic diet and do not have diabetes mellitus should not usually be affected by ketoacidosis, as their insulin production is normally sufficient to regulate blood glucose levels.

Another aspect is the **high protein content of the ketogenic diet**. Even if exceeding the recommended daily protein intake of 0.8 g per kilogram of body weight is still considered safe, a recent animal study advises caution and encourages further clinical studies on high-protein diets because the increased circulating **amino acid leucine** leads to a stronger **activation of the mTOR signaling pathway**, which in turn leads to increased **atherosclerosis (vascular calcification)**.[107]

Before considering calorie restriction, it is advisable to discuss this with a medical doctor or nutritionist so that diabetes mellitus is ruled out and **no adverse effects** occur due to other concomitant diseases. In addition, people who restrict calories should do so under **medical supervision** to ensure that they receive sufficient nutrients and maintain optimal health.

Meat vs. vegetarian or vegan diet

Meat consumption

Overall, meat in moderation is part of a balanced diet and can be an important source of essential nutrients. However, the quality of the meat and the preparation methods should be considered to improve the health effects.

Red meat

Red meat comes from mammals such as cattle, pigs and sheep. It is typically darker in color due to the higher content of myoglobin, a protein that stores oxygen in muscle tissue. Red meat is **rich in essential amino acids, iron, zinc, vitamin B12** and other B vitamins. Excessive consumption of red meat, particularly processed meat (sausages and bacon), has been linked to an increased risk of heart disease, stroke, type 2 diabetes and certain cancers.[108]

There are also concerns about the **Paleo diet,** a form of nutrition based on the Neolithic period, which is low in fiber by avoiding cereal products and which, due to the increased consumption of meat, produces metabolic products via intestinal bacteria that can be harmful to intestinal health and blood vessels (atherosclerosis).[109]

However, several meta-analyses have shown only very weak and uncertain health effects on overall mortality and cancer development when red meat is avoided, so that a general recommendation to avoid red meat is not possible.[110,111,112]

White meat

White meat usually comes from **poultry** such as chicken and turkey and **seafood** such as fish and shellfish. It is lighter in color due to the lower myoglobin content. White meat is also high in protein and also contains vitamin B12, zinc and other nutrients, although the **iron content tends to be lower** than red meat. White meat is generally leaner and contains less saturated fat. Skinless poultry meat in particular is a low-fat source of protein.

White meat, especially skinless poultry, is often considered a healthier alternative to red meat. It has not been associated with the same risks of heart disease and cancer. In fact, white meat is often recommended because it contains less saturated fat and may have a more favorable impact on cholesterol levels. But a recent review and meta-analysis came to the sobering conclusion that white meat is neither beneficial nor harmful to health in relation to the development of cardiovascular disease and type 2 diabetes mellitus.[113]

Vegetarian or vegan diet

A **vegetarian diet** does not include meat and fish products, but may include dairy products, eggs, honey and other animal products, while **vegan diets** exclude all animal products. A vegetarian or vegan diet can be beneficial to health, provided it is balanced and contains all the necessary nutrients. Careful planning is important to ensure that all nutritional needs are met.

Health risks of a vegetarian or vegan diet

Vitamin B12 deficiency: Vitamin B12 is mainly found in animal products such as meat, fish, dairy products and eggs. A vitamin B12 deficiency can lead to anemia and neurological problems. Vegetarians and vegans should therefore supplement vitamin B12 with fortified foods, food supplements or adequate portions of vitamin B12-rich plant foods such as fortified soy products or algae supplements.

Folic acid deficiency: Folic acid is rich in liver and eggs, and in plant-based foods such as **kale, spinach, tomatoes, pulses and oranges**.

A folic acid deficiency can have potentially serious consequences for the health of the baby, especially in pregnant vegans. Folic acid, sometimes referred to as vitamin B9, which is crucial for the development of the neural tube in the developing fetus. A deficiency of folic acid and vitamin B12 during pregnancy increases the risk of irreversible damage to the newborn due to **neural tube defects such as spina bifida and anencephaly**.[114]

Iron deficiency: Iron from plant sources is generally less efficiently absorbed by the body than iron from animal sources. People who follow a vegetarian or vegan diet should make sure to regularly consume iron-rich plant foods such as legumes, nuts, seeds, green leafy vegetables and fortified cereals and combine them with vitamin C-rich foods to improve absorption. A lack of iron can lead to a **reduced oxygen supply to the cells**, which can result in fatigue, weakness and reduced physical performance.[115]

Calcium deficiency: Dairy products are a major source of calcium in the diet. People who follow a vegetarian or vegan diet should include alternative sources of calcium in their diet such as fortified **plant-based milk, green leafy vegetables** (e.g. kale, broccoli), **tofu and almonds**. Symptoms of calcium deficiency can include cramps, muscle twitching, numbness, tingling, bone fractures, cardiac arrhythmias and fatigue.[116,117]

Lack of essential amino acids: Essential amino acids cannot be produced by the body itself and are usually found in large quantities in **meat** (beef, pork, poultry), **fish and seafood and dairy products**. For a vegetarian and/or vegan diet, the following plant-based protein sources are suitable, such as **pulses** (beans, lentils, chickpeas), **soy products** (tofu, tempeh, edamame), **wholegrain products** (brown rice, quinoa, oat flakes), **nuts and seeds** (almonds, walnuts, sunflower seeds, chia seeds). A lack of essential amino acids can weaken the immune system and increase susceptibility to infections, as proteins play an important role in immune function.[118] Some essential amino acids are precursors of neurotransmitters in the brain that are important for regulating mood, sleep and other neurological functions.[119]

While plant proteins can be a source of protein, it is important to consume a variety of protein-rich plant foods to ensure an adequate supply of **all essential amino acids**.

Other meat alternatives

Artificial meat

Artificial meat, also known as cultured meat or in vitro meat, is produced in a laboratory from animal cells without the need to slaughter animals. The production process is designed to promote the growth of muscle tissue in a controlled environment.

In the **production of artificial meat**, so-called **immortalization cells** are used, which are cells that have the ability to reproduce indefinitely, unlike normal cells, which undergo a limited number of cell divisions before they age and die.

Immortalization ("making immortal") of cells can occur naturally, for example in stem cells or cancer cells, or can be achieved by experimental methods. While cancer cells often have the ability to immortalize, not all immortalized cells are necessarily cancer cells.[120]

However, this also creates the following problems:"Attempts to sell cultured meat as normal meat and vice versa could lead to numerous **legal concerns**. Also, the possibility of mislabeling products and producing meat from non-animal species **could lead to serious health issues**, as research reports show that consumption of carcinogenic in vitro cell lines can transfer **DNA [deoxyribonucleic acid]**."[121]

Insects

In some cultures, insects are consumed as a source of protein. Products such as mealworms, grasshoppers or crickets are increasingly seen as a protein-rich alternative to conventional meat. Insect production generally requires less land, water and resources compared to livestock farming. Insects can also be bred on organic waste or agricultural by-products, which further reduces the environmental impact.

According to the **WHO** 's **Sustainable Development Goals**, edible insects such as mealworms, grasshoppers and crickets could serve as protein-rich meat substitutes.[122] But there are health concerns due to exposure to mycotoxins ("mold toxins"), which play an important role in beetle species, or due to intolerance to the chitin shell.[123]

In principle, alternatives to conventional meat represent an interesting approach for the future, but attention must be paid to food safety and possible health risks during production. A large number of studies and tests are still required for this.

Dilemma with salt in food

"Bread and salt" is a cultural symbol that has meaning in many parts of the world. It is often used as a gift on various occasions and symbolizes hospitality, prosperity and health.

The **World Health Organization (WHO)** recommends consuming no more than 5 g per day to maintain good health, which is only about a teaspoon.[124] It does not say how much is too little salt.

Salt is not unhealthy at all, but plays an important role in the human body. Sodium, one of the chemical components of salt, is required for various vital functions in the body, including the regulation of fluid balance, nerve function and muscle contraction. However, both excessive and insufficient salt consumption can be unhealthy.

More salt in food

Excessive salt consumption can cause a variety of health problems.

Some of the most common health harms associated with high salt consumption are:

Cardiovascular diseases: Through increased blood pressure and other mechanisms, excessive salt consumption can increase the risk of cardiovascular disease.[125] This includes **heart attacks, strokes, atherosclerosis (vascular calcification) and heart failure**. On a simulated **Mars mission over 105 days** in Russia, the **crew members locked in** a container were given food at the **WHO-reduced table salt level**, which the test participants did not notice in terms of taste and which led to a significant reduction in **systolic** ("upper") **blood pressure values**.[126]

Kidney problems: Kidneys have an important function in regulating sodium and water balance in the body. Excessive salt consumption can put a strain on the kidneys and increase the **risk of kidney stones**, kidney dysfunction and other kidney problems.[127]

Osteoporosis: A high salt intake can lead to the body excreting more calcium via the urine. In the long term, this can lead to a loss of bone mass and increase the risk of osteoporosis and bone fractures.[126] However, one study questions the disruption of the calcium balance caused by high salt consumption and considers **sugar** to be more **responsible**.[128]

Stomach health: Excessive salt consumption can irritate the stomach lining and increase the risk of stomach ulcers and even stomach cancer.[129]

Fluid retention and swelling: High salt consumption can cause the body to retain more water, which can lead to swelling in the extremities and other areas of the body.

Less salt in food

However, too little salt can also be harmful to health. Salt is important for the body as it provides sodium and chloride, which are needed for various vital functions. Too little salt consumption can lead to fluid imbalance and other health problems. Possible effects of low salt consumption are:

Hyponatremia: Too little sodium intake can lead to low blood sodium levels, which is known as hyponatremia. This condition can cause symptoms such as **fatigue, headaches, nausea, muscle cramps, confusion** and in severe cases even **seizures and unconsciousness**.

Dehydration: Salt plays a role in regulating fluid balance in the body. Too little salt consumption can result in the body not retaining enough water, which can lead to dehydration and an imbalance of electrolytes ("blood salts"). In severe cases, dehydration can lead to more serious problems such as **circulatory collapse, kidney failure, unconsciousness and even death** if not treated in time.

Cardiovascular disease: Low salt intake can increase the risk of cardiovascular problems with an increased risk of heart attack, stroke and heart failure.[130] This could be partly due to the effects on **blood pressure and fluid balance.**

Fluid retention and swelling: When blood sodium levels are too low, the body may have difficulty excreting excess fluid, leading to a buildup of fluid in the tissues. This fluid accumulation can manifest as **swelling (edema),** which can often occur in the legs, ankles or abdomen.

Kidney problems: Too little salt consumption could cause the kidneys to become overloaded, as they do not have enough fluid available to effectively filter breakdown products.[128] Insufficient fluid intake can lead to an increased concentration of substances in the urine, which can **promote** the **formation of kidney stones**. This can cause discomfort and lead to kidney damage over time.

Paradoxical reactions

The fact that **cardiovascular disease** occurs **with both high and low salt intake** seems to be a **paradox** at first. This may be due to conflicting reports of paradoxical reactions, e.g. that excessive salt consumption causes a reduction in blood pressure in clinical and animal studies, whereas low salt consumption can cause higher blood pressure values.[129] Attempts to explain this are based on **autonomic kidney function**, which reacts sensitively to a change in blood salts and blood pressure and then also counter-regulates in both directions.

A recent Chinese study has found that it is not the restriction of salt in the diet that contributes to lowering blood pressure and promoting health, but the use of **potassium chloride as a salt substitute** in comparison to sodium chloride ("table salt").[131]

Therefore, the generally accepted recommendation "A lot of salt is unhealthy, little salt is healthy!" does not go far enough and must even be called into question in some cases. It seems advisable to **achieve a balance**, which would probably have to be assessed differently for each individual. Further research should be carried out into the daily amounts of salt consumed to achieve this balance.

Intermittent fasting

Intermittent fasting is a dietary method that has become very popular in recent years, which involves alternating between periods of eating and fasting. There are different forms of intermittent fasting, but they all involve periods of not eating followed by periods of eating normally. The benefits of intermittent fasting can include weight loss, improved metabolic health, increased insulin sensitivity and possibly a longer lifespan.[132]

The most well-known forms of intermittent fasting are:

16/8 method: in this method, one fasts for 16 hours a day and then eats within an 8-hour window.[133]

5:2 diet: Here one eats normally on five days of the week and reduces one's calorie intake to around 500-600 calories per day on the other two days.[134]

Eat-stop-eat: This form of intermittent fasting involves fasting for 24 hours once or twice a week, consuming only water, tea or coffee without calories during the fast, or according to a recently published study, the water fasting interval has even been extended to a whole week.[135]

Alternate-day fasting: This pattern involves alternating between a day of normal eating and a day of fasting with significant calorie restriction.[134]

Caution:

However, there are some cases where intermittent fasting can be an issue. For example, underweight people or people with eating disorders such as anorexia or bulimia should avoid intermittent fasting, as this can lead to further weight loss and may be harmful to health. Pregnant or breastfeeding women should not fast either, as they and their babies need adequate nutrition. **Prolonged intervals of water fasting** could **also** promote **thrombosis, bone loss and heart failure** due to **changes in protein balance**.[135] People who are taking certain medications or have certain health conditions, such as **diabetes mellitus or hormonal disorders**, should speak to a medical doctor before starting intermittent fasting to ensure that it will not have a negative impact on their health. In 2024, a Chinese study based on US health data claimed to have found an alleged 91% increased risk of cardiac death with intermittent fasting, although this study data did not undergo a peer review process and appears to be "underpowered" for prognostic value with 31 deaths.[136]

Fake fasting

Fake fasting or **"Fasting Mimicking Diet"** is a fairly new dietary strategy that aims to mimic the health benefits of fasting while consuming food. Fake fasting is based on a specific composition of foods that are eaten during a set period of time to simulate a fasting-like state for the body.

The principle of fake fasting includes in detail:

Calorie restriction: during sham fasting, calorie intake is significantly reduced, typically to around **40-50% of normal calorie intake**.[137]

Nutrient composition: The sham fast consists of specific foods that provide certain nutrients in a specific composition to ensure that the body is adequately supplied with nutrients despite the reduced calorie intake. These foods include **unsaturated fats** such as olive oil or nuts accounting for **44-46%** of total calorie intake, **protein intake** is limited to around **9-11%** of total calorie intake, and **carbohydrate intake** is limited to around **43-47%** of total calorie intake.[138]

Controlled duration: Sham fasting is usually performed for a period of **5 consecutive days**.[139] This period has been chosen so that the body enters fasting mode and certain metabolic processes associated with the health benefits of fasting are activated.

Cyclical repetition: Sham fasting can be repeated cyclically, typically **every few months**.[139] It is recommended to perform sham fasting under medical supervision and to seek medical advice in advance, especially if one has certain health conditions or medical concerns.

Sham fasting aims to promote autophagy (cellular cleansing and re-generation), reduce inflammation, improve metabolism and promote longevity, while minimizing the risks of complete fasting.[139]

Exposure to cold

Cold exposure can help to lose body weight, but the effect of cold exposure alone is rather limited.

Cryotherapy

Cryotherapy involves exposing the body to extremely low temperatures for short periods of time, typically in a special cold chamber or through the local application of cold packs. Temperatures in cold chambers can be as low as -100°C (-148°F) or lower, while local cold therapy is usually applied at less extreme temperatures between -10°C (14°F) and -30°C (-22°F).[140] The duration of treatment usually varies from a few minutes to a maximum of 15 minutes per session, depending on the individual's tolerance and the therapist's instructions.

Cold water applications

Cold water treatments such as cold baths or cold plunge pools can also be used to promote recovery after exercise or for general health promotion. The water temperature here can typically be between 10°C (10°F) and 15°C (59°F).[141] The duration of the cold water application can vary, but typically short baths of around 5 to 10 minutes are recommended.

There are several mechanisms that could explain why cold exposure could indirectly contribute to weight loss:

Burning calories to produce heat: when the body is exposed to cold, it has to expend more energy to maintain its core temperature. This can lead to an increase in energy expenditure, which in turn leads to more calories being burned.[142]

Activation of brown adipose tissue: Brown adipose tissue is a type of fat that produces heat by burning fat and glucose. Cold exposure can increase the activation of brown adipose tissue, which increases energy expenditure.[143]

Appetite suppression: Some studies suggest that cold exposure can reduce appetite. This could lead to people eating less and therefore consuming fewer calories.[144]

Longevity through cold treatment?

The idea that cold treatment or cold exposure can lead to a longer life is based on various theories. Cold exposure can stimulate the metabolism and promote the activation of metabolic pathways such as the AMPK (adenosine monophosphate-activated protein kinase) signaling pathway (see chapter "Nutritional medicine in transition"; subchapter "mTOR signaling pathway - key to longevity").[144] Furthermore, cold exposure can increase the production of antioxidant enzymes that help to reduce oxidative stress and prevent cell damage.[144]

Caution:

However, cold treatments should be used with caution, especially for people with certain health conditions such as cardiovascular disease or Raynaud's syndrome (reflex vasoconstriction).[145] It is advisable to consult a medical doctor and/or qualified therapist before starting a cold treatment to determine the appropriate temperatures and application times to avoid health risks.

Conclusions

- Dogma about bad image of eggs, fat and salt partly not justified and distracts from the danger of sugar

- Aspects of longevity due to keto or low-carb diets supported by findings at molecular level

- Meat is not necessarily a bad food

- Cold treatments help with weight management

Chapter 4: Lifestyle supplements and superfoods for longevity

Lifestyle supplements to extend life are a complex subject and there is no clear evidence that certain products can actually extend life. However, there are some supplements associated with health and longevity that are worth mentioning.

Superfoods

"Superfoods" is a term used to describe certain foods that are particularly rich in nutrients and can supposedly provide a variety of health benefits. These foods often contain high concentrations of vitamins, minerals, antioxidants, omega-3 fatty acids, fiber and other important nutrients that are considered beneficial to the body's health, from boosting the immune system to preventing disease.

Some examples of superfoods include berries **(goji berries** and blueberries), green leafy vegetables **(spinach and kale)**, nuts and seeds **(chia seeds and walnuts)**, **quinoa, avocado, turmeric and ginger.**[146]

The terms "superfoods" or "functional foods" are not scientifically defined and are not recognized by official authorities such as the Food and Drug Administration (FDA) or the European Food Safety Authority (EFSA).[146] However, the term is often used in the media and marketing to refer to foods that are considered to be particularly beneficial to health. It should also be mentioned that superfoods alone cannot replace a balanced diet.

Antioxidants

Antioxidants such as **vitamin C, vitamin E, beta-carotene, flavonoids** and **polyphenols** are known for their ability to neutralize free radicals and reduce cell damage.

Free radicals

Free radicals are molecules that have an unpaired electron in their outer shell, which makes them unstable. To reduce this instability, free radicals search for another molecule from which they can steal an electron. This process is called oxidation. The molecule that is deprived of an electron then becomes a free radical itself, as it now has an unpaired electron.[146] This can lead to a chain reaction in which many molecules are damaged as they lose electrons and become free radicals themselves.[145]

Free radicals can arise in various ways: natural metabolic processes in the body as well as through external influences such as **UV rays, smoking, environmental pollution and poor nutrition**. They play a role in various diseases and ageing processes by damaging cells and tissues and **attacking DNA, proteins and lipids**, which can contribute to various diseases such as **cancer, cardiovascular diseases,**

neurodegenerative diseases (diseases in which nerve cells die) and a shorter life expectancy.[147]

However, the body has mechanisms to fight free radicals. Antioxidants are molecules that can capture and eliminate free radicals by donating an electron to them without becoming unstable themselves. A diet rich in antioxidant foods such as berries, green vegetables, nuts and spices can help reduce the damaging influence of free radicals and promote health and possibly contribute to longevity. This is through the **anti-cancer, cardioprotective** (cardiovascular protective) and **neuroprotective** (nerve cell protective) **properties of antioxidants**.

Vitamin C

Vitamin C is the second most widely used dietary supplement in the world. Also known as ascorbic acid, it is a water-soluble vitamin that plays an important role in biological processes in the body. A deficiency of vitamin C can lead to a serious condition called scurvy, which is characterized by fatigue, muscle weakness, joint pain, bleeding gums, tooth loss and impaired wound healing. Rare in developed countries today, **scurvy** was historically a **disease among sailors** because fresh fruits and vegetables, which are important sources of vitamin C, were often unavailable, a fact recognized by British naval surgeon James Lind in 1754.[148] On later voyages, the famous circumnavigator, **British Captain James Cook**, had his crew given "**beer** (made from an experimental concentrated malt extract)," **sauerkraut and fresh sea lion meat** to prevent and treat scurvy.[149]

Vitamin C acts as a powerful antioxidant in the body and can also contribute to longevity through the following biological functions:

Antioxidant action: vitamin C has a strong antioxidant effect by neutralizing free radicals and reducing oxidative damage to cells and tissues. By reducing oxidative stress, vitamin C can help slow down the ageing process and reduce the risk of age-related diseases such as heart disease, cancer and neurodegenerative diseases.

Immune function: Vitamin C plays an important role in supporting the immune system by strengthening the body's defenses against infection and disease, especially tumors.[151] By strengthening the immune system, vitamin C may help promote health and support longevity.

Collagen production: Vitamin C is crucial for the formation of collagen, a protein that plays an important role in the health of skin, bones, teeth and connective tissue. Adequate intake of vitamin C can help support collagen production and maintain the health of these tissues.[152]

Cardioprotective effect: Vitamin C may help to support cardiovascular health by improving blood vessel function, lowering blood pressure and reducing the formation of amyloid plaques in vascular dementia (Alzheimer's disease).[153,154] This may help to reduce the risk of cardiovascular disease and increase life expectancy.[155]

Neuroprotective effect: Some studies suggest that vitamin C may mediate neuroprotection, helping to reduce the likelihood of developing neurodegenerative diseases such as Alzheimer's and Parkinson's by reducing nerve cell damage and supporting brain function.[156]

Caution:

A balanced diet is sometimes considered the best source of vitamin C. Foods rich in vitamin C include fruit such as **oranges, grapefruit, strawberries and kiwis**, as well as vegetables such as **peppers, broccoli, spinach, chives** and **sauerkraut** made from white cabbage with lactic acid bacteria. Vitamin C supplements can also be used if necessary to ensure that the body is adequately supplied with this important nutrient. However, high doses can also cause side effects such as the formation of **kidney stones** (due to an increase in **oxalic acid**) or the development of **hemolysis** (dissolution of red blood cells).[157]

Zinc

Zinc is an essential trace element that acts as an antioxidant in the body. It protects the cells from oxidative stress by neutralizing free radicals and thus reducing inflammation and damage to the cells. Zinc plays an important role in various physiological processes in the body, including the immune system, wound healing, glucose metabolism and cell growth.[158] **Red meat such as beef, lamb and pork as well as poultry such as chicken and turkey, but also fish and seafood** are rich in zinc. Legumes (beans, lentils, chickpeas, peas), nuts **(cashew nuts, almonds, walnuts)**, seeds **(pumpkin seeds and sesame seeds)** and wholegrain products (oatmeal, wholegrain bread and brown rice) are also good sources.

In addition, milk, cheese and yogurt contain zinc as well as calcium. Fruit is not a particularly good source of zinc, while some vegetables such as **spinach, kale, broccoli and asparagus** contain zinc, albeit in smaller quantities compared to other sources. Zinc has a variety of positive effects on the human body.

Some of the most important effects are listed below:

Immune function: zinc is an important supporter of the immune system. Zinc helps regulate immune cells and the production of antibodies, which helps fight infection and improve resistance to disease.[159]

Wound healing: Zinc is essential for normal wound healing. It supports the formation of new cells and tissue, promotes **collagen production** and accelerates the healing process of injuries and wounds.[160]

Antioxidant effect: Like vitamin C, zinc has a strong antioxidant effect by protecting cells from the damaging effects of free radicals. This can help to reduce inflammation and slow down the ageing process.[158]

Hormone regulation: Zinc is involved in the regulation of many hormones, including insulin, which controls blood sugar levels, and sex hormones such as testosterone and estrogen.[161]

Healthy skin: Zinc can help regulate sebum production and **alleviate** skin problems such as **acne.** Zinc plays an important role in maintaining skin health and integrity.[162]

Neurological function: Zinc is essential for normal neurological function. It plays a role in signal transmission between nerve cells, can stabilize cognitive function and mood, and **stops premature aging**.[163]

DNA synthesis: Zinc serves as a **cofactor for a variety of enzymes** involved in DNA synthesis (the replication of nucleic acid molecules that carry a cell's genetic information). Enzymes are proteins that **catalyze ("fuel") chemical reactions in the body.** Without a sufficient supply of zinc, these enzymes cannot function properly, which impairs DNA synthesis. The zinc involved in DNA synthesis is important for cell growth, repair and cell function.[164]

Caution:

Excessive zinc intake can cause gastrointestinal complaints such as nausea, vomiting and stomach cramps. In the long term, **copper and iron absorption** can be **impaired**, which can lead to further health problems, such as iron deficiency anemia.[165] A medical doctor should therefore be consulted before planning regular zinc intake.

Vitamin E

Vitamin E is a fat-soluble compound and a powerful antioxidant found in various foods. It plays an important role in health and has potential benefits for longevity. Aspects of how vitamin E could affect longevity are:

Antioxidant action: vitamin E is one of the most important fat-soluble antioxidants in the body. It neutralizes free radicals and reduces oxidative stress, which helps prevent cell damage and slows down the aging process.[166]

Cardioprotective effect: Vitamin E can help support cardiovascular health by reducing the formation of plaque in the arteries, improving blood flow and supporting the function of blood vessels. This may help to reduce the risk of heart disease (demonstrated in obese women) and increase life expectancy.[167]

Immune function: Vitamin E plays a role in supporting the immune system and helps to strengthen the body's defenses against infection and disease. Adequate intake of vitamin E can help promote health and support longevity.[168]

Anti-inflammatory effect: Vitamin E has anti-inflammatory properties that can help to counteract chronic inflammation in the body. Chronic inflammation can cause a variety of age-related diseases, so some studies suggest that anti-inflammatory nutrients like vitamin E can help promote health and support longevity.[169]

Skin health: Vitamin E is also important for skin health and can protect the skin **from damage caused by UV rays and environmental toxins**. Adequate intake of vitamin E can help improve skin texture and reduce the appearance of skin aging symptoms such as wrinkles and fine lines.[170]

Caution:

As with vitamin C, a balanced diet is considered the best source of vitamin E. Vitamin E-rich foods include **nuts, seeds, vegetable oils, avocados, green leafy vegetables and whole grains**. Despite the promising results of individual studies, the US Preventive Services Task Force (USPSTF) 2022 has advised against vitamin E as a dietary supplement for the prevention of cardiovascular disease and cancer because the study data on positive or negative effects is inconsistent.[171] The USPSTF is an independent panel of health professionals established by the US government to develop evidence-based recommendations for clinical prevention to improve the health of the US population.

Beta-carotene

Beta-carotene is a **precursor of vitamin A** and a carotenoid found in various orange and dark green vegetables and fruits. It is a powerful antioxidant and has potential health and longevity benefits. Here are some of the ways beta-carotene may affect longevity:

Antioxidant action: beta-carotene is a powerful antioxidant that neutralizes free radicals and reduces oxidative damage to cells and tissues. By reducing oxidative stress, beta-carotene may help slow the aging process and reduce the likelihood of age-related diseases.[172]

Cardioprotective effect: Despite its antioxidant effect, beta-carotene does not appear to support the health of the cardiovascular system, contrary to previous assumptions, but even appears to contribute to the development of cardiovascular disease.[173]

Skin health: Beta-carotene is often used as a dietary supplement to improve skin health, as it can help to protect the skin from harmful influences such as **UV rays and environmental toxins**. An adequate intake of beta-carotene can help improve skin texture and reduce the appearance of skin aging symptoms such as wrinkles and fine lines.[174]

Eye health: Beta-carotene is important for visual function and can help support eye health. It is converted to vitamin A, which plays an important role in visual cells and adaptation to different light conditions.[175]

Caution:

Foods rich in beta-carotene include carrots, sweet potatoes, squash, spinach, mangoes and apricots. However, taking beta-carotene as a dietary supplement should also be viewed critically. A large study called the **Beta-Carotene and Retinol Efficacy Trial (CARET)** found that **smokers taking beta-carotene and vitamin A supplements** had an **increased risk of lung cancer**, so this study was stopped early when it was found that taking the supplements increased the risk of lung cancer.[176] As with vitamin E, the US Preventive Services Task Force (USPSTF) 2022 also advised against taking a beta-carotene supplement to prevent cardiovascular disease and cancer, especially since in case of doubt these diseases could even be promoted.[169] Historically, **polar explorers** in the Arctic had often consumed **vitamin A-rich polar bear liver** to cover their vitamin C requirements, causing an overdose of vitamin A, which led to **hair loss and tooth loss**, among other things.

Lutein

Lutein is also an antioxidant and belongs to the group of carotenoids, which are natural pigments. Lutein is found in **egg yolks** and in many fruits and vegetables, especially in green leafy vegetables such as spinach, kale, chard and arugula, as well as in **orange** (with carotenoid **beta-carotene**) and **yellow** (with carotenoid **zeaxanthin**) foods such as **carrots** and **corn**.

Antioxidant effect: Lutein helps to protect the body from the harmful effects of free radicals by neutralizing them. Free radicals are unstable molecules that can cause cell damage and have been linked to various health problems, including inflammation, premature ageing and the development of chronic diseases. For example, lutein has been shown to inhibit the **cell growth of breast cancer**.[177]

Eye health: Lutein is particularly well known for its role in protecting eye health. It accumulates in the macula of the eye, an area of the retina responsible for central visual acuity. There, lutein serves as a **filter for harmful blue-violet light** and protects the sensitive cells from oxidative stress, which helps **prevent age-related eye diseases such as macular degeneration**.[175]

Caution:

As with other antioxidants, it is recommended to take lutein preferably in its natural form, for example through eggs, rather than through food supplements, because eggs have **better bioavailability**, i.e. the amount of the active ingredient lutein is better absorbed and processed in the body for its biological effect.[73] Similar to the CARET study with beta-carotene and vitamin A supplements, the **"VITamins And Lifestyle (VITAL) Cohort Study"** showed that the long-term intake of lutein as a dietary supplement leads to **an increased risk of lung cancer** in smokers.[178]

Lycopene

Lycopene is a natural pigment and carotenoid found in various plants, mainly in **tomatoes**, but also in other red fruits such as **watermelons**, pink **grapefruits**, **red peppers** and **papayas**. It is known for its antioxidant properties and has potential health benefits. Some of the biological effects of lycopene are:

Antioxidant effect: Lycopene is a powerful antioxidant that helps to neutralize cell-damaging free radicals. Through this antioxidant effect, lycopene can help to reduce cell damage and thus prevent chronic diseases such as cardiovascular disease and certain types of cancer.[179]

Anti-cancer effect: Some studies suggest that lycopene has a positive effect against certain types of cancer, particularly prostate, lung and stomach cancer. It is thought that its antioxidant properties, as well as its ability to modulate cell growth and inflammation, may help to reduce the risk of cancer.[179]

Cardioprotective effect: Lycopene may also be beneficial for cardiovascular disease by supporting blood vessel health and helping to regulate blood pressure. It is thought that its antioxidant properties may help prevent the development of heart disease.[180]

Anti-inflammatory effect: Lycopene also has anti-inflammatory properties. Chronic inflammation is considered to be the underlying cause of many diseases, including metabolic diseases such as type 2 diabetes mellitus.[181]

Caution:

Once again, it is generally better to give preference to the natural form rather than the preparation. As cooking and processing tomatoes facilitates the release and absorption of lycopene from the cells, the intake of lycopene from cooked or processed tomato products can be higher than from raw tomatoes. As with lutein, the **"VITamins And Lifestyle (VITAL) Cohort Study"** also revealed with lycopene that there is an **increased risk of lung cancer** in smokers taking this dietary supplement in the long term.[178]

Selenium

Selenium is an essential trace element that is vital for the body. It is found in many foods such as **Brazil nuts, fish, seafood, whole grain products and meat** and plays an important role in various physiological processes.

Some important functions of selenium are:

Antioxidant function: selenium acts as a **cofactor for various enzymes**, particularly glutathione peroxidases, which help to neutralize free radicals in the body.[182] In this way, selenium helps to reduce cell damage from oxidative stress and maintain cellular health and improve life expectancy.[183]

Thyroid function: Selenium is important for the normal function of the thyroid gland. It plays a role in the **conversion of thyroid hormones (T4) into their active form (T3)** and helps balance thyroid hormone levels in the body.[184]

Cardiovascular disease: A meta-analysis found that low selenium levels lead to an increase in cardiovascular disease and overall mortality, and conversely higher levels can improve prognosis.[185]

Immune function: Selenium is important in the regulation of the immune system and the immune response. It supports the function of immune cells and helps to maintain the immune defense against infections and diseases.[186]

Anti-inflammatory effect: Selenium has anti-inflammatory properties and can help to reduce inflammation in the body. This can be particularly beneficial for chronic inflammatory conditions such as arthritis or inflammatory bowel disease.[187]

Anti-cancer effects: Some studies suggest that adequate selenium intake may be associated with a reduced risk of certain cancers, particularly cancers such as prostate, lung and colorectal cancer. However, the exact mechanisms by which selenium might prevent cancer are not yet fully understood.[188,189]

Caution:

Selenium poisoning, **selenosis**, occurs when the amount of selenium ingested exceeds the tolerable upper intake level ($\geq$200 µg per day); in severe cases, selenium poisoning can lead to life-threatening complications such as liver failure or kidney failure.[190]

Flavonoids

Flavonoids are a large class of antioxidants found in a variety of foods, including **berries** (blueberries, strawberries, raspberries), **citrus fruits, apples, onions, tea and dark chocolate**. Flavonoids belong to the superordinate group of polyphenols. Eating foods rich in flavonoids can help ensure an adequate intake of these important nutrients without the need to take additional supplements to promote health and support longevity. The flavonoids listed here provide only a broad overview of some of the most common antioxidants and the foods in which they are mainly found.

Quercetin

Quercetin is an antioxidant and anti-inflammatory flavonoid. It is found in many fruits and vegetables, such as apples, onions, garlic, berries, grapes, cabbage and kale. It has a variety of proven effects:

Cardioprotective effect: Quercetin may help improve cardiovascular health by lowering blood cholesterol levels, improving blood vessel function and preventing the formation of blood clots.[194,195]

Anticancer effect: There is evidence that quercetin may have anticancer properties by inhibiting the growth of cancer cells, preventing the formation of tumors and suppressing the spread of cancer cells in the body.[196]

Neuroprotective effects: Quercetin shows potential in supporting brain and nervous system health by protecting against neurodegenerative diseases such as Alzheimer's and Parkinson's.[194,197]

Metabolic diseases: Quercetin also appears to have treatment approaches in type 2 diabetes mellitus, which is particularly important for the prognosis of cardiovascular diseases.[197]

Caution:

Three problems of quercetin for use as a dietary supplement should be mentioned: 1) a **"low solubility"**, 2) the **"weak bioavailability"**, i.e. the amount of the active ingredient ingested and its biological effect then present turn out to be weak, and 3) it can **inhibit blood clotting** and increase the effect of blood-thinning drugs such as warfarin or phenprocoumon.[198,199] People who are taking **blood-thinning medication** or have other chronic health conditions should consult a medical doctor before taking quercetin supplements. Thus, according to the current state of science, expectations of quercetin as a strong candidate for longevity should be tempered.

Kaempferol

Kaempferol is a flavonoid found in many plants, including **spinach, kale, broccoli, tomatoes, arugula, tea** and certain fruits such as **apples and strawberries**. It has a number of biological effects, including:

Antioxidant effect: kaempferol is an antioxidant that can protect cells from oxidative stress by neutralizing free radicals.[200] This can help slow down the aging process and reduce the likelihood of developing various diseases such as heart disease, cancer and neurodegenerative diseases (Alzheimer's or Parkinson's).

Anti-inflammatory effect: Kaempferol can reduce inflammation in the body by inhibiting the production of pro-inflammatory molecules and activating anti-inflammatory signaling pathways.[201] This may help to reduce inflammation associated with various diseases such as arthritis, diabetes mellitus and heart disease.

Anti-cancer effects: Kaempferol-rich foods may have anti-cancer properties by inhibiting the growth of cancer cells, preventing the formation of tumors and suppressing the spread of cancer cells in the body. Kaempferol may also promote apoptosis (programmed cell death) of cancer cells.[202] Specifically, it may reduce the risk of developing cancers such as **skin, liver and colon cancer**.[203]

Cardioprotective effect: Studies have shown that kaempferol may help improve cardiovascular health by lowering cholesterol levels, regulating blood pressure, inhibiting blood clotting and improving blood vessel function.[195] This may help reduce the risk of heart disease and stroke.

Neuroprotective effect: Kaempferol may help to protect the health of the brain and nervous system by protecting against neurodegenerative diseases such as Alzheimer's and Parkinson's disease. It may also improve brain function and reduce the formation of amyloid-β plaques, which are associated with Alzheimer's disease.[204]

Caution:

As already mentioned for quercetin, kaempferol as a dietary supplement also has the problem of **low bioavailability**, i.e. the amount of the active ingredient absorbed and its biological effect are weak because kaempferol is absorbed to a lesser extent due to its "larger particle size and poor water solubility".[205]

Luteolin

Luteolin is a flavonoid with anti-inflammatory and anti-cancer properties, which was already known and used in **Traditional Chinese Medicine (TCM)**.[206] Luteolin is found in foods such as **peppers, celery, carrots, artichokes, rosemary and thyme**.

Antioxidant effect: Luteolin is an antioxidant and protects cells from oxidative stress. As a result, it develops anti-inflammatory, cardiovascular-protective, anti-cancer and nerve cell-protective properties.[207]

Anti-inflammatory effect: Luteolin can reduce inflammation in the body by inhibiting the production of pro-inflammatory molecules and activating anti-inflammatory signaling pathways.[201]

Anti-cancer effect: Luteolin has been shown to have anti-cancer properties in the following types of cancer: **Brain tumor** (glioblastoma)**, lung, breast, prostate, colon and pancreatic cancer**.[208] Furthermore, luteolin can **suppress** the spread of **metastases**.[209]

Neuroprotective effect: Luteolin may improve brain function, protect against Parkinson's disease and reduce the formation of amyloid-β plaques, which are associated with Alzheimer's disease.[210]

Caution:

In principle, luteolin is thought to have beneficial properties, including its neuroprotective role. However, in one study, luteolin was observed to inhibit neuronal differentiation of embryonic stem cells, contrary to expectations.[211] Therefore, more research is needed to make a definitive statement about its safe use.

Catechins

Catechins are flavonoids found in foods such as **green tea, red wine, dark chocolate, apples and berries**. They have strong antioxidant properties and can help promote health and support longevity.

Antioxidant effect: One of the outstanding properties of catechins is their ability to act as antioxidants. As powerful antioxidants, catechins scavenge free radicals.[212] Free radicals are non-stable chemical compounds that are produced by metabolic processes in the body and can damage cells, leading to various diseases and premature ageing.

Anti-inflammatory effect: Inflammation in the body is an underlying factor in many chronic diseases. Catechins have anti-inflammatory properties that can help reduce the development and impact of infections.[213] This can reduce the likelihood of inflammation-related diseases such as arthritis and certain cancers.[213]

Cardioprotective effect: Numerous studies have shown that the consumption of catechins, for example through the consumption of **dark chocolate**, can reduce the risk of cardiovascular disease.[214,215]

The cocoa contained in chocolate can lower blood pressure, relax blood vessels and improve blood flow, leading to overall healthier heart function.[216] However, the recently published results of the **COSMOS study** showed that **despite the daily administration** of **500 mg of cocoa flavonoids** (80 mg of which is epicatechin), the **risk of cardiovascular disease cannot be reduced**.[217,218]

Metabolic stimulating effect: Some studies suggest that catechins can boost the metabolism and increase fat burning. This may help to control body weight and reduce the **risk of obesity** and related diseases.[216]

Anticancer effects: Catechins may have anticancer properties by inhibiting tumor formation, growth and spread.[215] The following types of cancer may be prevented by green tea-derived catechins: **Lung, breast, esophageal, stomach, liver and prostate cancers.**[212] However, the **COSMOS study** conducted in relation to the administration of cocoa flavoinoids showed **no reduction in the risk of cancer.**[218]

Neuroprotective effect: Catechins also show neuroprotective properties, i.e. nerve cell-protective effects, by improving memory performance and reducing the risk of neurodegenerative diseases such as Alzheimer's and Parkinson's.[219] A **subgroup analysis of the COSMOS study** showed that older people benefit from the daily intake of cocoa flavonoids by **increasing their memory performance.**[220]

Caution:

As with all dietary supplements and bioactive compounds, it is important to consider potential drug interactions in liver metabolism. Some studies have indicated that higher concentrations of catechins from green tea may affect the effects of certain medications, particularly those that affect blood pressure or blood clotting.[221] Therefore, people who regularly take medication should monitor their catechin consumption and consult with their medical doctor.

Anthocyanins

Anthocyanins are flavonoids that give foods their red, purple or blue color. They are found in foods such as **berries** (blueberries, blackberries, blackcurrants, blueberries, raspberries, strawberries), **cherries,**

red grapes, beet, red cabbage and eggplants. Anthocyanins have strong antioxidant properties and are associated with various health benefits, including supporting **cardiovascular health and improving memory**. Specifically, anthocyanins have the following properties:

Antioxidant activity: anthocyanins are powerful antioxidants that reduce cell damage caused by free radicals. These antioxidant properties can reduce the risk of chronic diseases such as vascular diseases, cancer and nerve diseases.[222]

Anti-inflammatory effect: Anthocyanins can reduce inflammation in the body by inhibiting certain pro-inflammatory enzymes. This can help to alleviate inflammatory symptoms and reduce the risk of inflammation-related diseases such as inflammatory bowel disease (Crohn's disease or ulcerative colitis).[223]

Cardioprotective effect: Studies have shown that regular consumption of anthocyanin-rich foods such as blueberries can reduce the risk of cardiovascular disease by lowering **cholesterol levels**, lowering blood pressure and improving blood vessel function.[224]

Neuroprotective effects: Some research suggests that anthocyanins may help to improve memory and reduce the risk of neurodegenerative diseases such as Alzheimer's and dementia.[225] They may also help to improve mood and reduce the risk of depression.

Eye health: Some studies suggest that anthocyanins may help protect eye health by protecting against age-related eye diseases such as **macular degeneration and cataracts** (clouding of the lens).[226]

Metabolic diseases: Anthocyanins appear to be effective against the development of non-alcoholic fatty liver disease.[222] **Non-alcoholic fatty liver disease** is a common condition caused by the accumulation of fat in the liver in individuals who consume little or no alcohol. This disease is often associated with **obesity, type 2 diabetes mellitus, insulin resistance** and other metabolic disorders. Anthocyanins thus appear to help regulate blood sugar levels and improve insulin sensitivity, which reduces the **risk of diabetes mellitus** and its complications (cardiovascular, nerve, kidney and retinal eye diseases).

Caution:

Anthocyanins can influence the effect of various medications through the same enzymatic degradation pathways of the liver. Interactions have been described with drugs such as **antihypertensives, blood thinners, tranquillizers, immunosuppressants** (immune system suppressing drugs that patients with transplant organs need) and **antiepileptics** (drugs for the prevention and treatment of epileptic seizures).[227] People taking such drugs should therefore monitor their anthocyanin intake and consult their medical doctor.

Polyphenols

Polyphenols are a superordinate group of antioxidants found in many plant foods such as **berries** (blueberries, raspberries, strawberries, blackberries), **red grapes, apples, pears, citrus fruits** (oranges, grapefruits, lemons), **green and black tea, nuts** (walnuts, almonds, hazelnuts), **green leafy vegetables** such as spinach and kale, and other vegetables such as **artichokes, broccoli and onions.**

In addition to the subgroup already mentioned above, the flavonoids, the following representatives of the polyphenols are worth mentioning for their potential health benefits with possible slowing of the ageing process.

Tannins

Tannins (from the French word for "tanning") play an important role as vegetable tanning agents in leather production.[228] The process of tanning transforms animal hide into leather by chemically stabilizing it to make it durable, flexible and resistant.

In medicine, tannins have various applications and are intensively studied due to their diverse biological activities. Tannins are found in a variety of plant foods, including tea leaves, especially **black and green tea, in red wine** from the skins and seeds of grapes that enter the wine during the fermentation process, in **nuts** (walnuts, almonds, hazelnuts, pecans), in legumes **(beans, lentils, chickpeas)**, in **berries** (blueberries, raspberries, cranberries), in **persimmons, pomegranates, apples, pears** and in spices **(cloves, cinnamon, thyme)**.[228]

In terms of health, tannins are interesting due to their antioxidant properties and their ability to reduce inflammation, including protection against heart disease and cancer. The following effects have been described:

Antioxidant effect: Some tannins have antioxidant properties that help to trap free radicals that can cause cell damage. This can help to reduce inflammation and reduce the risk of cancer and cardiovascular disease.[229]

Anti-inflammatory effects: Some tannins have anti-inflammatory properties that can help reduce inflammation in the body. For example, strong antibacterial activity has been found against the very common pathogens Escherichia coli and Staphylococcus aureus.[230]

Blood pressure-lowering effect: Some studies suggest that tannins, especially those from tea, can have a blood pressure-lowering effect. This may help to regulate blood pressure and reduce the risk of cardiovascular disease.[231]

Lipid-modifying effect: Some studies suggest that tannins, especially those from red wine and tea, are lipid-modifying, i.e. have a beneficial effect on blood cholesterol levels, as has been described with **persimmon fruit**, for example.[232]

Cancer-inhibiting effect: Some studies have shown that tannins could inhibit the growth and spread of tumors. This could suggest that tannins could potentially play a role in slowing tumor progression. Some research suggests that tannins could trigger apoptosis (programmed cell death) in cancer cells, which helps to eliminate abnormal cells, which is being investigated as a therapeutic approach for **lung cancer**, for example.[233]

Incidentally, the **Californian red** wood trees, which grow up to 90 meters high, have a diameter of up to 7 meters and live up to **3000 years**, also contain tannins. **Tannins are found in the bark, needles** and other parts of redwood trees. These compounds serve to protect the plant from **predators, diseases and UV rays**.[234] Tannins are also responsible for the characteristic reddish color of many sequoia barks.

Caution:

However, consumed in large quantities, tannins can also have negative effects. This is why tannins are sometimes seen as **antinutrients**, which are natural molecules that can impair the absorption of nutrients in the body. Antinutrients are not necessarily harmful, but can reduce the bioavailability of nutrients or cause digestive problems. Excessive consumption of tannins can cause gastrointestinal discomfort such as stomach cramps, nausea and diarrhea.[235] In addition, **foods containing tannins** can **bind iron** and interfere with the absorption of iron in the intestines, especially when consumed at the same time as **iron-rich foods such as meat, kidney beans or iron supplements**.[236]

Lignans

The word "lignan" is derived from the Latin "lignum" for "wood". The discovery of lignans as components of plants goes back to research on lignin, another group of plant compounds also found in wood and plant cell walls. Scientists began to study the different components of plant materials in more detail and discovered that lignans have a variety of structures and biological activities. Lignans are found in a variety of plant foods. The main sources of lignans are **flax seeds and pumpkin seeds**, but also **sesame seeds, strawberries, olives and nuts**.

The potential health benefits of lignans include:

Antioxidant effect: Lignans can act as antioxidants and help fight cell damage caused by free radicals.[237]

Anti-inflammatory effect: Some studies suggest that lignans may have anti-inflammatory properties that reduce inflammation in the body.[237]

Anticancer effect: Lignans may have a hormonal effect and influence the activity of estrogen in the body. This can potentially have positive effects on women's health, particularly in terms of hormone balance and the risk of hormone-dependent diseases such as **breast cancer.**[238]

Cardioprotective effect: Some studies suggest that lignans may help reduce the likelihood of cardiovascular disease by lowering cholesterol levels and supporting blood vessel health.[239]

Gut health: Lignans may also play a role in promoting gut health by encouraging the growth of healthy gut bacteria and reducing inflammation in the digestive tract.[240]

Caution:

While consumption of lignans from natural foods is generally safe, excessive consumption of lignan supplements or isolated lignans may have undesirable side effects. Lignans are metabolized by the liver and can weaken the effect of other medications such as the pain and fever medication paracetamol.[241]

Ellagic acid

Ellagic acid is a polyphenolic compound found in foods such as **berries** (raspberries, blackberries, strawberries)**, pomegranates, walnuts and grapes**. It is known for its antioxidant and anti-inflammatory properties and is associated with various health benefits:

Antioxidant effect: Ellagic acid acts as a powerful antioxidant, helping to protect cells from oxidative stress as a **free radical scavenger**. This can help to slow down the ageing process and reduce the risk of cancer, vascular disease and liver disease.[242]

Anti-inflammatory effect: Ellagic acid can fight infections in the body and protect the immune system. Ellagic acid shows good antibacterial efficacy against Escherichia coli (coliform bacteria) and good antifungal efficacy against the fungus Candida auris.[243,244]

Anti-cancer effect: There is evidence that ellagic acid has anti-cancer properties. It can inhibit the growth of cancer cells, prevent the formation of tumors and suppress the spread of cancer cells in the body. Ellagic acid can also promote apoptosis (programmed cell death) of cancer cells and inhibit the formation of new blood vessels necessary for tumor growth. There are proven anti-cancer effects in **liver and colon cancer**, for example.[242,243]

Cardioprotective effect: Studies have shown that ellagic acid can help improve cardiovascular health by lowering cholesterol levels, boosting metabolism and promoting fat burning.[245]

Neuroprotective effect: Ellagic acid may also mitigate the damage that has occurred in nerve diseases such as Alzheimer's, Parkinson's and stroke.[246]

Caution:

While moderate intake of ellagic acid is generally safe and may even provide health benefits, there is no specific upper limit for intake. However, excessive intake could lead to gastrointestinal discomfort. As already mentioned for both quercetin and kaempferol, ellagic acid as a dietary supplement also has a **low bioavailability**, i.e. the amount of the active ingredient ingested and its biological effect are weak, whereby this is mainly due to "poor absorption capacity and rapid body excretion" in the case of ellagic acid compared to quercetin and kaempferol.[205]

Caffeic acid

Caffeic acid is a polyphenol that in nature is an antimicrobial, anti-inflammatory and antioxidant component of **honey bee resin** (propolis) to protect the hive from disease.[247] Otherwise, caffeic acid is found in **coffee beans, artichokes, potatoes, apples** and some herbs.

Caffeic acid has important biological effects such as:

Antioxidant effect: Caffeic acid is a powerful antioxidant and, as a radical scavenger, protects cells from oxidative stress.[248] Thus, alongside other antioxidants, caffeic acid can also contribute to health and longevity.

Anti-inflammatory effect: Caffeic acid can reduce various inflammations in the body. The anti-inflammatory effect has been proven for various classes of pathogens such as microbes, bacteria, fungi and viruses.[249]

Anti-cancer effect: Explained by its antioxidant properties, caffeic acid can have an anti-cancer effect on the following types of cancer: **liver, skin, lung, oral cavity and cervical cancer.**[250]

Cardioprotective effect: Studies have shown that caffeic acid helps to achieve a balanced cholesterol level and counteract the **metabolic syndrome** (combination of obesity, high blood pressure, sugar and fat metabolism disorders).[251,252] This reduces the risk of cardiovascular diseases and strokes.

Neuroprotective effect: by improving glucose utilization, caffeic acid can help protect the brain and nervous system to counteract the development of diseases such as Alzheimer's and Parkinson's.[253]

Caution:

Caffeic acid can stimulate the **stomach's G-cells** (gastrin-producing cells).[247] The G-cells, which are located in the stomach lining, produce the hormone gastrin, which in turn promotes the production and secretion of stomach acid. In addition to caffeic acid, **alcohol or caffeine** contained in coffee, for example, can also **stimulate gastric acid production** via the G cells. Therefore, the consumption of caffeinated drinks such as coffee can lead to an excessive production of stomach acid in some people, causing stomach complaints such as **heartburn** (gastroesophageal reflux).

Curcumin

Curcumin is a polyphenol found in **turmeric**, a spice used in **Indian cuisine**. Mustard also contains small amounts of curcumin, which helps give it its yellow color. Curcumin is associated with various health benefits and can potentially support longevity. The following biological properties are attributed to curcumin:

Antioxidant action: curcumin acts as an antioxidant that neutralizes free radicals and reduces cell damage caused by oxidative stress. By combating oxidative stress, curcumin contributes to a "healthy ageing process" and "human longevity".[254]

Anti-inflammatory effects: Curcumin is known for its powerful anti-inflammatory properties.[255] Chronic inflammation in the body is associated with a variety of age-related diseases, including heart disease, diabetes, cancer and neurodegenerative diseases. By reducing inflammation, curcumin can help reduce the risk of these diseases and extend lifespan.

Anti-cancer effect: Curcumin can have an anti-cancer effect by means of **epigenetic mechanisms**, i.e. biological processes that influence gene expression and thus the activity of genes without changing the underlying DNA sequence.[256] Epigenetic mechanisms involve controlling whether genes are switched on or off by **changing** the accessible **structure of the DNA and its interaction with proteins**.

Cardioprotective effect: Curcumin helps protect cardiovascular health by interacting with the enzyme **AMP-activated protein kinase (AMPK)** via the mTOR signaling pathway (see chapter "Nutritional medicine in transition"; subchapter "mTOR signaling pathway

- key to longevity").[257] This appears to help reduce the risk of heart disease and increase life expectancy.

Neuroprotective effect: Some studies suggest curcumin may counteract the development of neurological diseases such as Alzheimer's and Parkinson's by reducing neuronal cell damage and supporting brain function, although this would require curcumin to be administered in the form of nanoparticles in order to pass through the blood-brain barrier.[258] The **blood-brain barrier** is a physiological barrier between the bloodstream and the brain and spinal cord to protect the brain from potentially harmful substances present in the bloodstream. However, many molecules, including large proteins and certain drugs, are actively excluded from the barrier or require special transport mechanisms to pass through.

Caution:

Very high doses of curcumin may be used in supplements, far in excess of the amount normally ingested through the consumption of turmeric in food. In rare cases, very high doses of curcumin can cause gastrointestinal symptoms such as nausea, diarrhea or stomach discomfort in sensitive individuals. There are also some concerns about the interaction of curcumin with certain medications. Curcumin, as previously described with quercetin, may inhibit blood clotting and enhance the effects of **blood-thinning medication** such as warfarin or phenprocoumon.[199] Individuals who are taking blood-thinning medication or have other chronic health conditions should consult a physician before taking curcumin supplements. It should also be noted that most studies on curcumin to date have been conducted on cells and animals, and further research on humans is needed to confirm its potential longevity benefits. Nevertheless, a growing

number of studies suggest that curcumin may be a promising molecule to help promote health and extend lifespan.

Resveratrol

Resveratrol is a polyphenolic compound found in **red grapes, red
wine, dark chocolate and peanuts** and has been associated with
various health benefits. It has received a lot of attention in recent
years as a potential agent for promoting longevity and preventing
age-related diseases. Here are some potential ways resveratrol could
affect longevity:

Antioxidant properties: As an antioxidant, resveratrol provides
protection to cells from free radical damage caused by oxidative processes in the body. By neutralizing free radicals, resveratrol can help
prevent diseases caused by oxidative stress, such as heart disease,
cancer and premature aging.[259]

Anti-inflammatory effect: Resveratrol has anti-inflammatory properties to prevent chronic inflammation in the body. This could stop
the premature ageing process and prevent the development of age-
related diseases.[257]

Anti-cancer effect: Medical research is optimistic about resveratrol
as an anti-cancer agent, as it can reduce the incidence of cancer in a
variety of cancers, namely in **"breast, cervix, uterus, blood, kidney,
liver, eye, gallbladder, thyroid, esophagus, prostate, brain, lung,
skin, stomach, colon, head and neck and bone"**.[260]

Cardioprotective effect: Resveratrol is said to have a protective effect on the heart and blood vessels, particularly due to its lipid-modifying properties, i.e. its **cholesterol-lowering effect**. Resveratrol is also often cited as the responsible actor in connection with the "French paradox" (see above chapter "Nutritional medicine in transition"; subchapter "Mediterranean diet").[83] However, more recent meta-analyses dampen the initial euphoria about the supposed therapeutic effects of resveratrol on the cardiovascular system, as this has not yet been clearly proven in the human organism.[261]

Neuroprotective effect: There are therapeutic starting points for neurodegenerative diseases such as Alzheimer's, although further research is clearly needed to substantiate these aspects.[262]

Caution:

The effect of resveratrol on longevity and health is not yet fully understood, so further research is needed to confirm its long-term effects. In addition, the effects of resveratrol may depend on individual factors such as dosage, bioavailability and genetic differences.

Resveratrol has limited bioavailability because it is rapidly metabolized and has low oral absorption.[263] Much of the resveratrol is broken down in the intestine and does not enter the bloodstream. The **combination of resveratrol with** other compounds such as **piperine** (a component of black pepper), **quercetin or fatty acids** can **improve bioavailability** by increasing absorption or slowing down degradation.[264] **Despite its limited bioavailability**, there is evidence that **resveratrol, as a** non-specific **sirtuin activator, can promote longevity via the mTOR signaling pathway** (see chapter "Nutritional medicine in transition"; subchapter "mTOR signaling pathway - key to longevity").[265]

Individuals interested in using resveratrol should discuss this with a physician to ensure that it is appropriate for their individual needs and health conditions. Resveratrol is present in natural foods such as **red grapes, peanuts and dark chocolate,** and a balanced diet rich in these foods can be a good source of resveratrol.

Saponins

Saponins are a large group of plant substances with a wide range of biological activities. Their name is derived from the Latin ("soap") because of their foamy structure, which exhibits soap-like properties on contact with water. Saponins are amphophilic in their chemical properties, i.e. they can be both **hydrophilic** (water-loving) and **lipophilic** (fat-loving), which makes them interesting for a variety of applications in medicine, the food industry and agriculture.[266]

In the plant world, saponins serve as a defense mechanism against pests and diseases. The pungent taste and odor properties of some saponins make them unattractive to insects and other herbivores and protect the plant from them. In addition, saponins can inhibit the **growth of pathogenic microorganisms** and thus help to maintain plant health.

In addition to their role as defense substances in plants, saponins also have a wide range of health benefits for humans. In traditional medicine (especially in **Traditional Chinese Medicine**), they have been used for centuries to treat various ailments. Some saponins have anti-inflammatory, antioxidant and immunostimulant properties that can help relieve inflammation, strengthen the immune system and protect against oxidative stress.[266] In addition, some saponins also show potential antitumor activities and are being investigated as promising candidates for cancer therapy.

Another important aspect of saponins is their importance in the food industry. Some saponins, such as the soy saponins found in soybeans, are used in the production of emulsifiers and foaming agents. They help to stabilize foods and improve their shelf life. They are also in demand as **natural bitter substances and foaming agents** in beverages such as **beer and sparkling wine**. The following is a selection of plants that contain saponins and their uses.

Soybeans

Soybeans belong to the legume family. Soybeans and soy products such as **tofu and soy milk** contain saponins known as soy saponins. The word "soy" is originally Japanese and is derived from the word 醤油 Shōyu, which means "soybean oil or sauce".[267] Soy is known to have various health benefits:

Protein source: soybeans are rich in fiber and protein, which can help increase satiety and control appetite. This can help people control their weight or lose weight by reducing overeating and **snacking** (eating at uncontrolled intervals between planned main meals). Soy contains **all 9 essential amino acids** and can help meet protein needs, especially for people on a vegetarian or vegan diet.[268]

Anti-cancer effect: The anti-cancer effect is attributed to the isoflavones in soy, which have antioxidant and anti-inflammatory properties. Some studies suggest that regular consumption of soy products may reduce the risk of certain cancers such as **stomach, ovarian,**

breast, colon, uterine and lung cancer and the associated mortality.[269] Soybeans appear to be particularly helpful in preventing breast cancer.[270] In cancer patients, soybeans appear to sensitize cancer cells to chemotherapy and/or radiation and protect healthy cells from the treatments.[271]

Cardioprotective effect: Soy contains unsaturated fatty acids and is free of saturated fats and cholesterol. Regular consumption of soy products can help to lower cholesterol levels and reduce the risk of heart disease.[272]

In addition, soy proteins, such as the curcumin mentioned above, interact with the enzyme **AMP-activated protein kinase (AMPK)**, which leads to improved glucose regulation and insulin sensitivity (responsiveness of cells to insulin) and thus reduces the risk of type 2 diabetes mellitus and heart disease.[273] In people without pre-existing heart disease, soy consumption ≥4 days per week can significantly reduce mortality.[274]

Osteoporosis prevention: Soy products can help improve bone health as they are rich in calcium and vitamin D, both of which are important for strong bones.[275]

Menopause: Isoflavones in soybeans can help menopausal women as they have some similarity to estrogen and so can relieve some of the symptoms, such as hot flashes and vaginal dryness.[276]

Caution:

A moderate intake of soybeans is generally safe and may provide health benefits, especially for heart health. However, excessive intake could cause digestive problems and trigger allergic reactions in some people who are allergic to soy.[277]

Quinoa

Quinoa is a grain from **the Andean region** that also contains saponins in its outer husk.[278] At around 40 mg/g dry weight, **saponins in quinoa have a sweet taste, but at higher concentrations they tend to have a bitter taste,** so the outer husk of quinoa should be thoroughly rinsed or removed before consumption.[279]

Quinoa is naturally **gluten-free**, making it an important **alternative for people with coeliac disease** or **gluten intolerance**.[280] In addition to saponins, quinoa contains a variety of micronutrients, including iron, magnesium, potassium, zinc, copper and manganese. These minerals are important for various bodily functions, including supporting the immune system.

Source of protein: Quinoa is an excellent plant-based source of protein and, like soybeans, contains **all 9 essential amino acids**.[279] This makes it an essential source of protein for vegetarians and vegans. Due to its high fiber and protein content, quinoa can help promote a feeling of satiety and support weight loss.

Antioxidant effect: Quinoa contains a variety of antioxidant molecules, including flavonoids, polyphenols and vitamin E.[281] These compounds can help fight cell damage caused by free radicals and reduce the risk of diseases such as cancer, cardiovascular disease and premature ageing.

Anti-inflammatory effect: Quinoa has proven anti-inflammatory properties with the help of mono-desmosidic (linked to a single sugar chain) saponins, which could help with a variety of chronic diseases.[279]

Anticancer effect: Animal experiments have shown that quinoa appears to alleviate symptoms of **colon/rectal cancer** and restore the gut microbiome (natural gut flora).[282]

Cardioprotective effect: Quinoa's antioxidant properties have a potential positive effect on heart health and may help reduce cardiovascular disease risk markers, although the exact therapeutic mechanisms require further research.[278]

Caution:

Although rare, some individuals may be allergic to quinoa.[283] Allergic reactions to quinoa may include skin rashes, itching, facial swelling, or difficulty breathing.[284] Individuals with known food allergies should be cautious and avoid quinoa if necessary.

Amaranth

The name amaranth Αμάραντος comes from the Greek and means "imperishable". Amaranth, whose origins date back to ancient civilizations in Central and South America, was a fundamental food source for pre-Columbian peoples such as the **Aztecs, Mayas and Incas.**[285] It was revered as a sacred plant and used in religious ceremonies. Its ability to grow in adverse conditions and produce abundant harvests made it a symbol of immortality and abundance. Due to the Spanish conquistadors ("conquistadors"), the cultivation of amaranth declined significantly as the Spanish recognized its cultural significance in the Americas and associated it with pagan rituals.[286] Nevertheless, amaranth survived as a traditional crop in some regions and is now experiencing a renaissance in the modern diet.

Amaranth is rich in protein, fiber, iron, magnesium, calcium and has a lower proportion of saponins compared to quinoa, but is also **gluten-free**, making it an option **for people with celiac disease or gluten intolerance**.[280,287]

Antioxidant effect: Amaranth contains antioxidants such as vitamin E, which can help fight cell damage caused by free radicals and thus reduce the likelihood of cancer and premature ageing.[287]

Anti-inflammatory effect: Some studies suggest that amaranth may have anti-inflammatory properties that could help in the prevention and treatment of inflammatory diseases.[280]

Cardioprotective effect: The fiber, calcium, potassium and other nutrients in amaranth may help lower cholesterol levels and thus reduce the **risk of heart disease**.[288] The cardiovascular risk profile may also be lowered because fibre in amaranth helps to **stabilize blood sugar levels**, which may be particularly beneficial for people with diabetes mellitus.[288] Amaranth may also **lower blood pressure** by inhibiting the hormone renin in the **renin-angiotensin-aldosterone system**.[289]

Caution:

Amaranth contains oxalic acid, which, when consumed in large quantities, can promote the formation of kidney stones.[290] People who are susceptible to **kidney stones** or already suffer from them should possibly limit their consumption of amaranth in combination with other **foods containing oxalic acid** (e.g. **spinach, rhubarb, soybeans, beet, cocoa or dark chocolate**) and consult their medical doctor.

Ginseng

Ginseng, the name is derived from the Chinese 人参 rénshēn "human-like root", the name "Panax ginseng" used in botany goes back to the ancient Greek word Πανάκεια "panacea".[291] Ginseng has been used as a medicinal plant in **Traditional Chinese Medicine (TCM)** for over 5,000 years.[292] Ginseng contains **saponins called ginsenosides**, which are valued for improving physical and mental performance, reducing stress and promoting general well-being.[292]

The following biological effects of ginseng have been scientifically proven:

Antioxidant effect: One of the outstanding biological effects of ginseng is its antioxidant activity. Ginseng contains a variety of bioactive compounds, including ginsenosides, flavonoids and polysaccharides, which can increase the activity of antioxidant enzymes and help reduce oxidative stress.[291]

Stress-reducing effect: Ginseng can help the body to adapt to stress and alleviate the stress response. Ginseng has been shown to favorably influence the release of stress hormones such as serotonin and cortisol, which helps to improve general well-being.[293]

Performance-enhancing effect: Ginseng is often considered a natural stimulant and can improve mental and physical performance. Ginseng can boost energy, increase stamina and reduce fatigue, for example by "helping muscles to regenerate and renew" after exercise.[294]

Anti-inflammatory effect: Ginseng also has anti-inflammatory properties that help to strengthen the immune system and improve the body's own defense mechanisms against infections. For example, ginseng root extracts have been shown to mitigate the effects of injury and the production of pro-inflammatory messengers (cytokines).[295] This improves the body's response to infection and increases resistance to disease.

Anti-cancer effect: A large number of studies have found anti-cancer properties in ginseng, particularly in colon cancer.[296] But **ginsenosides** also offer hope for therapeutic approaches to other cancers such as **liver, esophageal, ovarian, cervical, breast and lung cancer.**[297]

Cardioprotective effect: Some studies suggest that ginseng could have positive effects on heart health by lowering cholesterol levels, regulating blood pressure and improving blood circulation.[298] This could help to reduce the risk of cardiovascular disease and prolong life.

Neuroprotective effect: Furthermore, neuroprotective effects of ginseng are being intensively researched. Ginseng extracts may have neuroprotective properties that help to protect the brain from age-related changes and neurodegenerative diseases.[299] **Ginsenosides**, the main active ingredients of ginseng, have shown that they can promote neurogenesis (the formation of new nerve cells), synaptogenesis (the formation of new connections between two nerve cells) and neuroplasticity (changes in the structure and function of nerve cells), which can lead to improved learning and cognitive functions, so that ginseng is also known as a **nootropic** ("smart drug").[300]

In addition, the antioxidant properties of ginseng can help reduce oxidative stress in the brain and reduce damage to nerve cells.

Caution:

Ginseng may interact with certain medications, particularly **blood-thinning medication** and some antidiabetic drugs such as metformin, so consult with one's medical doctor before taking ginseng.[301,302]

Jiaogulan

Jiaogulan, also known as Xiāncǎo 仙草 "immortality herb", belongs to the gourd family. The botanical name is Gynostemma pentaphyllum. Jiaogulan is used in **Traditional Chinese Medicine (TCM)** and is also being researched in Western medicine for its potential health benefits to slow down the ageing process, as it contains a considerably high proportion of **ginsenosides** (saponins from ginseng), the highest proportion of ginsenosides is best extracted (drawn out) before flowering.[303]

Some of the researched biological effects of Jiaogulan are:

Antioxidant effect: Jiaogulan contains a variety of bioactive compounds, including flavonoids, saponins and polysaccharides, which have strong antioxidant and also antidiabetic properties (i.e. directed against diabetes mellitus).[304]

Anti-inflammatory effect: Inflammation can play a role in the development of cancer, and some studies suggest that jiaogulan has anti-inflammatory properties.[304] By reducing inflammation in the body, jiaogulan could help to reduce the risk of cancer.

Anti-cancer effects: Some studies have shown promising results suggesting that extracts from jiaogulan can kill cancer cells or inhibit their growth. For example, saponins were able to **trigger programmed cell death (apoptosis)** of **renal cell tumor cells by involving the mTOR signaling pathway** (see chapter "Nutritional medicine in transition"; subchapter "mTOR signaling pathway - key to longevity").[305]

Overall, cancer research with jiaogulan has made progress in recent years, with positive effects also being seen in **breast, lung, stomach and skin cancer.**[306] However, the hopeful results still need to be substantiated in further studies.

Stress-reducing effect: As previously mentioned with ginseng, jiaogulan is also said to be able to help the body adapt to stress and mitigate stress reactions, as shown by the determination of **stress hormones such as cortisol.**[307]

Cardioprotective effect: Some research suggests that jiaogulan may have positive effects on heart health by lowering cholesterol levels, improving blood flow and supporting arterial function.[308,309] However, there is still a lack of clinical data that clearly demonstrates therapeutic benefits for cardiovascular disease.[310]

Neuroprotective effect: Jiaogulan is also classified as a candidate for a neurodegenerative disease such as Alzheimer's, which has the potential to improve the disease, although this has also only been proven in animal experiments so far.[311]

Caution:

Jiaogulan may interact with certain medications, particularly **blood-thinning medication** (e.g. antiplatelet drugs) and also antidepressants (e.g. the serotonin-norepinephrine reuptake inhibitor duloxetine).[312,313] People taking these medications should therefore speak to their medical doctor to discuss possible side effects. As this book goes to press, there is a legal problem **in the European Union**, as the sale of jiaogulan **as a food or food supplement** is **prohibited**, as it is a "novel food subject to authorization within the meaning of Article 3(2) of Regulation (EU) 2015/2283".[314]

Ginkgo

"This tree leaf, which from the east
Entrusted to my garden,
Gives secret meaning to taste,
As it edifies the knowing."[315]

This is the first verse of the poem "Ginkgo biloba" in **Johann Wolfgang von Goethe**'s "Divan" and a kind of homage to one of the oldest tree species in the world, which has long been used in **Traditional Chinese Medicine (TCM)**.[315] The name ginkgo is derived from the Japanese 銀杏 **Ginkyō** ("silver apricot").[316] The effects of ginkgo have been the subject of many scientific studies, and although not all effects have been clearly proven, there are some potential health benefits associated with taking ginkgo:

Antioxidant effect: Ginkgo contains compounds with antioxidant properties to scavenge free radicals in the body and thus prevent cell damage.[317]

Anti-inflammatory effect: As with other representatives of this group with antioxidant properties, ginkgo also has an anti-inflammatory effect, which is used as a therapeutic approach for rheumatoid arthritis, for example.[318]

Anti-cancer effect: Ginkgo exerts an anti-cancer effect via its anti-oxidant and anti-inflammatory properties: via "programmed cell death (apoptosis), inhibition of tumor cell formation and invasion of cancer cells" and appears to be effective in the following types of cancer: **"lung, liver, stomach, breast, colon and cervical cancer"**.[319]

Cardioprotective effects: Ginkgo can improve peripheral blood flow, which may help to alleviate symptoms of **peripheral arterial disease (PAD),** such as pain when walking.[320] A recent study found that the **anti-atherosclerotic** effects are due to the ginkgolides B contained in ginkgo.[321] Despite the apparent vasoprotective effect, reviews and meta-analyses have shown only limited therapeutic benefit in cardiovascular disease.[322]

As already mentioned for jiaogulan, there is still a lack of clinical data for ginkgo that clearly demonstrates the therapeutic benefits for cardiovascular disease and survival.[320]

Neuroprotective effect: Some studies suggest that ginkgo can improve cognitive function, especially in older adults who suffer from memory problems. Some research suggests that ginkgo may help prevent or treat age-related diseases such as **Alzheimer's disease and macular degeneration in the eye**, although more research is needed here as well.[323]

Caution:

Although ginkgo is considered safe, there may still be side effects and interactions with other medications. Some possible side effects of overdose attributed to the **neurotoxin 4'-O-methylpyridoxine (MPN)** or **ginkgotoxin** contained in ginkgo include **nausea, vomiting, seizures and allergic reactions**.[324] It may also interact with **blood-thinning medication**, so affected individuals should consult their treating physician.[325]

Q10

Coenzyme Q10, also known as **ubiquinone-10**, is a fat-soluble molecule that is found in every cell of the human body and plays a crucial role in energy metabolism. It is provided on the one hand by food and on the other by the body's own synthesis, whereby endogenous production can decrease with increasing age. In recent years, Q10 has attracted increasing interest as a dietary supplement, as it offers numerous potential health benefits. Q10 is now the **third most widely used dietary supplement in the world after vitamin D and vitamin C**.[326]

One of the main benefits of Q10 as a dietary supplement is its role in energy production in the cells. Q10 is a key component of the mitochondrial respiratory chain, which is responsible for converting nutrients into adenosine triphosphate (ATP), the cells' main source of energy.[327] An adequate supply of Q10 can therefore help to **support cell function and energy metabolism**, which is particularly important for organs with **high energy requirements such as the heart**.

Antioxidant effect: Q10 has antioxidant properties that protect cells from oxidative stress. By neutralizing free radicals, Q10 can help reduce the risk of diseases associated with oxidative stress.[328]

Cardioprotective effect: In terms of heart health, Q10 has become particularly important as a dietary supplement. Numerous studies suggest that Q10 can improve heart function and alleviate the symptoms of heart failure (cardiac insufficiency).[327] It supports the energy supply of the heart muscle and can help to reduce oxidative damage to heart muscle tissue, thereby reducing the likelihood of cardiovascular disease and cardiovascular death.[329]

Anti-cancer effect: Q10 is said to have an anti-cancer effect. Even though the majority of studies have shown a favorable prognosis, "overall the **results are not consistent**".[330] So too much expectation should not be placed in the dietary supplement for cancer treatment at present.

Immune function: Another potential benefit of Q10 as a dietary supplement lies in its role in supporting the immune system. Q10 can improve the function of immune cells and boost immune defenses, which can help fight infections and thus maintain overall health.[331]

Skin health: Q10 is also used in many skin care products as it has antioxidant properties and can help protect the **skin from premature ageing caused by UV rays** and pollution.[332]

Caution:

In addition to these potential benefits, however, there are also important considerations when using Q10 as a dietary supplement. Although Q10 is generally considered safe, side effects can occur if taken in excess, especially in people taking **blood-thinning medication** or suffering from certain medical conditions.[333] In addition, the bioavailability of Q10 varies depending on the dosage form, and not all products on the market are of high quality.

Vitamin D

The most commonly used dietary supplement worldwide is vitamin D. The vitamin plays an important role in **bone health**, the **immune system** and the **regulation of inflammation**. Vitamin D deficiency has been linked to a variety of health problems, and supplementing with vitamin D can help improve health and potentially extend lifespan, especially in people with low vitamin D levels.

Vitamin D, often referred to as the **"sunshine vitamin,"** is a fat-soluble vitamin that plays a critical role in the body's health and can potentially support longevity.[334] In a world increasingly dominated by technology and indoor activities, it is important to recognize the importance of sunshine in the context of preventing rickets. Historically, **rickets,** also known as "English disease", was a common health disorder among growing children and adolescents.[335] Sunshine is the main source of the body's own production of vitamin D. When UVB rays hit the skin, the body begins to produce vitamin D, which in turn is necessary for the absorption of calcium and phosphorus from food, so it is critical for bone mineralization and normal bone growth.[335] Here are some examples of how vitamin D could affect longevity:

Osteoporosis prevention: vitamin D is important in maintaining bone health by increasing intestinal absorption of calcium and phosphorus and regulating bone metabolism. Adequate vitamin D levels can help reduce the risk of **osteoporosis** (bone loss) and fractures in old age.[336]

Immune function: Adequate vitamin D levels can help to reduce the risk of infections and improve immune function. This is because low vitamin D levels increase the risk of autoimmune diseases such as **psoriasis, type 1 diabetes mellitus** and **multiple sclerosis (MS).**[337] According to the recently published **VITAL extension trial**, a long-term intake of vitamin D can apparently **prevent autoimmune diseases in the long term.**[338]

Cardioprotective effect: According to the findings of observational studies, **vitamin D can reduce** the risk of **high blood pressure, vascular calcification** (atherosclerosis) and **heart** failure and thus improve heart health and increase life expectancy, whereas more recent intervention studies no longer see these correlations.[339]

Mood regulation: Some studies suggest that vitamin D plays an important role in the regulation of mood and that low vitamin D levels are associated with an increased risk of psychiatric disorders such as anxiety disorders, depression and schizophrenia.[340,341] Adequate vitamin D levels can help to improve emotional well-being and promote quality of life.

It should be noted that vitamin D is mainly synthesized in the body itself through exposure to sunlight on the skin, but it can also be obtained through the diet from foods such as **fatty fish and egg yolks**. In some cases, vitamin D supplementation may be necessary, especially in regions with little sunlight or in people with an increased risk of vitamin D deficiency. However, before taking supplements, this should be discussed with a medical doctor or nutritionist, as vitamin D hypervitaminosis is also an issue.

Caution:

Vitamin D hypervitaminosis occurs when the body absorbs too much vitamin D, which leads to an accumulation of vitamin D in the blood. This can be caused by excessive supplementation (intake of food supplements). In severe cases, vitamin D hypervitaminosis can lead to hypercalcemia, a condition in which the calcium level in the blood is too high, which can then lead to serious complications such as **kidney stones, kidney failure and cardiac arrhythmias.**[342] Untreated hypercalcemia can lead to bone loss (osteoporosis), which increases the risk of bone fractures, thus even reversing the originally desired effect of vitamin D for osteoporosis prophylaxis through excessive intake.

Niacin

Niacin, also known as vitamin B3, is an essential nutrient that plays a significant role in numerous biological processes in the human body. Its importance extends far beyond its role as a vitamin, and it influences various aspects of health, including metabolic regulation, cell function and energy production.

A deficiency of niacin can lead to a condition known as **pellagra**. Pellagra is characterized by symptoms such as skin inflammation, dementia, diarrhea and depression and can be fatal if left untreated. Historically, pellagra was common in poorer populations with a **diet** heavy in **corn**, as corn has relatively low levels of niacin and the bio-available form of niacin in corn (niacinamide) is poorly absorbed.[343]

The main sources of niacin in the diet are foods such as meat, fish, poultry, legumes, nuts and whole grains. In addition, the body can produce niacin from the **amino acid tryptophan**, which is found in protein-rich foods.[344]

The health effects and therapeutic applications of niacin are listed below:

Energy metabolism: Niacin is an essential component of the **coenzyme** nicotinamide adenine dinucleotide **(NAD+),** which plays a key role in energy metabolism (see chapter "Lifestyle supplements and superfoods for longevity"; subchapter "Nicotinamide adenine dinucleotide").[345]

Lipid-modifying effect: Niacin influences lipid metabolism, particularly through its ability to stimulate the breakdown of fatty acids and increase the release of fats from adipose tissue. In addition, niacin can inhibit the breakdown of triglycerides in the liver and reduce the release of fats into the bloodstream, which leads to a reduction in **LDL cholesterol ("bad cholesterol")** and triglycerides while increasing **HDL cholesterol ("good cholesterol")**.[346]

Anti-inflammatory effect: Niacin has anti-inflammatory properties that can reduce the likelihood of inflammation in the body.[347]

Vasodilator effect: In addition, niacin has a vasodilator effect, which means that it promotes the dilation of blood vessels. This could be useful in the treatment of circulatory disorders such as peripheral arterial disease (PAD).[348]

DNA repair: Niacin is involved in DNA repair and may help to repair damage to DNA caused by oxidative stress, highlighting its potential role in cancer prevention and fighting ageing processes.[349]

Neuroprotective effect: Niacin plays a role in neurotransmitter synthesis and neurological function. A lack of niacin can lead to neurological symptoms such as depression, memory impairment and headaches.[350]

Skin health: Niacin can promote skin health by increasing the production of skin lipids, strengthening the skin barrier and improving skin hydration. This may help alleviate skin conditions such as eczema and acne.[351]

Caution:

The therapeutic potential of niacin especially for the treatment of hyperlipidemia (dyslipidemia) has been accepted for decades. Although niacin is generally considered safe, high doses can lead to side effects such as flushing symptoms (reddening of the skin, itching, feeling of heat).[352]

These side effects and also the results of two large **studies from 2011 and 2014 showed no advantage over classic cholesterol-lowering monotherapy with statins** (see chapter "Lifestyle supplements and superfoods for longevity"; subchapter "Statins"), so that there is now limited use of niacin as a lipid-lowering agent.[346] In addition, a newly published study shows that a **vitamin B3 excess** apparently **as a paradox** even **increases** the **risk of cardiovascular disease** through increased inflammatory reactions in the blood vessels.[353] It should therefore be emphasized that **"vitamins" do not always** have to be **good for the body**. As can also be seen with vitamin D, it all depends on the right dose.

Omega-3 fatty acids

Fatty fish such as salmon, mackerel and sardines are an important source of omega-3 fatty acids, but vegetarian and vegan sources such as **flaxseed, chia seeds, walnuts and algae oil** can also provide these fatty acids.

The following biological properties have been investigated in studies:

Anti-inflammatory effect: omega-3 fatty acids have anti-inflammatory properties that can reduce the occurrence of inflammatory (inflammatory) diseases in the body. This can help to reduce the risk of various diseases such as **rheumatoid arthritis, bronchial asthma** and **chronic inflammatory bowel disease (Crohn's disease and ulcerative colitis)**.[354,355,356] In particular, an **imbalance**

with a high excess of omega-6 fatty acids compared to omega-3 fatty acids in the diet (e.g. in safflower oil) significantly increases the likelihood of chronic inflammatory bowel disease.[356]

Immune function: In addition to vitamin D, omega-3 fatty acids were also examined in the recently published **VITAL extension trial** and it was found that even two years after the end of therapy there is still a prophylactic effect against autoimmune diseases.[338]

Cardioprotective effect: Omega-3 fatty acids have anti-inflammatory properties and for decades they were (and still are, depending on the study source) said to be able to significantly reduce the risk of heart disease, cancer and general mortality, thus promoting health and possibly extending lifespan.[357,358] In contrast, a review of 79 randomized studies in 2018 produced disappointing results, and a meta-analysis from 2022 also found no positive effects on heart health or overall mortality, even in a dose-dependent manner, meaning that taking omega-3 fatty acids as a dietary supplement does not appear to bring any survival benefits.[359,360]

Mood regulation: There is evidence that omega-3 fatty acids can help to improve mood and reduce the risk of mental illnesses such as depression and anxiety. One possible explanation for mood enhancement appears to be that omega-3 fatty acids **improve nerve cell communication by increasing the synthesis of neurotransmitters (messengers in the synapses).**[361]

Skin health: Omega-3 fatty acids can help improve skin health by increasing skin hydration, reducing inflammation and strengthening the skin barrier.[362] This can help alleviate skin conditions such as **acne, eczema and psoriasis.**

Eye health: Omega-3 fatty acids are an important component of the retina in the eye. They can help support eye health and reduce the risk of **age-related eye diseases such as macular degeneration.**[363]

Caution:

The legend of the **Inuit ("Eskimos"),** who had better heart health due to heavy fish consumption, seems to have been literally put on ice since the **Diet And Reinfarction Trials (DART-1 and DART-2),** as people with pre-existing heart disease who regularly took **fish oil capsules** or ate **fish** intensively as secondary prophylaxis even died more frequently.[364] **Evidence-based medicine remains contradictory with regard to omega-3 fatty acids.** A clear, conclusive result is still pending.

Omega-9 fatty acids

Omega-9 fatty acids are essential fatty acids that the body needs to function properly, but does not need to obtain completely from food, as the body can synthesize them itself and are therefore referred to as "partially essential".[365]

Omega-9 fatty acids such as **oleic acid and nervonic acid** are found in various vegetable oils such as **olive, rapeseed, macadamia and avocado oil, mustard** as well as in animal sources such as **salmon.**[365,366]

Omega-9 fatty acids play an important role in various processes in the body:

Anti-inflammatory effect: Chronic inflammation is associated with many diseases, and a diet rich in omega-9 fatty acids appears to help reduce the risk of inflammatory diseases.[365]

Anti-cancer effect: In connection with the anti-inflammatory effect, possible anti-cancer properties have been described, for example breast, esophageal, tongue and colon cancer.[365]

Lipid-modifying effect: Omega-9 fatty acids, particularly oleic acid, may help to lower cholesterol levels, especially LDL ("bad") choles-terol.[365] Nervonic acid is important for nerve cell production and may reduce the risk of cardiovascular disease.[366]

Neuroprotective effects: Omega-9 fatty acids are important for brain health and may help support cognitive function and reduce the risk of neurodegenerative diseases.[367]

Skin health: Omega-9 fatty acids may help maintain skin health by preserving skin moisture and strengthening the skin barrier. This can help relieve dry skin and keep skin supple and healthy, which is also important for conditions such as **psoriasis**.[368]

Caution:

Despite the promising health benefits of omega-9 fatty acids such as oleic acid and nervonic acid in terms of cholesterol levels and heart health, a prognostic heart study from Ludwigshafen contradicts pre-vious studies by finding **concentration-dependent negative effects on cardiovascular risk and death**.[369] There are also controversial views on **erucic acid,** a monounsaturated omega-9 fatty acid found in the oil-rich seeds of plants such as **mustard and rapeseed**.[370] Ex-cessive consumption of erucic acid could potentially have negative effects on health, particularly in relation to the cardiovascular system.[368] Thus, once again, **"the dose makes the poison"**, following the 16th century Swiss physician **Paracelsus**.[371]

Nicotinamide adenine dinucleotide

Nicotinamide adenine dinucleotide (NAD+) is a **coenzyme of niacin (vitamin B3)**, which is found in all living cells and plays an important role in metabolism. In recent years, NAD+ has received much attention as a potential means of promoting longevity and preventing age-related diseases, thanks in part to the media coverage and numerous publications by **Professor David Andrew Sinclair** and his research group at **Harvard**.[372]

How NAD+ could affect longevity is listed below:

Energy metabolism: NAD+ is critical for the conversion of nutrients such as carbohydrates, fats and proteins into energy needed for cell function and metabolism. An adequate supply of NAD+ can help maintain energy production in cells and support metabolism.[373]

DNA repair: NAD+ plays an important role in the repair of DNA damage caused by **environmental toxins, UV rays** and other harmful influences.[374] A sufficient supply of NAD+ can help to maintain the integrity of DNA and slow down cell ageing.

Activation of sirtuins: NAD+ is an essential **cofactor for sirtuins**, a group of proteins that play a key role in the regulation of metabolism, cell function and longevity.[375] Adequate NAD+ supply is required to maintain the activity of sirtuins and maximize their health benefits.[376]

Anti-inflammatory effect: NAD+ has anti-inflammatory properties and can therefore help to reduce chronic inflammation in the body.[377] Chronic inflammation is considered to be one of the main factors contributing to the ageing process and the development of age-related diseases.

Ageing processes: NAD+ may be able to slow or reverse the process of cellular senescence (the end of cell divisions) by supporting the activation of sirtuins and improving the function of **mitochondria** ("energy powerhouses" in cells).[375,376] Senescence is a state in which cells are no longer capable of dividing, allowing age-related diseases to develop.

Caution:

Despite the worldwide "aggressive marketing" of **NAD+ as a kind of panacea against ageing**, exaggerated expectations should nevertheless be tempered at this stage, as "long-term safety and clinical efficacy of **anti-aging effects** [effects against ageing] in humans are scarce".[378] Research on NAD+ and its role in longevity is still in its infancy. Further studies are needed to better understand its long-term effects and potential health benefits. In addition, the effects of NAD+ may depend on individual factors such as dosage, bioavailability and genetic differences. There is a lack of reliable information on the target concentration of circulating NAD+ in the body and the use of skin care products that are already on the market appears to be inappropriate, as NAD+ cannot pass through the skin barrier due to its high water solubility.[377]

Individuals interested in using NAD+ to promote longevity should discuss this with a medical doctor to see if it is tailored to them individually. Finally, it should be noted that NAD+ is found in natural foods such as **meat, fish, dairy products, legumes and vegetables** and a balanced diet with these foods can be a good source of NAD+.

Metformin

Metformin is a drug derived from the **French lilac plant** that is commonly used to treat **type 2 diabetes mellitus**. In recent years, however, it has attracted increasing interest as a potential means of promoting longevity and preventing age-related diseases. This interest is based on a number of research studies and observations suggesting that metformin may have some beneficial effects on health beyond the treatment of diabetes mellitus. Here are some possible mechanisms by which metformin could affect longevity:

Improved insulin sensitivity: Metformin works by improving insulin sensitivity and increasing glucose uptake in cells.[379] This may help to lower blood glucose levels and reduce the risk of type 2 diabetes mellitus, which in turn has been linked to a longer lifespan.

Anti-inflammatory effect: Metformin has been associated with anti-inflammatory properties that help reduce the incidence of inflammation, which may also be a building block for longevity.[380]

Anticancer effect: In recent years, metformin has been shown to **inhibit** both the growth and survival of malignant tumor cells as well as the **development of metastases**.[381] The exact mechanisms of action still need to be further investigated; in **colon cancer**, for example, **influencing the function of T-killer cells** appears to play an important role.[382] Positive effects have been demonstrated in cancer of the colon, breast, bone, endometrium and skin (melanoma).[381,382,383]

Ageing processes: Some studies suggest that metformin may have senescence-preventing effects by slowing or reversing the process of cellular senescence (end of cell division). Metformin activates an enzyme called **AMP-activated protein kinase (AMPK)**, which plays an important role in the regulation of energy metabolism and cell function.[384] Activation of AMPK has been associated with various health benefits, including improved metabolic health and a possible increase in lifespan.

Improvement or prevention of various diseases: Favorable effects can be demonstrated with the administration of metformin in **cardiovascular disease, obesity, liver disease and kidney disease**, thus also decisively counteracting the aging process.[381]

Caution:

Although there is promising evidence of the potential **anti-aging effects** of metformin, it is important to note that further research is needed to better understand its long-term effects on longevity and health. Metformin is a drug that can have side effects, interactions and contraindications and is therefore not suitable for everyone. For example, long-term therapy with metformin can also cause **vitamin 12 deficiency**.[385] Individuals interested in using metformin to promote longevity should discuss this with a physician to determine if it is appropriate for their individual health condition. The diabetes drug requires a prescription and should not be used in pregnant or breastfeeding women.

Semaglutide

Obesity is a common and complex condition that is associated with a variety of health risks, including **heart disease, type 2 diabetes mellitus, stroke and certain cancers**. Despite many weight loss efforts, many people face challenges in controlling their weight. In this context, semaglutides for the **treatment of obesity** have attracted attention in recent years.

The semaglutide class of drugs, which are currently administered in the form of subcutaneous injections, mimic the action of the **natural hormone GLP-1 (glucagon-like peptide 1)**, which stimulates the release of insulin, lowers blood sugar levels and increases the feeling of satiety.[386] Semaglutide has the potential to reduce appetite, reduce food intake and promote weight loss.[386]

The efficacy of semaglutide has been extensively studied in clinical trials. One study, known as the **STEP program**, examined the effect of semaglutide in **overweight or obese participants with or without diabetes mellitus**.[386,387] The results were impressive: participants receiving semaglutide lost significantly more weight compared to the placebo group; some participants **even** achieved **a weight loss of more than 15%** of their initial weight.[387]

In a subsequent study, the use of semaglutide was found to reduce the **incidence of cardiovascular death, heart attack or stroke** in obese patients without diabetes mellitus.[388]

Caution:

With regular use of semaglutides, there are reports of increased diarrhea, which can then lead to a shift in electrolytes ("blood salts").[389]

Furthermore, there are contradictory reports on the occurrence of suicidal thoughts due to the use of semaglutides.[390,391] Overall, there appears to be a 1.2% risk of psychiatric events such as depression, anxiety and **suicidal ideation**.[392] Further research is therefore needed on this class of medication, because not only body weight and heart health, but also mental health is a decisive factor for a long life (see chapter "Elimination of noxious substances"; subchapter "Mental health").

Acetylsalicylic acid

Acetylsalicylic acid (ASA), better known as Aspirin®, is a widely used and well-researched drug that has a number of effects on the human body.

The saying **"An aspirin a day keeps the doctor away!"** is common, which is a variation of the well-known English proverb: "An apple a day keeps the doctor away!" ("An apple a day keeps the doctor away!").[393]

In terms of medical history, ASA extends far beyond its original discovery in 1897, when **"willow bark was used by Sumerians and Egyptians over 3500 years ago"** and later by **"physicians in ancient Greece and Rome to reduce pain and fever"**.[394]

Here are some of the most important positive effects of ASA:

Analgesic effect: ASA is a non-steroidal anti-inflammatory drug (NSAID) that is effective in relieving pain of varying intensity. It is often used to treat headaches, toothache, menstrual cramps and muscle pain.[395]

Anti-inflammatory effect: ASA has an anti-inflammatory effect by inhibiting the production of inflammatory messenger substances such as prostaglandins. This has made it an effective treatment for inflammatory diseases such as rheumatoid arthritis for decades.[396]

Antipyretic effect: ASA has antipyretic properties, which means that it can reduce fever by regulating body temperature. It is often used for fevers such as flu and colds.[397]

Cardioprotective effect: ASA inhibits the formation of blood clots by blocking the action of the prostaglandin thromboxane A2, a molecule involved in blood clotting.[398] For this reason, ASA is often used to **prevent heart attacks and strokes** in people at high risk of these conditions.

Anti-cancer effects: There is evidence that regular use of ASA can reduce the risk of certain cancers, **particularly colon cancer** and possibly other cancers.[398] This is thought to be due to the anti-inflammatory and anti-proliferative (stopping uncontrolled cell growth) properties of ASA.

Caution:

Even though the regular use of ASA is undisputedly an important prognostic therapy in **secondary prophylaxis,** i.e. after a heart attack or stroke, it has not yet become established in **primary prophylaxis,** i.e. when there is no cardiovascular disease.[399] Although the risk of heart attack and stroke is reduced in primary prophylaxis, the general risk of **bleeding** (from gastric to cerebral bleeding) is too high.[400] Particular attention must be paid to the increased risk of bleeding when taking **other blood-thinning medication** at the same time, due to the irreversible platelet inhibition of ASA. This effect can last for up to a week, which is why ASA is paused accordingly before planned operations by surgeons.[401] ASA can irritate the mucous membrane of the stomach and lead to **stomach ulcers, gastric bleeding** or stomach pain.[402] This occurs due to the inhibition of prostaglandin production, which has a protective function for the stomach lining. In addition, ASA can trigger bronchial **asthma attacks** in people with asthma.[403]

ASA may increase the risk of **Reye's syndrome**, a rare but potentially life-threatening condition that causes liver and brain dysfunction, in children and adolescents with viral infections, particularly influenza or chickenpox.[404]

Statins

Statins are a class of drugs used to **lower blood cholesterol levels**. Statins are thought to have **pleiotropic effects**, meaning that in addition to lowering cholesterol, they have a range of biological effects.[405]

Here are some of the most important effects of statins:

Lowering LDL cholesterol: Statins inhibit an enzyme called HMG-CoA reductase, which plays a key role in the production of cholesterol in the liver. By reducing cholesterol synthesis, statins effectively lower the **level of "bad" LDL cholesterol** in the blood, which reduces the risk of atherosclerosis and cardiovascular disease.[406]

Increase in HDL cholesterol: Statins can also help to slightly increase the **level of "good" HDL cholesterol** in the blood.[406] HDL cholesterol can help to remove excess cholesterol from artery walls and transport it to the liver where it is broken down, providing additional protection against cardiovascular disease.

Cardioprotective effect: By lowering LDL cholesterol levels, statins can **reduce** the **risk of heart attack, stroke and cardiovascular death by 22%,** according to a meta-analysis of 170,000 individuals from 26 studies.[407]

Stabilization of plaques: Statins can help stabilize atherosclerotic plaques in the arteries, which can reduce the risk of dangerous plaque ruptures and related complications such as heart attacks and strokes.[408]

Anti-inflammatory effect: Apart from their cholesterol-lowering effects, statins also have anti-inflammatory properties. They can reduce inflammation in the arterial walls, which is involved in the development of arteriosclerosis, and help to slow down the progression of cardiovascular disease.[409]

Anti-cancer effect: Statins may also appear to have an anti-cancer effect, as demonstrated in studies of pancreatic and liver cancer.[410,411]

Caution:

Overall, statins are considered important drugs for lowering cholesterol and preventing cardiovascular disease. Their positive health effects generally outweigh the potential risks and side effects, especially in individuals at high risk for cardiovascular disease.[406] However, statins can still carry some negative side effects and risks. It is important to understand and consider these, especially with long-term use or in certain individuals with specific health conditions.

Here are some of the most common negative effects of statins:

Muscle pain and weakness: One of the best known side effects of statins is muscle pain, muscle weakness and muscle damage, which can be referred to as myopathy.[412] In rare cases, statins can lead to serious muscle disorders such as rhabdomyolysis, which can lead to life-threatening complications, prompting one manufacturer to withdraw its product from the world market in 2001.[413]

Liver dysfunction: Although liver problems due to statins are rare, they can occasionally lead to abnormal liver function tests with increases in transaminases (liver enzymes).[412] In rare cases, severe liver damage can occur, requiring monitoring of liver function during treatment.[414]

Increased risk of diabetes: Meta-analyses of randomized control trials indicate that statins increase the risk of new-onset diabetes mellitus by 9-13%.[415] In diabetics, statin therapy may unfavorably promote progression of diabetes.[416]

Neurological side effects: Some studies have suggested a link between statin use and neurologic side effects such as memory impairment, confusion, sleep disturbances, and peripheral neuropathies, although this link is not clear and needs further study.[417]

Although most people tolerate statins well, individuals taking or considering statins should do so under medical supervision. Careful monitoring and regular check-ups can help identify potential side effects early and, if necessary, move onto alternatives such as **ezetemib** (inhibition of cholesterol absorption in the gut), **bempidoic acid** (inhibition of the enzyme ATP citrate lyase in endogenous cholesterol production) and/or **PCSK9 inhibitors** (inhibition of the aforesaid enzyme that reduces the number of LDL cholesterol receptors on the liver cell envelope). Statins are only available on prescription and must not be administered to pregnant or breastfeeding women.

Methylxanthines

Caffeine and theobromine are methylxanthines, which are found in many foods and drinks, especially coffee, tea, chocolate and cocoa. Both methylxanthines have similar, but also some different biological effects. The caffeine in tea is also referred to as theine, but chemically speaking, caffeine and theine are the same molecule, namely 1,3,7-trimethylxanthine.[418]

Caffeine

Caffeine is the better known stimulant and is consumed in a variety of foods and beverages, including coffee, tea, energy drinks, coke and some medications.

The effects of caffeine are relatively rapid and can cause increased alertness, increased attention, increased energy and improved cognitive function. The biological effects in detail are:

Stimulant effect: caffeine is known for its stimulant effect on the central nervous system. It blocks adenosine receptors in the brain, leading to an increased release of **neurotransmitters such as dopamine and noradrenaline.**[419] This can lead to increased alertness, improved attention, increased energy and reduced feelings of fatigue.

Increased metabolic rate: Caffeine is also known as a **"fat burner"** because it stimulates metabolism and increases fat burning, which leads to improved physical performance and supports weight loss.[420]

Memory performance: Caffeine can improve cognitive function, including memory, reaction time and concentration, which in turn also improves physical performance according to the current position paper of the International Society for Sport and Nutrition (ISSN).[421]

Cardiovascular disease: Caffeine may temporarily increase heart rate and raise blood pressure, especially in susceptible individuals or in high doses.[422]

Caution:

When consumed in excess, caffeine can lead to cardiac arrhythmias such as atrial fibrillation, increased blood pressure, insomnia, anxiety, gastrointestinal discomfort.[422] However, caffeine has a relatively short half-life in the body, which means that its effects wear off relatively quickly.[423]

Theobromine

Theobromine is a stimulant found mainly in cocoa and chocolate products, but in smaller quantities than caffeine.[424] The effect of theobromine is generally less strong than that of caffeine and is slower to kick in. It can cause mild stimulation, improved mood and a feeling of relaxation. The biological effects in detail are as follows:

Mild stimulation: theobromine has a milder stimulant effect than caffeine, but similar to caffeine, it also blocks adenosine receptors in the brain and can lead to increased alertness and improved focus.[425]

Dilation of blood vessels: Theobromine can dilate blood vessels and improve blood flow, which can lead to an improved oxygen supply to the tissues and a reduction in blood pressure.[426]

Diuretic effect: Theobromine acts as a weak diuretic and can increase diuresis.[427]

Cardioprotective effect: Theobromine has been shown to have a beneficial effect on the risk factors for cardiovascular disease in patients with **metabolic syndrome** (combination of obesity, high blood pressure, sugar and lipid metabolism disorders).[428]

Neuroprotective effect: In the case of circulatory disorders in the brain, theobromine can apparently help to compensate for neurological deficits, motor and memory disorders, as animal experiments on rats have shown.[429]

Caution:

Excessive consumption of theobromine can also lead to cardiac arrhythmias (such as atrial fibrillation), nausea, vomiting, tremors and other unpleasant symptoms, although these are usually less pronounced than with caffeine.[430] Theobromine has a longer half-life than caffeine, which means that its effects can last longer in the body.[423]

Taurine

Taurine is a sulphur-containing amino acid that is found in many animal products such as **meat and fish** and is "present in **tissues in higher concentrations than any other amino acid**".[431]

The biosynthesis of taurine occurs mainly in the liver and involves a series of enzymatic reactions that start from methionine. Methionine is first converted to cystathionine and then to cysteine, and cysteine is then converted to glutathione and taurine.[431]

Recently, there has been growing evidence that taurine offers some health benefits that may be associated with longevity.[432]

Cardioprotective effects: Taurine has been associated with improved cardiovascular health, including lowering blood pressure, reducing the risk of heart disease and protecting against oxidative stress in the heart muscle.[433,434]

Antioxidant effects: Taurine acts as an antioxidant in the body, meaning it can neutralize free radicals and reduce cell damage.[435] This could help slow the aging process and promote longevity.

Neuroprotective effect: Taurine may also have neuroprotective properties, meaning that it protects the brain from damage and reduces the likelihood of neurodegenerative diseases such as Alzheimer's and Parkinson's.[436]

Anti-inflammatory effect: Taurine has anti-inflammatory properties that can reduce inflammation in the body. The positive effect of taurine on inflammation could be used to tackle premature ageing and various health problems.[434]

Anti-cancer effect: Taurine can mitigate the side effects of chemotherapy and also has an anti-cancer effect, for example in **breast, kidney and colon cancer**.[437]

Caution:

The effectiveness of the small amounts of taurine in **energy drinks** is the subject of scientific debate and controversy.[438] Some energy drink manufacturers make promotional claims that the addition of taurine to their products helps to improve performance, stamina and memory and reduce fatigue, but this is more likely due to the extremely **high levels of caffeine**, which have contributed to cardiac arrhythmias and, in some cases, sudden cardiac arrest.[438] Thus, the combination of high doses of taurine and caffeine appears to have a negative effect.[439]

In addition, taurine consumption in **combination with alcohol**, which is particularly popular among young people, can be **toxic** because taurine **mimics** the **neurotransmitter GABA (γ-aminobutyric acid)** and alcohol promotes GABA excretion at nerve receptors, which leads to impaired motor function (muscle control in the body).[440]

Alliin

Alliin is formed when the enzyme alliinase meets cysteine. This happens when **fresh garlic** is cut or crushed. The alliin is then enzymatically converted to allicin, which is responsible for the characteristic smell and taste of garlic.[440] The use of garlic extracts to treat pain and parasite infections was described **in cuneiform writing** on clay tablets **in Mesopotamia** as early as 2600 BC and documented **in hieroglyphs** on papyrus **in Ancient Egypt** in the **"Codex Ebers"**.[441] Although alliin is a compound derived from an amino acid, it is not itself an amino acid and does not have the characteristic properties of amino acids, such as the ability to form proteins.[441]

Although alliin itself is not directly bioactive, its conversion into allicin and other compounds has various biological effects:

Antimicrobial effect: allicin exhibits antimicrobial properties and appears to be effective against various bacteria, viruses, fungi and parasites.[442,443] Allicin is thought to damage the cell membranes of microorganisms, impairing their ability to multiply.

Antioxidant effect: Allicin and other sulfur compounds produced from alliin have antioxidant properties that reduce cell damage caused by free radicals. This can help to reduce inflammation and lower the risk of cardiovascular disease and **metabolic syndrome** (a combination of obesity, high blood pressure, sugar and fat metabolism disorders).[444]

Cardioprotective effect: Alliin and its transformation products can have a protective effect on the cardiovascular system. They can lower blood pressure, improve blood lipid levels, inhibit blood clotting and improve vascular function, which could reduce the overall risk of cardiovascular disease.[445]

Caution:

By inhibiting liver enzyme activity, allicin and other sulfur compounds formed from alliin may interact with other medications; blood thinners in particular should then be used with greater caution.[446]

Mistletoe

Mistletoe (Viscum album), with its characteristic green foliage and white berries, has long been a fascinating symbol in numerous cultures and traditions. Even in ancient times, the **Roman natural history writer Pliny the Elder** reported that **druids of the Celtic culture** harvested mistletoe from oak trees at the winter solstice, revered it as a sacred plant and used it in their rituals, as they believed that mistletoe **possessed magical powers** and served as a protective agent against evil spirits and diseases.[447]

Over time, mistletoe retained its symbolic meaning and was associated with various festivals and customs. In Europe in particular, mistletoe is an integral part of **Christmas decorations** and is often seen as a symbol of **love, happiness and friendship**.[447]

Mistletoe is not only valued for its symbolic meaning, but also for its potential medicinal applications. In traditional medicine, mistletoe has been used for centuries to treat various ailments.

The following biological effects have been proven:

Immune function: Mistletoe preparations had interesting targets for boosting the immune system and averting disease, which occurs via the mediation of natural killer cells, **T-helper (CD4+)** and **T-killer (CD8+) cells.**[448]

Anti-inflammatory effect: Some laboratory tests and animal studies have shown that various components of mistletoe can have anti-inflammatory effects, including viscotoxin, lectins and polysaccharides.[449] These substances can influence anti-inflammatory reactions in the body by inhibiting the release of pro-inflammatory molecules or modulating the activity of inflammatory cells.

Anticancer effects: Some studies suggest that mistletoe may help in the treatment of cancer, particularly cancers such as breast and colon cancer.[450,451] This is thought to occur through stimulation of the immune system via T-cells and direct cytotoxic effects against cancer cells.[452]

Cardioprotective effect: Mistletoe may also have a mild antihypertensive effect and improve blood circulation.[453]

Caution:

"Most consumers consider complementary and alternative medicine products to be basically safe" because these substances are of "natural" origin.[454,455] But it is a delusion to believe that "natural" plant products have no pharmacological effects or side effects. For example, certain components of mistletoe, such as viscotoxins and phoratoxins, can cause nausea, vomiting, diarrhea, headaches, dizziness, skin rash, itching, bradycardia (slowing of the heartbeat) and negative inotropy (reduced heart pumping power) in higher doses.[455,456] Pregnant women, nursing mothers, children and people with certain medical conditions should discuss the use of mistletoe preparations with a medical doctor, as their safety and efficacy may not have been adequately studied.

Hawthorn

The hawthorn or **hawthorn** (botanical name Crataegus) with its delicate flowers and red berries, has long been a fascinating plant valued in folk medicine and traditional medicine. Its history is characterized by a multitude of **cultural** and **medicinal** applications.

The "Twilight of the Gods" from **Richard Wagner's** tetralogy "The Ring of the Nibelung" states:

"Great happiness and salvation now laughs upon the Rhine,
since Hagen, the Grim, may be so merry!
The hawthorn no longer stings;
he was ordered to be the wedding caller."[457]

Symbolically, "hawthorn" here stands for "**the mythical sign of death**."[457]

As previously described for mistletoe, natural products are not always harmless to health, but can still have some beneficial effects.

Possible health benefits of hawthorn are:

Antioxidant effect: Hawthorn is rich in antioxidants, which can help reduce cell damage caused by free radicals and strengthen the immune system, as well as apparently having a **longevity** effect, as demonstrated by experiments with fruit flies (Drosophila melanogaster).[458] For example, hawthorn also has therapeutic potential for various liver diseases.[459]

Cardioprotective effect: Hawthorn can help to lower blood pressure and **prevent atherosclerosis** (vascular calcification).[460,461] Furthermore, numerous studies have shown hawthorn to **support** the treatment of **heart failure**.[462,463,464]

Relaxing effect: Hawthorn has a calming effect that helps to reduce stress, depression and anxiety and improve general well-being.[465]

Improving sleep quality: Hawthorn can help improve sleep quality and alleviate sleep disorders, which can lead to more restful sleep.[466]

Caution:

Although it has been reported rather rarely, taking excessive amounts of hawthorn can lead to adverse side effects such as gastrointestinal discomfort, nausea, headaches, **palpitations (heart stumbling), and allergic skin reactions (rash).**[467] It is important to adhere to recommended dosages and not to overdo the use of hawthorn.

There is limited information on the safety of hawthorn during pregnancy and breastfeeding. Pregnant or breastfeeding women should discuss the use of hawthorn with their medical doctor before taking it to avoid potential risks to themselves and their baby.

Camomile

The word "chamomile" comes from the Greek and goes back to the word χαμαίμηλον, which literally means "ground or earth apple".[468] This name could refer to the characteristic smell of the plant, which is reminiscent of apples. Chamomile is one of the most commonly used medicinal plants worldwide and was already valued in the ancient world ("**Egypt, Greece, Rome**") for the treatment of "**stomach complaints, cramps, skin inflammations and minor infections**".[469]

Here are some of the most important biological effects of chamomile:

Anti-inflammatory action: chamomile contains compounds such as flavonoids and terpenes that have anti-inflammatory properties.[470] They can help reduce inflammation in the body and relieve symptoms of inflammatory diseases such as rheumatoid arthritis and skin irritation.[469,471]

Digestive benefits: Chamomile has antispasmodic properties that can help relieve digestive symptoms such as bloating, cramping and gastrointestinal discomfort.[469] Chamomile tea is often taken for gastrointestinal discomfort and can also aid digestion.[472]

Antioxidant effect: The antioxidant ingredients in chamomile, such as flavonoids, can neutralize free radicals in the body. This can help to reduce the risk of chronic diseases and have an anti-cancer effect on **stomach, colon, liver and cervical cancer**.[469,473]

Relaxing effect: Chamomile has calming and relaxing properties that can help reduce stress and anxiety.[468] Chamomile tea is often used as a natural sedative and can help fight insomnia and improve sleep quality.[474]

Caution:

People with allergies to plants of the daisy family should avoid chamomile, as allergic reactions such as **skin rash, hay fever, bronchial asthma or anaphylactic shock** may occur.[475] In addition, pregnant women and people taking **blood-thinning medication** should consult a medical doctor before using chamomile.[476]

Goji berries

Goji berries, also known as wolfberries, have gained popularity worldwide in recent years thanks to their rich nutritional composition and multiple health benefits, so much so that they are also prized as the 'fruit of longevity'.[477]

Goji berries (derived from the Chinese name 枸杞 gǒuqǐ) are traditionally grown in the mountainous regions of China and the Himalayas.[477,478] Originally used in **Traditional Chinese Medicine (TCM)**, goji berries have become sought-after "superfoods" that are consumed in various forms, from fresh berries to dried fruit, juices and supplements.[477,478]

The following health benefits have been described for regular consumption of goji berries:

Antioxidant effect: goji berries contain a high concentration of vitamin C, beta-carotene and other antioxidants, which can strengthen the immune system and improve the body's defenses against infection and disease.[479]

Anti-cancer effect: With their antioxidant properties, goji berries are able to act against tumor maturation and cancers such as **breast, cervical, colon, oral cavity and prostate cancer**.[480,481,482,483,484]

Eye health: Goji berries are rich in **beta-carotene**, which is **converted into vitamin A** in the body and plays an important role in improving vision.[479]

Cardioprotective effect: The antioxidant properties of beta-carotene contained in goji berries are said to be responsible for reducing inflammation, lowering cholesterol levels and stabilizing blood sugar levels, which can reduce the risk of cardiovascular disease.[485]

Skin Health: The antioxidant properties of goji berries may support skin health by protecting the skin from free radical damage and minimizing the appearance of signs of aging with wrinkling.[486] In addition, the high levels of **vitamin B1** may contribute **to collagen production**, resulting in firmer and more youthful skin.[479]

Caution:

Some people may have an allergic reaction to goji berries, especially if they already have allergies to other berries or plants.[487] Symptoms of an allergic reaction may include skin rash, itching, swelling or difficulty breathing. People with known allergies should therefore be careful when eating goji berries.

Furthermore, the excessive intake of beta-carotene is problematic when consuming large amounts of goji berries (see chapter "Lifestyle supplements and superfoods for longevity"; subchapter "Beta-carotene").

Ginger

Ginger was cultivated in India and ancient China around "5000 years ago as a strengthening root for all ailments".[488] Ginger is known for its bulbous root and is used in a variety of ways in both cooking and traditional medicine. The name ginger comes from the **classical Indian language Sanskrit** from the word शृङ्गवेर "sringavera (**sringam=horn+vera=body)**".[489]

Ginger is used in **Traditional Chinese Medicine (TCM)** to treat digestive problems, nausea and inflammation.[490] In **Ayurvedic medicine**, ginger is considered a **"universal medicine"** and is recommended to strengthen the immune system, relieve headaches and promote digestion.[487] Not only were trade goods exchanged along the historic **Silk Road**, but also medical knowledge. For this reason, ginger was also used to treat digestive disorders in **ancient Persian medicine.**[491]

Modern scientific studies have confirmed some of the traditional uses of ginger and further investigated its potential health benefits.

Here are some of the most important effects of ginger:

Anti-inflammatory effects: fresh ginger contains bioactive compounds such as **gingerols**, and dried ginger roots contain **shoagols**, which may have anti-inflammatory properties.[491] This can help to reduce inflammation in the body, which may be particularly beneficial for conditions such as rheumatoid arthritis and other inflammatory conditions.[492]

Digestive benefits: Ginger is traditionally used to aid digestion and relieve stomach complaints such as nausea, vomiting, gas and indigestion.[493] It can also help to speed up the movement of the stomach, which can promote the emptying of stomach contents.[494]

Antiemetic effect: Ginger can relieve nausea and vomiting, whether from motion sickness, morning sickness or the side effects of chemotherapy.[495,496]

Pain relief: Due to its anti-inflammatory properties, ginger can also help relieve pain, be it arthritis, muscle pain or menstrual cramps.[497,498]

Immune function: Ginger can support the immune system by stimulating the production of immune cells and having anti-inflammatory effects that help ward off disease.[498]

Cardioprotective effect: Ginger also appears to reduce the risk of cardiovascular disease by lowering cholesterol levels, lowering blood pressure and promoting platelet inhibition.[499]

Antioxidant effect: Ginger is said to have strong antioxidant properties and can both attenuate and prevent the formation of free radicals that cause cell damage.[500]

Anti-cancer effect: Due to the anti-inflammatory and antioxidant properties of ginger, the anti-cancer effect is plausible and has been found, for example, in **colon or breast cancer**.[490,501]

Caution:

Although ginger is generally considered safe to take, in rare cases ginger can cause allergic reactions, especially in people who are already allergic to other plants in the ginger family (Zingiberaceae).[502] Although ginger is often used to relieve stomach discomfort, in some cases it can cause stomach irritation or heartburn, especially if ≥ 2 g of ginger powder is taken per day or if someone already suffers from stomach problems.[490] Taking ginger in larger amounts could increase the risk of bleeding due to its platelet-inhibiting effect, especially in people already taking **blood-thinning medication**.[498] If ≤ 4 g of ginger powder is taken, no significant platelet inhibition is expected.[490] While smaller amounts of ginger are generally considered safe, there is insufficient data to confirm the safety of ginger in larger amounts during pregnancy and lactation. It is recommended that pregnant or breastfeeding women consult their physician before taking ginger.

Resistant starch

Resistant starch refers to the property of starch (carbohydrates) that is resistant (resilient) to digestion, especially digestion in the human intestine. This type of starch is not completely broken down and absorbed by enzymes in the small intestine, but enters the large intestine unchanged.[503]

Resistant starch is found naturally in some foods, such as unprocessed **whole grain products, green bananas and pulses**. However, it can also be produced artificially by subjecting foods such as **potatoes or rice** to certain processing procedures by cooking, cooling and reheating them.[503]

Resistant starch has a variety of positive effects on health:

Improved gut health: resistant starch acts as a **prebiotic**, meaning that it improves the growth conditions for healthy bacteria in the gut. It promotes the growth of beneficial bacteria such as bifidobacteria and lactobacilli, which leads to healthier gut flora and supports digestive health.[504]

Blood sugar regulation: Regular consumption of resistant starch can improve insulin sensitivity, which means that cells respond better to insulin and the body can process glucose more efficiently, which could be particularly beneficial for diabetes patients.[505]

Weight management: Through its ability to increase satiety and regulate blood sugar levels, resistant starch can help reduce hunger and control calorie intake. This can help with weight management, for example to bring about a desired reduction in body weight.[504]

Anti-cancer effect: Adequate intake of resistant starch can reduce the risk of colorectal cancer by improving gut health and reducing inflammation.[506]

Caution:

Although resistant starch has many health benefits, there are also potential risks and side effects, especially when consumed in large quantities. A sudden increase in resistant starch intake can lead to digestive discomfort such as bloating, gas and diarrhea, especially in people whose digestive systems are not accustomed to it.[507] People with certain digestive tract conditions such as irritable bowel syndrome or Crohn's disease may be sensitive to resistant starch intake and may exacerbate symptoms. While resistant starch can help stabilize blood glucose levels, people with diabetes mellitus or insulin resistance should carefully monitor their blood glucose levels as unexpected effects may occur.[505]

Vanillin

Vanilla, especially vanillin, which is extracted from vanilla pods, is known for its typical sweet and spicy aroma and taste. The name is derived from the Spanish **vainilla** for "pod" or "small sheath".[508] It has a number of health benefits:

Antioxidant effect: vanillin, the main component of vanilla, can scavenge free radicals and reduce oxidative stress.[509]

Anti-inflammatory effect: Vanillin has an anti-inflammatory effect through the downregulation of cytokine expression (reduced formation of pro-inflammatory messenger substances).[509]

Neuroprotective effect: Vanillin appears to protect against neurodegenerative diseases by reducing cell damage and inflammation, and appears to relieve pain.[510]

Caution:

Heavy vanillin consumption can lead to nausea, vomiting and headaches.[511] Some products contain **synthetically produced** vanillin derived **from petroleum derivatives**, which is considered safe but raises concerns among consumers about its origin.

Capsaicin

Capsaicin is a vanilloid, structurally **similar to vanillin**, is a natural compound found in many hot peppers, especially **chili peppers**. Capsaicin is responsible for the **pungency of peppers** and may offer some health benefits:

Weight loss: capsaicin, also advertised as a "weight loss capsule," can improve **gut health with the microbiome** (the body's own micro-organisms) and work as a **"fat burner",** which can help with desired weight loss.[512]

Cardioprotective effect: Capsaicin can lower cholesterol levels and reduce the risk of cardiovascular disease.[512]

Antioxidant effect: Capsaicin is also an antioxidant that can protect cells from free radical damage.[513]

Neuroprotective effect: Capsaicin can either **relieve nerve pain topically** (i.e. through local application of creams) (like vanillin) or **improve neurodegenerative diseases** by means of capsules.[514,515]

Caution:

Excessive consumption of capsaicin in the form of highly concen-trated food supplements or hot sauces can lead to stomach irritation, heartburn or diarrhea. A case of sudden cardiac death has even been described in a 41-year-old with no previous illnesses who consumed "cayenne pepper pills".[512]

Conclusions

- Lifestyle supplements are promising for a long and
  healthy life

- Not all dietary supplements, vitamins and superfoods are
  useful and could even be dangerous in some cases

- Better a dose of nutrition from regional foods than lifestyle
  supplements and exotic plant products

Chapter 5: Eliminating noxious substances

Noxious elimination refers to the process of removing or neutralizing harmful substances or stimuli that are potentially harmful to the body. "Noxious" is a term that refers to any toxic or harmful substance or stimulus that can affect the body. Here are some examples of measures to eliminate noxious substances:

Detoxification: this involves the process of removing harmful substances from the body, either through natural elimination via organs such as the liver and kidneys, or through targeted medical interventions such as the administration of drugs to detoxify.

Avoidance: An important step in eliminating noxious substances is to avoid exposure to harmful substances. This can mean avoiding harmful chemicals in the environment such as smoke, pollutants or toxic fumes, as well as avoiding the consumption of contaminated food or drink.

Treatment of diseases and infections: Some diseases or infections can be considered noxious agents because they can harm the body. Treating these diseases and infections is therefore crucial to eliminate the noxious agents and restore health.

Removing harmful substances from the diet: Certain foods or ingredients can be harmful to the body. Eliminating noxious substances from the diet can mean reducing the consumption of processed foods.

Eliminating noxious substances from the diet can mean reducing the consumption of processed foods high in additives, sugar or trans fats and instead promoting a healthy, balanced diet.

Reducing stress: Chronic stress and **poor sleep hygiene** can also be considered noxious substances, as they put a strain on the body and can weaken the immune system. (see chapter "Sleep, relaxation and music: underestimated pillars of health"). The introduction of stress management strategies such as meditation, yoga or regular exercise can help to eliminate noxious substances and improve general health (see chapter "Physical activities"; subchapters "Calisthenics" and "Yoga").

Solanine

As already mentioned several times, plant substances can have potentially health-promoting effects, but they can also serve as defense **substances against predators** in the plant and therefore also be harmful to human health (see chapter "Lifestyle supplements and superfoods for longevity"; subchapter "Saponins").

Solanine is a naturally occurring toxin found in certain plants of the **nightshade** family such as **potatoes, eggplants, tomatoes and peppers**. It is particularly high in unripe or green parts of these plants, such as **green potatoes** or **green tomatoes**. The **Greek philosopher Socrates** was condemned to death with the nightshade plant hemlock (toxic substance contained: **coniin**).[516]

In small quantities, solanine is normally not dangerous to humans, as the body is able to process and excrete it. However, large amounts of solanine can cause symptoms of poisoning, such as nausea, vomiting, diarrhea, headaches, dizziness and in severe cases even seizures or unconsciousness.[516]

To minimize the risk of solanine poisoning, **green or unripe parts of nightshade plants** should be avoided.[516] It is recommended to remove these parts and consume only ripe, well-processed products.

Mushrooms

Mushrooms can be both healthy and harmful, depending on the type of mushroom and how it is prepared or consumed.

Healthy mushrooms such as button mushrooms, shiitake, chanterelles and many others contain important nutrients such as protein, fiber, vitamins and minerals.[517] They are also often a good source of antioxidants, which can help fight cell damage and boost the immune system.[517]

However, there are also many types of mushrooms that are toxic and can cause serious health problems such as liver and kidney failure or even death if eaten. In a 19-year review of hospital data from Germany, more than 90% of fatal mushroom infections were found to be caused by **tuber leaf mushroom poisoning**, a mushroom that looks **very similar to a button mushroom**.[518] It is therefore extremely important to only buy mushrooms from safe sources or have them collected by experienced people who know how to identify edible mushrooms.

Additionally, although rare, **mold poisoning** can play a harmful role in health, especially for those with allergies or respiratory illnesses, and they can also be potentially carcinogenic.[519]

However, the increasingly popular consumption of **psilocybin mushrooms ("magic mushrooms")**, which are consumed as **hallucinogenic drugs** due to their psychoactive substances, has also become problematic for public health in recent years.[518] Anxiety disorders, panic attacks and delusions (paranoia), which can also degenerate into so-called "horror trips", can be triggered by consumption.[520]

In addition to a socially critical discussion about the causes of drug use, drug counseling and therapy are usually required for those affected. Abuse for intoxication purposes as well as trafficking, import, sale and distribution are also relevant under criminal law in Germany (§ 1 BtMG and § 29 BtMG "Narcotics Act") and in many other countries.

Cannabis

Cannabis (hemp) has a long history as a useful plant, medicine and psychoactive substance. **Thousands of years ago**, it was **used** in various civilizations **(China, Egypt, Greece, Rome) for religious, medicinal and craft purposes**.[521] In some ancient societies, cannabis was considered a sacred plant, while in others it was used as a versatile raw material for textiles, ropes and even as a remedy.[521]

Today, cannabis is used all over the world for various purposes. Medicinal cannabis (cannabidiol) is used to relieve pain, nausea, muscle spasms and epileptic seizures.[522] Recreational cannabis is also common as a quasi-**'lifestyle drug'**, with people enjoying cannabis for its psychoactive effects, particularly due to its main constituent **tetrahy-**

drocannabinol (THC), with over 100 cannabinoids now identified in the plant.[523]

The effects of cannabis can be varied and depend on a number of factors, including the type of cannabis strain, dosage, method of use and individual sensitivity. Short-term effects include euphoria, relaxation, heightened cognition and altered perception of time. However, long-term and excessive use can lead to **dependence**, cognitive impairment and mental health problems.[524]

In addition, consumption can increase the risk of atrial fibrillation, a cardiac arrhythmia that is associated with an increased risk of stroke.[525] Furthermore, a recent study from the USA found that **regular cannabis use increases the risk of stroke by 42% and the risk of heart attack by 25%.**[526]

The **cannabis variant hexahydrocannabinol (HHC), "legal high"**), which in contrast to THC has 6 and not 4 H atoms and circumvents the law in many countries, is also freely available for sale as sweets or gummy bears, which is to be viewed critically from a medical point of view, especially due to the easy access for children and adolescents, because **HHC is also attributed dangerous "neurological, cardiovascular, gastrointestinal and psychiatric effects".**[527]

Attitudes towards cannabis have changed significantly over time and remain **a controversial topic in many parts of the world.** While some countries have legalized cannabis or adopted more liberal policies, others maintain strict prohibition.[523] The debate over cannabis legalization revolves around issues of public health, road safety, crime, personal freedoms and economic impact.

Cannabis remains a hot topic that raises a wide range of social, cultural, medical, legal and political issues. As research into the effects of cannabis continues to advance, it is important to take a balanced perspective and consider the potential benefits and harms. The future of cannabis depends on informed debate, evidence-based policy and responsible use.

Fentanyl

Fentanyl, a synthetic opioid, has attracted worrying global attention in recent years. It is extremely dangerous and poses significant risks to public health.

First of all, the **potency of fentanyl** is extremely high. **Compared to** other opioids such as **heroin, fentanyl is up to 50 times stronger**.[528] Even in small amounts, it can lead to a strong and often fatal effect.[528] This extreme potency makes it particularly dangerous for people who may abuse or accidentally use it.

Another reason for the **dangerousness of fentanyl** is its widespread use as a **street drug**.[528] Fentanyl is often produced illegally and introduced into the drug trade, often in the form of counterfeit pills or as an additive to other drugs such as heroin or cocaine to enhance their effects. Users may not be aware that the product they are consuming contains fentanyl, which can lead to an unpredictable and potentially fatal overdose.

In addition, fentanyl can also be **prescribed legally** to treat **severe pain**.[529] Although it can be effective in this regard, it still carries a significant risk of **dependence and abuse**. Individuals who are prescribed fentanyl may accidentally overdose, particularly if they exceed the prescribed dosage or use the medication in unintended ways.

Another issue related to fentanyl is its role in the current **opioid crisis,** as the abuse of fentanyl and other synthetic opioids has led to a dramatic increase in overdose deaths.[530] This crisis has a devastating impact on families, communities, and society as a whole, as it not only costs lives but also requires significant resources to deal with the consequences.[530]

Finally, the difficulty of treating an overdose with fentanyl contributes to the dangerous nature of this opioid. Due to its extreme potency, a fentanyl overdose often requires immediate medical intervention with the opioid antagonist naloxone. Even if **naloxone** is administered in time as an **antidote**, it can be difficult to prevent the life-threatening effects of a fentanyl overdose, especially if it is not recognized in time.[531]

Overall, fentanyl is an extremely dangerous substance that poses serious risks to public health. Its extreme potency, its prevalence as a street drug, its role in the opioid crisis, and the difficulty in treating overdoses make it a significant concern for society. It is vital that governments, healthcare institutions and communities work together to take action to curb the abuse and spread of fentanyl and support those affected by its danger.

Alcohol

Alcohol has been a fixture in human life for thousands of years, whether as a social drink or for cultural reasons. Early documents of

Western historiography show that **"beer and wine, not water**, were favored as daily thirst quenchers" by "Egyptians, Babylonians, Hebrews, Assyrians, Greeks and Romans".[532] Nevertheless, it is important to recognize that alcohol also poses a significant risk to health and well-being.

First of all, alcohol is a psychoactive substance that affects the central nervous system.[533] In small amounts, alcohol consumption can be relaxing and lower social inhibitions. But even in moderate amounts, alcohol can impair cognitive function, which can lead to impaired judgment, coordination problems and slow reaction time.[534] This significantly **increases the risk of accidents and injuries**, especially on the road **when driving under the influence of alcohol.**

Another serious health risk associated with alcohol is the possibility of **addiction.**[533] Alcoholism is a chronic disease that can severely affect the lives of those affected.

This can lead to a range of health problems, including liver damage, heart disease, mental disorders and social problems.[533] People who are addicted to alcohol have difficulty controlling their drinking and often suffer severe withdrawal symptoms when they try to stop.

Another health risk associated with alcohol consumption is the possibility of serious physical harm. Long-term excessive alcohol consumption can lead to **liver diseases** such as **fatty liver, cirrhosis and liver cancer.**[535]

In addition, alcohol consumption increases the risk of various cancers, including **breast cancer, pancreatic cancer, oral cavity cancer, throat cancer, esophageal cancer and colon cancer.**[536] The risk of cardiovascular disease, stroke and neurological problems such as dementia also increases with alcohol consumption.

Furthermore, alcoholism can also have a considerable impact on the social and family environment. Relationship problems, job difficulties and financial problems are common consequences of excessive alcohol consumption.[537] Children of alcoholic parents can also suffer from emotional neglect, abuse or other forms of trauma that can last a lifetime.[538] Alcohol consumption by the pregnant mother can also have fatal effects on the unborn child's "heart, kidneys, liver, gastrointestinal tract and hormonal system".[539]

In recent years, easier access to high-proof alcohol through sweetened mixed drinks such as alcopops has played a role in addiction medicine among children and adolescents and could be curbed, for example, through increased sales prices and restricted availability.[540]

It is also important to note that alcohol can be dangerous not only for the individual, but also for society as a whole. The **costs of alcohol-related accidents, disease and criminal behavior are enormous** and place a burden on health systems and law enforcement agencies worldwide.

Alcohol is an extremely dangerous substance that poses significant risks to health, well-being and society as a whole. It is important to understand the risks of alcohol consumption and to be aware of how it can affect people's lives. Prevention measures, education campaigns and support for people with alcohol problems are crucial to minimizing the negative effects of alcohol and creating safer communities.

Smoking

Tobacco (Nicotiana), a plant from the **nightshade** family, originated in the Americas.[541] After the discovery of America by European explorers in the 15th century, tobacco was brought to Europe, where it was initially considered a medicinal product, and later people began to smoke tobacco.[541]

In the following centuries, tobacco smoking spread worldwide, partly due to trade and colonization. It developed into a widespread social habit found in different cultures and social classes.

Smoking is one of the leading preventable causes of disease and premature death worldwide. One reason for the widespread lifestyle of smoking over the decades was the increased media presence on television and in film productions and the **very successful advertising campaigns of the tobacco industry, which even used US doctors for media-effective product advertising in the years 1930-1953**.[542]

Despite the wide availability today of information about the harmful effects of smoking and anti-smoking campaigns by governments, many people still choose to smoke or take up smoking. Reasons for this may be that in some **social circles and cultural environments**, smoking is seen as normal behavior or even positively reinforcing. People may succumb to peer pressure or their social environment and start smoking to fit in or to identify with others who smoke.[543]

Some people use smoking as a **means of coping with stress**, relaxation or as a way of dealing with emotional distress.[544] They may see smoking as a form of self-medication to find temporary relief.

Despite extensive awareness campaigns, there are still **misconception or trivialization of the health risks** of smoking.[545] Some people may ignore or misjudge the long-term effects of smoking and believe that they will not be affected by the negative effects.

The fact is that the health risks of smoking are very well documented and extremely serious. Smoking is a major cause of several diseases, including chronic obstructive pulmonary disease **(COPD), heart attacks, strokes** and various types of cancer such as **lung, oral cavity and bladder cancer.**[546] The chemicals in tobacco smoke, such as nicotine, tar and carbon monoxide, damage the respiratory tract, impair lung function and increase the risk of serious diseases. The long-term effects of smoking can be life-threatening and significantly impair quality of life.

Another reason why smoking is dangerous is its negative impact on public health. **Passive smoking,** the inhalation of tobacco smoke by non-smokers in the vicinity of smokers, can also cause serious health problems, especially in children and non-smoking adults.[546] Passive smoking also increases the risk of cardiovascular disease, respiratory disease and cancer.[547]

In addition, smoking also has a **significant social and economic impact** worldwide. Smoking places a burden on global health systems through the treatment of smoking-related diseases **(direct medical costs)** and the loss of productive working hours **(indirect costs)** due to illness or premature death.[548] It can also lead to financial burdens for smokers and their families, as smoking is expensive and can result in significant long-term costs for cigarettes and medical treatment.

Another aspect of the danger of smoking is the powerful addiction it causes. Nicotine, an addictive substance in tobacco, can lead to a **physical and psychological dependence** that makes it extremely difficult for smokers to quit.[549] Many people struggle for years trying to quit smoking, and even after successfully quitting, **the addiction can return**, especially during times of stress or other challenges.

It is important that individual smokers, society and governments work together to reduce smoking and offer smokers support to help them cope with their addiction. Effective **tobacco prevention and cessation programs** (courses financed by companies or health insurance companies or contribution refunds), comprehensive **smoking bans** in public spaces (in public buildings, on airplanes and other means of transport) and the **promotion of healthy lifestyles** (in Germany, the **Prevention Act** introduced in 2015 as an article in the **Social Code** §§ 20 ff SGB V) make a decisive contribution to reducing the burden of smoking and improving public health.

It's never too late to quit!

When smoking is stopped, the **risk of developing" lung, liver, stomach and bowel cancer"** is reduced **to the level of non-smokers after around 15 years**, as a recently published Korean study showed.[550] Even an immune system damaged by smoking can return to normal immune cell responses in ex-smokers.[551] If **smoking** is **stopped before the age of 40, overall mortality** can **fall to the level of non-smokers after three years** of abstinence from nicotine.[552]

Smoking during pregnancy is dangerous and can cause serious health problems for the unborn child, which is why expectant mothers should stop smoking. Smoking can lead to low birth weight or premature birth, which is associated with increased susceptibility to disease and developmental problems.[553,554] **Children of smokers have an increased risk** of "sudden infant death syndrome, neurological and behavioral developmental disorders, obesity, hypertension, type 2 diabetes mellitus, impaired lung function and asthma".[554]

The **"Harm Reduction"** campaign introduced by the tobacco industry in recent years through the use of **e-cigarettes and vaporizers** should also be viewed critically, as according to a meta-analysis from 2024, these alternatives are at least as dangerous as traditional cigarettes.[555] Moreover, **analogous to the sugar industry** (see chapter "Changing nutritional medicine"; subchapter "Explosive revelation of conflicts of interest"), **conflicts of interest with the tobacco industry** also play a decisive role in the emergence of research results, some of which claim to have found alleged "harmless" effects.[556]

It is better not to try half-hearted attempts at "harm reduction", which seem to be anything but harmless, but to stop smoking completely - immediately!

Glutamate

Glutamate is one of the main components of umami flavor and is therefore often used as a flavor enhancer. Alongside sweet, sour, salty and bitter, **umami** is the **fifth flavor** that was discovered in Japan in 1908 and was created as an artificial word meaning "delicious" and "taste".[557] It describes a taste that is perceived as meaty, savory, spicy and pleasant.

The question of whether glutamate is healthy or unhealthy as a flavor enhancer is a contentious issue of long-standing debate and scientific research. There are three important points to make here:

1. **safety:** Glutamate, particularly in the form of monosodium glutamate (MSG), has been extensively studied by various food regulatory agencies, including the US Food and Drug Administration (FDA) in 2012 and the European Food Safety Authority (EFSA) in 2017, and has been found to be safe for human consumption when consumed in the recommended amounts (maximum 3.2 g per kilogram of body weight per day).[558,559] A limit on the amount for food safety came about because there have been animal studies that have described a link between glutamate intake and the development of neurodegenerative diseases.[556] More recent studies also see **neurotoxicity (nerve cell damage)** with glutamate-rich foods and can see the "onset and progression of psychiatric symptoms".[560,561]

2. **sensitivity:** Some people may be sensitive to glutamate and experience symptoms such as headaches, nausea, dizziness or flushing (temporary reddening of the skin around the face due to dilation of blood vessels). This reaction is sometimes referred to as "**Chinese restaurant syndrome**", although it has no specific relationship to Chinese food.[562] However, individual sensitivity can vary and not all people experience these symptoms.

3. **natural occurrence:** Glutamate is a naturally occurring amino acid found in many foods, including meat, cheese, tomatoes, and mushrooms.[563] Consumption of foods naturally containing glutamate is

generally safe and is not associated with side effects related to "Chinese restaurant syndrome".[563]

Glutamate is safe for consumption as a flavor enhancer in most cases, but individuals who are sensitive to it should limit or avoid consumption of foods high in glutamate.[563] It is also important to be aware that many food additives, not just glutamate, can trigger a hypersensitivity reaction.

Environmental toxins

The modern world faces an invisible yet devastating threat: environmental toxins. These harmful substances are present in air, water, soil and food and pose a serious threat to human health and the environment. Environmental toxins can be produced in a variety of ways, whether through industrial processes, agricultural activities, waste disposal or the daily use of chemicals. Their effects are diverse and can be far-reaching, ranging from acute health problems to long-term environmental damage.

Air pollution

One of the biggest threats from environmental toxins is air pollution. The burning of fossil fuels, industrial emissions, vehicle exhaust and other sources release harmful pollutants such as nitrogen oxides, sulphur dioxide, carbon monoxide and particulate matter into the air.

Particulate matter

Particulate matter is a term used to describe small particles suspended in the air. Particulate matter consists of various materials such as dust, soot, smoke, pollen, and other organic or inorganic substances. **Particulate matter particles have a diameter of less than 10 micrometers (µm) or 0.01 millimeters.** They are so small that they are invisible to the naked eye. These extremely small particles can penetrate deep into the lungs and can cause a variety of health problems, including **respiratory diseases, cardiovascular diseases and cancer.**[564] According to a study of over 600 cities worldwide, a direct link between particulate matter pollution and mortality was found.[565]

Caution: electric cars!

Even if vehicles with electric drives are marketed as "emission-free" compared to vehicles with combustion engines, the environmentally friendly aspect is limited, as considerable particulate matter pollution is also generated during **battery production, energy generation** and, finally, **during operation due to tire and brake wear** (cars are generally heavier than combustion engines due to the batteries).[566]

Benzene

Benzene is a component of gasoline and can be released during vehicle refueling and other activities at gas stations, such as refueling gasoline tanks or handling benzene products. This exposure can pose a potential health risk, particularly for service station employees and people who refuel frequently. Benzene can affect the central nervous system and cause neurological symptoms such as dizziness, headaches, drowsiness and, in severe cases, loss of consciousness.[567] Benzene is also a known **carcinogen**, which means that it can cause cancer, such as **lung and bladder cancer**.[568,569] Long-term exposure can increase the risk of blood cancer (especially **acute myeloid leukemia**).[567]

Lead

In addition to the harmful effects of benzene, gasoline fumes have also led to a significant **reduction in intelligence** (measured by **IQ tests**) in more than 170 million Americans who had high levels of lead in their blood during childhood, as lead in gasoline was not banned until 1996.[570]

Noise pollution

As early as 1910, Nobel Prize winner **Robert Koch** predicted:"One day, man will have to fight noise as relentlessly as cholera and the plague."[571]

Exposure to noise also plays a significant role in the development of diseases, particularly in urban environments. It has been proven that **city noise is associated with an increased incidence of high blood pressure, heart attacks and strokes**, because noise emissions increase stress hormone levels such as adrenaline in the body and have an unfavorable effect on vascular function.[571]

Water pollution

Water is another vital resource that is threatened by environmental toxins. Pollution from **industrial effluents, agricultural fertilizers and pesticides, household waste** can affect water quality and **endanger** both **human health** and the **aquatic environment**. Pollutants such as heavy metals, pesticides, herbicides and organic chemicals can accumulate in rivers, lakes, oceans and groundwater and cause damage to ecosystems and biodiversity.

Microplastics

Microplastics, **tiny plastic particles less than five millimeters in size**, pose an increasing threat to the marine environment and human health. These particles enter the water in a variety of ways, whether through direct inputs such as **plastic waste** or through the **degradation of larger plastic parts such as packaging, bottles and nets**.

As fish and other seafood are an important source of protein for many people, **eating contaminated fish** can result in microplastic particles entering the human food chain. Although the exact effects of this exposure are not yet fully understood, there are concerns about potential health risks, particularly long-term chronic exposure to microplastics. For example, the **ingestion of microplastics via the gut** can lead to "oxidative stress, cell damage and translocation to other tissues".[572] It is therefore not surprising that microplastics have been shown to have a carcinogenic effect.[573]

Soil pollution

Soil is also vulnerable to environmental toxins caused by **industrial pollution, mining activities, uncontrolled waste disposal and the use of pesticides and fertilizers** in agriculture. These substances can impair soil fertility, endanger the health of plants, animals and humans and cause long-term damage to agricultural ecosystems and livelihoods.

Pesticides

Pesticides are chemicals used to control pests such as weeds, insects, fungi and other organisms that can damage crops. **Glyphosate** is one of the most commonly used herbicides (weed killers) in the world.[574]

Glyphosate and some other pesticides can be toxic and cause health problems with prolonged or excessive exposure. Studies have shown that glyphosate can be linked to various health problems, including cancer, kidney damage, liver damage, nerve damage, endocrine disruption and reproductive problems.[574,575]

UV rays

UV or "ultraviolet" rays are a form of electromagnetic radiation emitted by the sun. They are invisible to the human eye as their wavelengths lie outside the visible light spectrum.

UV rays, especially UVA rays, can promote the formation of free radicals in the skin through various mechanisms (see chapter (see chapter "Lifestyle supplements and superfoods for longevity"; subchapter "Free radicals"). In contrast to UVA rays, UVB rays do not penetrate as deeply into the skin, but mainly affect the upper layers of the skin.[576] UVB rays play a decisive role in the production of vitamin D in the skin (see chapter "Lifestyle supplements and superfoods for longevity"; subchapter "Vitamin D").

Although UVB rays from the sun outdoors or from tanning salons help to achieve a desired skin tan or to medically treat patients with psoriasis, they can also be harmful with excessive exposure. UVB rays are the main cause of sunburn and UVB, but especially UVA rays, increase the risk of skin cancer and premature skin ageing.[576] For this reason, it is recommended to protect oneself from excessive UV radiation by using sunscreen (but beware: see **phthalates**), wearing protective clothing and limiting sun exposure at peak times of the day.

Phthalates

Phthalates are chemicals that can be found in many different products, including plastics, cosmetics, cleaning products and much more. They are **often used as plasticizers** to make plastics more flexible and durable.

In sunscreens, there are studies suggesting that some sunscreens may contain phthalates, particularly those containing chemical UV filters.[577] Studies have shown that phthalates can be detected in urine after people have applied sunscreens containing phthalates to their skin.[577,578] This means that exposure to phthalates **via sunscreens** can lead to absorption of these chemicals into the body. However, not all sunscreens contain phthalates, and many brands now offer phthalate-free options.

The potential **health risks** of phthalates are a topic of intense research. Some of the potential risks associated with phthalates include:

Hormonal disruption: Some phthalates have estrogen-like properties and can act as endocrine disruptors, meaning they can disrupt hormonal balance in the body.[579] This may be of particular concern during fetal and child development.[579]

Reproductive and developmental toxicity: Studies have shown an association between exposure to certain phthalates and reduced fertility and developmental problems in children.[580,581]

Respiratory and allergic reactions: Some phthalates can cause respiratory irritation (bronchial asthma) and trigger allergic reactions, especially in people who are sensitive to certain chemicals.[582]

Toxicity to liver and kidneys: There is evidence that some phthalates can cause liver and kidney damage with overexposure.[583]

Phosphates

Phosphates are a group of chemical compounds found in many foods. They play an important role in biological processes and are often used as food additives. Some common foods that may contain phosphates are:

Meat and poultry: Processed meats such as **sausages and sausages** may contain phosphates, which are used as humectants and to improve texture.[584]

Prepared foods: Many prepared foods and frozen products such as **pizza** contain phosphates to improve texture and extend shelf life.[584]

Cheese and dairy products: Some cheeses and dairy **products** may contain phosphates, which act as emulsifiers and stabilizers.[584]

Baked goods: In baked goods such as **breads, pastries and cakes**, phosphates can be used as leavening agents to loosen the dough and increase volume.[584]

Soft drinks and processed beverages: Phosphates are sometimes used in soft drinks, **colas** and other processed beverages as acidity regulators and flavor enhancers.[585]

However, excessive consumption of phosphates can be **problematic**, especially **for people with kidney problems** or other health conditions.[585] Some studies have also found a link between high phosphate consumption and health problems such as **cardiovascular disease and osteoporosis**.[584,585,586] It is therefore advisable to reduce the consumption of processed foods and food additives or to switch to a diet of fresh, unprocessed foods.

Nitrates and nitrites

Nitrates and nitrites are naturally present in many foods, especially in vegetables such as spinach, rocket, beet and celery. In the food industry, they are used as **preservatives in the form of pickling salts**, particularly in processed meats such as sausages, bacon and ham.[587] **Nitrates and nitrites counteract food spoilage** by inhibiting the growth of bacteria, particularly **Clostridium botulinum**, which **grow** in preserved foods such as **canned** foods and **produce botulinum toxin**, which is extremely dangerous and can lead to life-threatening diseases such as **botulism** with severe paralysis, speech disorders and breathing difficulties.[588]

Nitrates can be converted to nitrites by enzymes in the body. The potential danger of nitrates and nitrites in drinking water and food is mainly related to their **conversion to carcinogenic nitrosamines**, especially under certain conditions such as high temperatures (e.g. during cooking or frying) and under acidic conditions (such as in the stomach).[587]

Furthermore, nitrites can promote the **conversion of hemoglobin to methemoglobin in the red blood cells**.[587] In methemoglobin, the iron in hemoglobin is present in its oxidized form instead of its normal reduced form, so that hemoglobin is no longer able to transport sufficient oxygen. This can lead to tissue damage and, in severe cases, to life-threatening conditions such as hypoxia.

This **methemoglobinemia** can be countered, for example, with methylene **blue** as an **antidote**. Methylene blue is an artificially produced chemical compound that is used in industry as a dye, but whose medical importance was recognized as early as 1891 by Nobel Prize winner **Paul Ehrlich**.[589] In addition to its antidote properties, it is also used as an **antimalarial agent** and has **antioxidant, neuro-protective and anti-aging** effects (especially on the skin).[590]

Caution:

Even though methylene blue is often advertised as a longevity drug, high doses can cause nausea, vomiting, dizziness, breathing difficulties, drop in blood pressure, loss of consciousness and even organ failure **(acute methylene blue poisoning)**.[591] It can also lead to **life-threatening conditions such as serotonin syndrome** in patients taking antidepressants or **hemolytic anemia**, e.g. in patients with glucose-6-phosphate dehydrogenase deficiency.[591]

Acrylamide

Acrylamide is formed when carbohydrate-rich foods are **heated (above 120°C;248°F)**, in particular when **starchy foods such as potatoes and cereal products are prepared by roasting** (coffee beans, nuts), **baking** pasta made from cereals (cookies, puff pastry, crusty bread) or **deep-frying** (chips, potato chips).[592]

Although the heat-induced chemical reaction of sugars with amino acids **(Maillard reaction)** is responsible for the golden brown color ("roux") and rich taste of food, acrylamide can be formed to a greater extent at high temperatures and low humidity.[592,593] Acrylamide is considered harmful to health in higher quantities as it is **carcinogenic, neurotoxic** (damaging to nerve cells), **hepatotoxic** (damaging to the liver) and **teratogenic** (causing developmental and reproductive damage).[592,593,594] Controlling the temperature and time of cooking and baking is therefore important, but **preheating treatments such as soaking and blanching can** also **reduce the formation of acrylamide**.[593] The European Union already set legal requirements for the food industry in 2017 to limit the amount of acrylamide in industrially produced food.[592]

Benzpyrenes

Benzpyrenes are mainly formed during the incomplete combustion of organic materials such as coal, oil, gas, wood, tobacco and other organic substances. They can also be formed during the preparation of food by cooking, frying, grilling or roasting at high temperatures, especially when fat or meat juices drip onto a hot surface and smoke is produced. Like the acrylamide described above, benzpyrenes are **carcinogenic, neurotoxic and teratogenic.**[595] **Care** should therefore be taken when **using barbecues and open fires** and the consumption of heavily **roasted or charred food should be avoided**.

Infections

Infectious diseases have always been a challenge for mankind. Historically, they have decimated entire populations and changed the social fabric. The importance of infectious diseases became particularly clear during the **conquest of the New World** by the Spanish conquistadors ("conquistadores") and the impact on the indigenous population of the Americas as a tragic chapter in history.[596] When the Europeans arrived in the Americas in the 15th and 16th centuries, they brought with them a variety of infectious diseases to which the indigenous population had no immunity. Among the most devastating of these diseases were **smallpox, measles, influenza, typhoid**

and tuberculosis.[595] According to a new hypothesis, however, **leptospires (Weil's disease)**, bacteria found in many different animals such as rodents, dogs, cattle and pigs, were also involved in the fatal infection.[596] The disease is usually transmitted through contact with water or soil contaminated with urine from infected animals.

Infectious diseases spread rapidly, causing epidemic outbreaks that wiped out entire communities. Mortality rates were extremely high, with estimates of up to 90% of the indigenous population of the Americas dying from disease within a few decades of the arrival of Europeans.[597]

Over time, humanity has learned to understand, combat and control many of these diseases, for example through hygiene measures. However, despite advances in medicine and public health, infectious diseases remain a serious threat to global health.

Plague

The plague, also known as "the black death", is one of the most devastating infectious diseases in human history. It was caused by the bacterium Yersinia pestis and was rampant in Europe during the Middle Ages, killing up to a third of Europe's population, according to estimates.[598] The disease was transmitted to humans mainly by **fleas from rodents** such as rats.[599] Although plague is rare today, outbreaks still occur in some parts of the world, particularly in parts of Africa, Asia and the Americas.[598,599]

Aspergillosis

Another infectious disease, aspergillosis, is caused by fungi of the genus Aspergillus. **Air conditioning systems** can both serve **as a source** of Aspergillus spores and contribute to the spread of these spores, increasing the risk of infection, especially for those with weakened immune systems.[600] Aspergillosis can take a variety of forms, from a harmless allergic reaction to life-threatening pneumonia.[601] To minimize the risk of aspergillosis from air conditioning systems, proper maintenance and cleaning of equipment is essential. This includes regular inspections, cleaning of air filters and removal of moisture from the system to prevent mold and fungus growth. In addition, air purifiers and UV light systems can be installed in air conditioning systems to reduce the spore load in the air.

Legionellosis

Legionnaires' disease, caused by the bacterium Legionella pneumophila, is a potentially fatal infectious disease transmitted by **inhalation of water droplets** or aerosols containing the bacterium.[602] The disease can cause severe pneumonia, which primarily affects the elderly and people with weakened immune systems.[603] Prevention of legionellosis focuses on the control and elimination of Legionella bacteria in the environment, particularly in artificial water systems. This includes **regular cleaning and disinfection of air conditioning systems, showerheads, hot tubs** and other water sources, maintaining appropriate water temperatures (at least 60°C;140°F in hot water systems), and the use of biocides to disinfect water.[604]

Hepatitis

Another important topic in the area of infectious diseases is hepatitis, an inflammation of the liver that can be caused by various viruses. **Hepatitis B and C** are among the most common forms of viral hepatitis and represent a serious health problem worldwide.[605]

These viruses are mainly transmitted through **contact with infected blood or body fluids**, e.g. through unsafe medical procedures, sharing needles or unprotected sexual intercourse.[605] Although hepatitis B and C can often be asymptomatic, they can cause long-term complications such as **cirrhosis and liver cancer**. Fortunately, effective vaccines are now available to prevent hepatitis B and antiviral drugs are available to treat hepatitis C.[605] Nevertheless, the prevention and treatment of these diseases remains a challenge, especially in countries with limited resources and inadequate healthcare.[606]

HIV/AIDS

HIV/AIDS is one of the most well-known infectious diseases of modern times. HIV, the human immunodeficiency virus, weakens the body's immune system and makes it susceptible to various infections and diseases.

The virus is mainly transmitted through **unprotected sexual intercourse,** the exchange of **infected needles** and **from mother to child during pregnancy, childbirth or breastfeeding**.[607] Since the discovery of AIDS (Acquired Immunodeficiency Syndrome) in the 1980s, medical research has developed considerably, leading to better prevention and treatment of the disease. The introduction of antiretroviral drugs has significantly improved the life expectancy of people with HIV and reduced the risk of transmitting the virus to others.[608] In addition, education campaigns and measures to promote safe sexual behavior have helped to curb the spread of HIV.[608]

Influenza

Flu, also known as **influenza**, is a **highly contagious viral disease** that leads **to severe outbreaks every year**, has a **high mortality rate** and affects **around 10% of people worldwide**.[609] Flu is easily transmitted from person to person, **mainly through droplets** that become airborne when infected people cough, sneeze or speak and are inhaled by others. Symptoms include fever, chills, cough, sore throat, muscle aches, headache, fatigue and general malaise.[609] In some people, particularly the elderly, pregnant women, young children or those with weakened immune systems, flu can cause serious complications such as **pneumonia** and can **even** be **life-threatening**.[609] In addition to the direct health impact, there is also a significant economic impact due to sick days, hospitalizations and lost productivity. **Despite** the availability of **vaccines**, influenza is **not completely eradicated** as the virus is constantly changing (mutating) and new strains can emerge.[610]

COVID-19

Finally, COVID-19, caused by the SARS-CoV-2 virus, which was first identified in the Chinese city of Wuhan at the end of 2019, is the most recent global pandemic.[611]

Since its discovery, the coronavirus disease has spread rapidly around the world and led to millions of deaths.[612] As a result, global life expectancy has suffered due to **excess mortality** caused by the infections, i.e. the number of deaths during the pandemic has exceeded the usual number of expected natural deaths.[613]

COVID-19 is characterized by symptoms such as fever, cough, difficulty breathing and fatigue and can lead to pneumonia and death in severe cases.[614] To contain the spread of COVID-19, governments around the world have taken measures such as **lockdowns, social distancing, mandatory masks and vaccination campaigns**.

An ongoing problem is **post-COVID-19 fatigue syndrome**, or **long-COVID**, which is the persistent and often severe symptoms that people experience after an acute COVID-19 illness.[615] These symptoms can persist for several weeks or months after recovery from the acute infection and severely affect the quality of life of those affected: persistent fatigue, shortness of breath, chest pain, muscle weakness, joint pain, headaches, memory problems, concentration problems, sleep disorders, depression, persistent loss of sense of taste and smell and gastrointestinal complaints.[615]

The exact causes of post-COVID-19 fatigue syndrome are not yet fully understood, there are no specific diagnostic tests and treatment focuses primarily on relieving symptoms and improving the quality of life of those affected. This may involve a combination of medical therapies, physiotherapy, psychological support and nutritional advice.

Tick-borne infections

Tick-borne infections are a serious health threat that has continued to increase significantly in recent years.[616] These tiny, often overlooked spider-like parasites can transmit serious diseases, including Lyme disease and tick-borne encephalitis (TBE), which can affect both humans and animals.

Lyme borreliosis, a multisystemic disease, is caused by the bacterium Borrelia burgdorferi and is transmitted through the bite of infected ticks. Although the disease is **treatable with antibiotics** in most cases, untreated cases can lead to serious and long-term health complications such as joint inflammation and heart problems **(cardiac arrhythmias and conduction disorders)**, nerve disorders with symptoms of sensation and paralysis **(polyneuropathy)** and **meningitis**. The symptoms can vary from person to person and are often non-specific, which makes diagnosis difficult.[616]

In addition to the bacterial infection caused by Borrelia, **TBE** is a viral infection that attacks the central nervous system and can cause meningitis. Although vaccines for TBE are available, the disease remains a risk in some regions, particularly in certain parts of Europe and Asia.

The spread of ticks is influenced by various factors, including climate change, changes in the landscape, human activities and the spread of wild animals that serve as hosts. Climate change in particular has contributed to increasing tick populations in some regions, as warmer temperatures and changing precipitation patterns create ideal conditions for their survival.[617] **Ticks are true survivors**; in 2022, a tick was reported in the lab to have **survived 27 years without feeding!**[618]

To reduce the impact of tick infections, a holistic strategy based on prevention, early detection and medical treatment is required. Preventive measures include **wearing long-sleeved clothing, using repellents** (insect repellents), **regularly checking the body** after spending time outdoors and avoiding dense undergrowth and tall grass. Timely removal of ticks can significantly reduce the risk of infection.

Hygiene

The word hygiene comes from the Greek goddess of health and cleanliness Ὑγίεια (Hygieia), practices such as hand washing used to have more of a ritual or religious significance, but it was not until the 19th century that the connection between the development of disease due to a lack of personal hygiene and poor environmental conditions was understood and behavior was adapted accordingly.[619]

Good hygiene practices can help to prevent the spread of disease. Bacteria, viruses and other pathogens can accumulate on the skin and in the oral cavity. Regular hand washing and washing of the body and cleaning of the teeth can remove these pathogens, reducing the risk of infection. Oral hygiene is particularly important as the mouth is an entry point for many pathogens. **Tongue brushing, regular tooth brushing,** the use of **dental floss** and **mouthwashes** can prevent plaque and tooth decay. Good oral health is also important to prevent gum disease such as gingivitis and periodontitis. **Regular hand washing and cleansing of the body** can help prevent skin problems such as acne, eczema and skin infections. Hygiene measures are important for **diabetics**, as these people are **highly susceptible to infections**. The **use of condoms** and other protective measures can help to prevent sexually transmitted diseases.

Quarantine (isolation of infectious people) is an important hygiene measure. If one has symptoms of illness, one should stay at home to prevent the spread of infection. Moreover, pathogens should be contained by covering the mouth and nose when coughing and sneezing and by using disposable handkerchiefs and private toilets.

Cetylpyridinium chloride

Cetylpyridinium chloride (CPC) is a chemical compound that is often used as an antiseptic in mouthwashes, toothpastes, chewing gums and lozenges. In higher concentrations, CPC may be harmful: apart from mucous membrane irritation and allergic reactions, CPC is also toxic **1) by disrupting microtubule polymerization (formation of small molecules into large tubular structures) with a risk of cancer** and **2) by damaging the oligodendrocytes that form the nerve fibres and the myelin protective layer** (nerve insulation), which can lead to **brain developmental disorders in children**.[620,621]

Sugar substitutes

A key benefit of sugar substitutes is their ability to reduce the calorie content of foods, as many of these substances are **low in calories** and have a **minimal effect on blood sugar levels**. This can be beneficial for people with diabetes or those who are losing weight. In addition, **sugar alcohols** such as xylitol and sorbitol are often used in **tooth-friendly products** such as chewing gum, as they are not easily fermented by oral bacteria and can therefore reduce the risk of tooth decay. However, there are also health concerns.

Xylitol

Xylitol, also known as **birch sugar**, is a sugar alcohol derived from plant sources such as corn or birch wood. In large amounts, xylitol can cause gastrointestinal discomfort such as bloating or diarrhea.[622] Consumption of xylitol by dogs can lead to serious health problems such as a rapid drop in blood sugar levels and liver damage. It is therefore extremely important to keep xylitol away from pets.[623]

Aspartame

Aspartame is an artificial sweetener made from the amino acids aspartic acid and phenylalanine and is **about 200 times sweeter than sugar**.[624] There are concerns about the potential health effects of aspartame, especially in people with the metabolic disorder **phenylketonuria**.[624] There has also been discussion about whether aspartame can cause headaches or other neurological effects, but this is controversial and not clearly proven. Based on the current study situation, especially after the publication of a French observational study with over 100,000 people, the **World Health Organization (WHO)** classified aspartame as **"possibly carcinogenic"** in 2023.[625,626]

Erythritol

Erythritol is a calorie-free sugar alcohol obtained by fermenting glucose or starch. Some people report a cooling effect in the mouth when they consume erythritol. Of health concern is the proven link between erythritol and an **increased risk of thrombosis, heart attack, stroke and death**.[627]

Stevia

Stevia, also known as sweet leaf or honey herb, which is derived from the leaves of the South American plant Stevia rebaudiana, which is perceived to be **up to 300 times sweeter than sugar**.[628] For some people, stevia can have a bitter aftertaste. There are some concerns about the effect of stevia on fertility, but this has not yet been sufficiently researched.[628]

Sorbitol

Sorbitol, also known as glucitol, is a **sugar alcohol** that is often used as a sugar substitute in sugar-free or diabetic-friendly foods. It is made from glucose. In large quantities or in people with **sorbitol intolerance**, sorbitol can lead to gastrointestinal complaints such as flatulence or diarrhea.[629]

Accidents

Road traffic

Road traffic accidents are one of the most common causes of injuries and deaths worldwide.[630] **After the terrorist attacks on the World Trade Center and the Pentagon** on September 11, 2001, the **fear of flying was simply rampant in the USA**, so that the population traveled more by car, which led to a **significant increase in traffic fatalities**, as the behavioral psychologist **Professor Gerd Gigerenzer** and his team have found out.[631]

Traffic accidents can result in a variety of injuries, including traumatic brain injuries, spinal cord injuries, fractures, internal injuries and lacerations. The severity of injuries often depends on the speed of the collision, the type of vehicle and other factors. The **risk of fatal injury** is influenced by the following:

1. Speed
2. Driving under the influence of alcohol or drugs
3. Severity of the accident
4. Presence of safety measures such as seat belts, airbags, bicycle and motorcycle helmets.[632]

Various measures are needed to reduce the risk of traffic accidents, such as promoting safe driving practices, improving road infrastructure and promoting safety measures such as seat belts, airbags and child seats.[633] The promotion of public transport, bicycles and pedestrian zones (major exception: **e-scooters** with currently high accident figures) can also help to reduce the number of traffic accidents.

Recreational and extreme sports

Recreational and extreme sports offer undeniable benefits for physical fitness, self-confidence and personal development. However, it should not be overlooked that these activities are also associated with significant risks that can cause serious injury or even death.

First of all, it should be noted that recreational and extreme sports often take place in challenging environments that carry an increased risk of injury. Examples include **mountaineering, rafting, diving, skiing, skydiving/parachuting** (especially **wingsuit** or **BASE jumping,** i.e. from buildings **"Building"**, transmission masts **"Antenna"**, bridges **"Span"**, elevations such as rocks **"Earth"**), **kitesurfing and mountain biking**.[633] In these activities, unforeseen situations such as steep terrain, weather changes or unexpected obstacles can lead to serious accidents.

One of the most common injuries in recreational sports are falls, which can lead to fractures, sprains, strains and concussions.[634] Similarly, sports such as **scuba diving or surfing** pose **risks of drowning or water accidents**, while extreme sports such as **BASE jumping, bungee jumping or free climbing** pose a **higher risk of fatal injury** due to equipment failure or human error.[633]

The risks of recreational and extreme sports are often compounded by a lack of experience, inadequate training or a lack of adequate safety precautions. Many people **plunge into these activities un-**

prepared, without the basic skills or knowledge to recognize and manage potential dangers.

To minimize the risk of injury, adequate safety precautions are critical, including for spectators at sporting events, which are disproportionately common in racing.[635] For athletes, the **use of protective equipment** (e.g. helmets, goggles, knee pads and back protectors), **regular maintenance and inspection of equipment**, and **adherence to safety protocols** and **recommendations from experienced athletes or coaches** are necessary. In addition, it is important that athletes understand the importance of **risk assessment** and **risk management**.[636]

Mental illness

Mental illnesses are invisible shackles that limit the lives of many people in unimaginable ways. From the pervasive burden of depression to the shattering reality of schizophrenia and the insidious poison of loneliness, these illnesses shape the experiences and tragically limit the quality of life of those affected.

Depression

Depression, often referred to as the **"silent killer"**, is a disorder that is far more than temporary sadness or melancholy.[637] It affects every aspect of life and often leaves sufferers trapped in an endless vortex of hopelessness and despair. The simplest tasks can become insurmountable hurdles, and the feeling of emptiness can be so over-whelming that it calls existence itself into question. The joy of life fades and every day becomes a struggle to even get up and carry on.

People suffering from depression have a **significantly increased risk of suicidal ideation and attempts**.[638] The overwhelming hope-lessness and despair that can accompany severe depression can lead to the thought that suicide is the only solution to escape the emo-tional pain.

Depression can also have serious effects on physical health. People with depression have an increased risk of **cardiovascular disease, hypertension, diabetes mellitus, obesity** and other chronic diseas-es, as depression can affect lifestyle by leading to poor eating and sleeping habits and a lack of exercise.[639]

Psychotherapy: Cognitive behavioral therapy, interpersonal therapy and mindfulness-based therapies are effective approaches to treating depression.[640] These therapies can help identify and change negative thought patterns, improve coping with stressful life events and de-velop effective coping strategies.

Drug therapy: Antidepressants are a common drug treatment op-tion for depression. **Selective serotonin reuptake inhibitors (SSRIs)** and **serotonin-norepinephrine reuptake inhibitors (SNRIs)** are some of the most commonly prescribed medications for the treatment of depression and have greatly displaced previously established **tricyclic antidepressants** and **monoamine oxidase (MAO) inhibitors**.[641]

Light therapy: Light therapy can be particularly effective for seasonal affective disorder. This form of therapy involves exposure to bright light to regulate hormone levels and improve mood.[642]

Exercise therapy: Regular physical activity can have a positive effect on mood and contribute to the treatment of depression. Exercise can promote the release of endorphins and other neurotransmitter-regulating substances that increase well-being.[643]

Loneliness

Loneliness is another grim reality that many people, whether with with or without a diagnosed mental illness. It is not a temporary feeling of isolation, but a deep-rooted, long-lasting sense of separation from others and from oneself. Loneliness can have both physical and mental effects, undermining self-esteem, destroying confidence and increasing the risk of further mental health problems.[644] Even in a crowded world, someone can feel profoundly lonely, trapped in an endless maze of self-isolation. A **new therapeutic approach** is the use of **social media platforms** to reach patients for medical and psychological intervention programs.[644] The evaluation of accelerometers, electronic diary and brain imaging data showed that regular physical activity has a positive effect on the mental state of those affected by loneliness.[645]

Schizophrenia

Schizophrenia, on the other hand, is a complex disorder that distorts the perception of reality and destroys self-image. Sufferers can be plagued by **hallucinations** (such as hearing voices that others do not hear) and **delusions** (false beliefs held despite evidence to the contrary) that isolate them from the outside world and plunge them into a frightening **world of paranoia and chaos**.[646,647]

Individuals with schizophrenia have **disorganized thinking,** meaning they may have difficulty organizing their thoughts or expressing themselves coherently. This may manifest as fragmented speech or difficulty following a conversation.[648]

Schizophrenic individuals lose the ability to function normally, resulting in diminished emotional expression, social withdrawal, and a lack of motivation or interest in daily activities. Schizophrenia can rob individuals of a sense of control over their own lives and keep them trapped in a permanent state of confusion and anxiety.[649] In acute psychotic states, there is also a risk of **danger to oneself and others**.[650]

The following treatment options are available:

Antipsychotic medication: Antipsychotics are the main treatment for schizophrenia.[651] They help to control positive symptoms such as hallucinations and delusions by affecting the activity of certain neurotransmitters in the brain.

Psychoeducation: Psychoeducation involves the provision of information about the illness, treatment options and coping strategies for those affected and their families. This improves understanding of the illness and promotes adherence to treatment.[652]

Psychotherapy: In addition to drug treatment, psychotherapy can be helpful, particularly in coping with negative symptoms, social difficulties and improving quality of life.[653]

Supportive therapy: Supportive therapies such as occupational therapy, music therapy and art therapy can help to promote social integration, improve communication skills and boost self-esteem.[654]

Anxiety disorder

Anxiety is a normal human emotion that helps us react to potential threats and protect ourselves. It occurs when we feel in danger or are faced with stress. But for some people, this natural reaction develops into something overwhelming and paralyzing. Anxiety disorders are serious mental illnesses that can have a significant impact on the lives of those affected.

The impact of anxiety disorders on an individual's life can be devastating. People suffering from anxiety disorders **often** experience **significant impairment** in various areas of life, including **work, school, social relationships and leisure activities**. The constant stress of anxiety can lead to sleep disturbances, concentration problems, physical discomfort and a restricted lifestyle.[655] In addition, the constant tension and worry can increase the **risk of** other mental illnesses such as **depression**.[656]

The social impact of anxiety disorders should also not be underestimated. Anxiety disorders can lead to significant **economic burdens** by reducing productivity in the workplace, placing a strain on the healthcare system and placing a strain on public resources.[657]

In addition, the **stigmatization of mental illness** can lead to sufferers being reluctant to seek help and their symptoms going unrecognized or untreated.[658]

Anxiety disorders are complex and multifaceted, which can have various causes, including genetic predisposition, neurobiological factors, environmental factors and life experiences.[659,660] The treatment of anxiety disorders therefore requires a comprehensive approach that includes medical, therapeutic and supportive interventions. Medications such as **antidepressants and benzodiazepines** can be used to alleviate symptoms, while **cognitive behavioral therapy, exposure therapy** and other psychotherapeutic approaches can help to change negative thought patterns and behaviors.[660]

Stress

Stress is a natural response of the body to challenges we face in everyday life. While stress is often seen as negative, there are two main types of stress: distress and eustress. **Distress** is **negative stress** that can affect health and well-being, while **eustress** is **positive stress** that can motivate and increase performance.[661]

Distress

Distress can have a variety of negative effects on health. Distress occurs when we feel overwhelmed, overwhelmed or unable to cope with the challenges we face. For example, financial problems, interpersonal conflicts or professional pressure can trigger distress. Distress can lead to feeling stressed, anxious or depressed. It can also cause physical symptoms such as **headaches, sleep disturbances and stomach problems**.[662,663]

Long-term distress can have serious effects on health. Chronic stress can weaken the immune system, increase the **risk of cardiovascular disease, chronic obstructive pulmonary disease (COPD), arthritis, diabetes mellitus** and lead to a deterioration in mental health.[664,665] In addition, distress can increase the **risk of burnout** and other work-related stress consequences.[666]

Eustress

In contrast to distress, **eustress** is a form of stress that is seen as positive or productive. It occurs when facing a challenge that is perceived as manageable and rewarding. For example, preparing for an exam, planning a wedding or striving to achieve professional goals can trigger eustress. Eustress can help to improve performance, promote creativity and boost self-confidence.

The health effects of eustress can be positive as long as it is experienced in appropriate amounts and for limited periods of time. **Eustress can** help to **strengthen mental and emotional resilience** by helping to cope with challenges and develop skills.[667] In addition, eustress can **strengthen immune function** and improve overall well-being by triggering positive emotions such as joy and fulfillment.[668]

However, a growing number of people consider eustress to be critical for "longevity" and therefore recommend abolishing the term "eustress".[669] This was impressively demonstrated, for example, at the 2006 **Soccer World Cup** in Germany: whenever the German national team played, **the rate of heart attacks increased significantly.**[670]

In order to minimize the health effects of eustress and distress, it is important to **learn** and apply **stress management techniques**. These include **regular exercise, relaxation techniques such as meditation and breathing exercises, a balanced diet**, sufficient sleep and maintaining social relationships. Learning how to deal with stressors and develop healthy coping mechanisms should improve health and well-being and achieve a balance between eustress and distress.

Wars, terrorism and street violence

Reduced life expectancy due to wars, terrorism and street violence in urban areas is a serious problem that threatens the health and well-being of millions of people worldwide. Both wars and street violence lead to direct and indirect effects that influence life expectancy and severely affect life in urban communities.

Wars

Wars, whether through armed conflict between states or internal civil wars, have a devastating impact on populations. The immediate threat of bombing, rocket attacks, shelling, mines and shooting leads to a direct loss of life. Civilians, including children, women and the elderly, are often **victims of violence, resulting in increased mortality rates and reduced life expectancy.**

In addition, wars lead to the destruction of infrastructure, including hospitals, schools and public facilities. The lack of medical care, clean water and food **exacerbates existing health problems and increases the risk of disease and malnutrition.**[671] The interruption of healthcare and access to life-saving treatment further contributes to high mortality rates and shortens the life expectancy of the population.

In order to combat the **reduced life expectancy caused by war** at the international level, both short-term emergency aid and long-term peace and reconciliation processes should be implemented. The international community must commit to promoting peace, security and stability through **diplomatic efforts** and **conflict prevention.**[672] Furthermore, it is important to address the root causes of conflict, reduce inequality and promote socio-economic development in order to ensure long-term sustainable peace stability and a better quality of life for all.

Terrorism

Terrorism is one of the most threatening and harrowing realities of our time. The devastating effects of acts of terrorism go far beyond the immediate physical damage and can have a life-limiting impact on individuals, communities and societies.

First of all, it is important to recognize that terrorism not only endangers physical health, but can also have a massive impact on mental health. Victims of terrorist attacks often face severe traumatic experiences that can lead to a variety of mental health problems, including **post-traumatic stress disorder, anxiety, depression and sleep disorders**.[673] These mental health problems can severely affect the daily lives of those affected and significantly limit their ability to lead a normal life.

Furthermore, terrorism can also cause a significant restriction of individual freedoms and social life. Faced with the threat of terrorist violence, people may tend to restrict their activities, avoid public places and avoid travel. These restrictions can lead to a **feeling of loneliness, isolation and fear**, which significantly affects the quality of life of those affected.

In addition, terrorism also has a life-limiting effect on society as a whole. The threat of terrorist violence can lead to an atmosphere of fear and insecurity that corrodes the social fabric and undermines trust between people. This can lead to a division in society, weakening social cohesion and affecting the ability to overcome challenges together.

In addition to the **direct impact on individual and social health** and well-being, terrorism also has long-term consequences for the **political, economic and cultural development of communities** and nations. Terrorist attacks can lead to a hardening of political attitudes, a restriction of civil liberties and a deterioration of economic conditions. They can also lead to tensions between different population groups and make intercultural dialog more difficult.

Given these **life-limiting effects of terrorism**, it is critical that governments, communities and individuals take appropriate measures to combat terrorism and minimize its impact. This includes **strength-**

ening security measures, promoting intercultural understanding and dialog, providing **psychosocial support for victims and witnesses,** and **promoting resilience** (the ability to cope with challenges in difficult situations) **and cohesion in society.**[674]

Ultimately, terrorism is not only a threat to physical life, but also a serious threat to the foundations of society and human existence. It is therefore crucial to work together to combat terrorism in all its forms and create a world where peace, security and prosperity are possible for all.

Street violence

Street violence in urban areas is another significant factor that affects life expectancy. Youth gangs, criminal organizations and social unrest can lead to an increase in violence on the streets, including shootings, rapes, robberies and murders. The fear of violence and crime restricts people's freedom of movement, especially after dark, and affects their social participation and general well-being.

Street violence also has an indirect impact on the health and life expectancy of the population. Frequent acts of violence can lead to psychological stress, trauma and anxiety, which have long-term effects on physical and mental health. The **prevalence of illicit drugs** and the **abuse of alcohol,** which are often **associated with street violence, increase the risk of addiction and overdose, which can also lead to premature death.**

To combat the **reduced life expectancy caused by street violence** in urban areas, comprehensive measures are needed that include

strengthening the rule of law and public safety.[675] In addition, it is important to address the socio-economic causes of violence, such as poverty, inequality and lack of social integration, in order to achieve a sustainable improvement in living conditions in urban communities and increase life expectancy. This is because a strong socio-economic divide has a direct impact on physical health, as a significant increase in cardiovascular disease has been documented in economically weak regions, for example.[676]

Conclusions

- With a sensible lifestyle, long life is not magic

- Be aware of the health risks of sunscreens and
food additives

- A simple mantra for treating addiction: stop drinking, taking drugs and smoking **immediately,** with professional help if necessary

- Be mindful of oneself, one's fellow human-beings and the environment

Chapter 6: Recipes

Nutritional recommendations often refer to a "healthy, balanced diet". But what does this actually mean? Based on the current findings of nutritional medicine, which are, however, as described above, also controversial and constantly changing, the following **50 recipes** for starters, main courses and desserts can be used to provide incentives for a hopefully **healthy, balanced diet.**

The cooking suggestions show that cooking can be done quickly and does not have to be complicated. Compared to frozen pizza, ready meals and eating out, cooking at home for oneself is usually healthier, cheaper and makes one happier, because cooking is also fun!

Starters

Greek salad with tomatoes and cucumber

Preparation time: approx. 15 minutes

Servings: 4

Ingredients:

2 large ripe tomatoes

1 cucumber

1 red onion

1 green bell pepper

100 g feta cheese

1/4 cup pitted Kalamata olives (optional)

2 tablespoons extra virgin olive oil

1 tablespoon fresh lemon juice

1 teaspoon dried oregano

Salt and pepper to taste

Fresh parsley or basil for garnish (optional)

Instructions:

Preparation of the ingredients:

Rinse and dice the tomatoes and place in a large bowl.

Peel the cucumber, cut in half and remove the seeds with a spoon. Cut the cucumber into thin slices and add to the tomatoes.

Peel the red onion and cut into thin half rings. Remove the seeds from the pepper and cut into strips. Add both to the tomatoes and cucumber.

Cut the feta cheese into small cubes and sprinkle over the vegetables.

Optionally, add the pitted kalamata olives.

Prepare the dressing:

In a small bowl, mix together the olive oil, lemon juice, dried oregano, salt and pepper.

Assemble the salad:

Pour the dressing over the salad and gently mix everything together until the ingredients are evenly coated with it.

Garnish:

Garnish with fresh parsley or basil leaves, if desired.

Allow the Greek salad to stand in the fridge for at least 15 minutes before serving so that the flavors combine well.

Serve and arrange on plates.

Serve:

Serve the Greek salad as a healthy starter before the main course.

This Greek salad is not only healthy, but also refreshing and full of flavor. It is perfect as a light starter for a summer meal or as a side dish with grilled meat or fish.

Roasted chickpeas with spices

Preparation time: approx. 30 minutes

Servings: 4

Ingredients:

2 tins of chickpeas (400 g each), drained and rinsed

2 tablespoons olive oil

1 teaspoon ground cumin

1 teaspoon paprika powder

1 teaspoon garlic powder

1 teaspoon onion powder

1/2 teaspoon ground turmeric

Salt and pepper to taste

Fresh herbs for garnish (optional)

Instructions:

Preheat the oven and prepare the chickpeas:

Preheat the oven to 200°C (392°F) (top/bottom heat).

Pat the drained and rinsed chickpeas dry between two kitchen towels to remove any excess moisture.

Season the chickpeas:

Place the dry chickpeas in a large bowl and drizzle with olive oil.

Add the spices (cumin, paprika, garlic powder, onion powder, turmeric, salt and pepper) and mix well until the chickpeas are evenly coated with the spices.

Roast the chickpeas:

Spread the spiced chickpeas on a baking tray lined with baking paper, making sure they are not touching.

Bake the chickpeas in the preheated oven for about 20-25 minutes, turning occasionally, until golden brown and crispy.

Serve:

Remove the roasted chickpeas from the oven and leave to cool slightly.

Garnish with fresh herbs as desired, e.g. chopped parsley or coriander.

Serve the roasted chickpeas as a healthy and crispy starter.

These roasted chickpeas are rich in fiber, protein and healthy fats. They are a delicious and crunchy starter that is ideal for nibbling on before the main course. They can also be enjoyed as a healthy snack between meals.

Chicory with oranges and slivered almonds

Preparation time: approx. 15 minutes

Servings: 4

Ingredients:

4 chicory heads

2 oranges

50 g slivered almonds

2 tablespoons olive oil

1 tablespoon honey

1 tablespoon lemon juice

Salt and pepper to taste

Instructions:

Prepare the chicory:

Remove the outer leaves of the chicory. Cut the heads in half and remove the stalk.

Cut the chicory halves into thin strips and place in a large salad bowl.

Prepare the oranges:

Peel the oranges and cut into thin slices. Make sure to remove the seeds.

Pour the juice from the slicing over the chicory.

Toasting the almond slivers:

Toast the slivered almonds in a dry pan over a medium heat until golden brown. Stir occasionally so that they brown evenly.

Preparing the salad dressing:

In a small bowl, mix together the olive oil, honey and lemon juice. Season to taste with salt and pepper.

Assembling the salad:

Sprinkle the toasted almond slivers over the chicory and oranges.

Pour the dressing over the salad.

Mix carefully:

Mix everything carefully until the ingredients are evenly coated with the dressing. Be careful not to mash the salad.

Serve:

Arrange the chicory salad with oranges and slivered almonds on plates.

Sprinkle with freshly ground black pepper to taste.

Serve immediately and enjoy.

This chicory salad with oranges and slivered almonds is a refreshing yet hearty salad creation. It makes an excellent starter or accompaniment to various main courses.

Basil, mozzarella, tomatoes in olive oil (Caprese salad)

Preparation time: approx. 15 minutes

Servings: 2-3

Ingredients:

2-3 large tomatoes, cut into slices

1-2 balls of mozzarella, sliced

Fresh basil leaves

2 cloves of garlic, thinly sliced or chopped

Extra virgin olive oil

Salt and pepper to taste

Optional: balsamic glaze or balsamic vinegar for drizzling

Instructions:

Preparation of the ingredients:

Wash and slice the tomatoes.

Cut the mozzarella into slices too.

Peel the garlic cloves and cut or chop into thin slices.

Pluck the basil leaves from the stalks and set aside.

Serve the salad:

On a large serving plate, arrange the tomato slices, mozzarella slices and basil leaves alternately.

Scatter the thin slices of garlic over the salad or spread the chopped garlic evenly on top.

Season and drizzle:

Drizzle the salad generously with extra virgin olive oil.

Season with salt and pepper to taste.

If desired, drizzle a little balsamic glaze or balsamic vinegar over the salad to give it additional flavor nuances.

Serve:

Serve immediately, ideally at room temperature to make the most of the flavors.

This Caprese salad is a simple yet elegant dish that captures the freshness and flavors of Mediterranean cuisine. It is perfect as a starter or as a side dish to main courses. The combination of juicy tomatoes, creamy mozzarella, fresh basil and spicy garlic in olive oil creates a taste experience that is to be enjoyed again and again.

Avocado salad

Preparation time: approx. 15 minutes

Servings: 2-3

Ingredients:

2 ripe avocados, pitted and cut into cubes

1 large tomato, diced

1/2 red onion, finely chopped

1/2 cucumber, seeded and diced

1 handful of rocket or baby spinach

juice of one lime or lemon

2 tablespoons olive oil

Salt and pepper to taste

Optional: fresh herbs such as coriander or parsley, chopped

Optional: Feta cheese, crumbled

Instructions:

Preparation of the ingredients:

Cut the avocados in half, remove the stone and carefully remove the flesh from the skin with a spoon. Cut into cubes and place in a large bowl.

Dice the tomato and add to the avocado in the bowl.

Finely chop the red onion and add to the bowl.

Deseed the cucumber and cut into cubes. Add to the bowl with the other ingredients.

Wash the rocket or baby spinach and pat dry.

Prepare the dressing:

Drizzle the juice of a lime or lemon over the avocado and vegetables in the bowl.

Add the olive oil.

Season to taste with salt and pepper.

Optionally add chopped herbs.

Serve:

Carefully mix everything in the bowl until the dressing and ingredients are evenly distributed.

Sprinkle with feta cheese if desired.

Serve immediately and enjoy!

This avocado salad is easy to prepare and offers a refreshing and healthy option for a meal or as a side dish to other dishes. The combination of creamy avocado, fresh vegetables and a simple dressing makes it a tasty and balanced dish.

Tomato and mozzarella skewers with basil pesto

Preparation time: approx. 15 minutes

Servings: 4

Ingredients:

2 large tomatoes

1 ball of mozzarella cheese

Fresh basil leaves

olive oil

Balsamic glaze

Salt and pepper to taste

Wooden skewers or cocktail sticks

For the basil pesto:

2 cups fresh basil leaves

2 cloves of garlic, roughly chopped

1/4 cup toasted pine nuts

1/4 cup freshly grated Parmesan cheese

1/2 cup extra virgin olive oil

Salt and pepper to taste

Instructions:

Prepare the tomatoes and mozzarella:

Wash the tomatoes and cut into slices about 1 cm thick.

Cut the mozzarella into slices of a similar thickness to the tomatoes.

Prepare the basil pesto:

Place all the ingredients for the basil pesto (basil leaves, garlic, pine nuts, parmesan, olive oil, salt and pepper) in a blender or food processor.

Blend everything to a smooth paste. If necessary, add more olive oil to achieve the desired consistency. Season to taste with salt and pepper.

Assemble the skewers:

Thread a slice of tomato, a slice of mozzarella and a basil leaf alternately onto each wooden skewer or cocktail stick until the skewer is full.

Arrange the finished skewers on a serving plate.

Serve:

Drizzle the skewers with olive oil and balsamic glaze.

Season with a pinch of salt and pepper.

Serve the basil pesto in a small bowl next to the skewers.

Serve the tomato and mozzarella skewers with basil pesto as a healthy and refreshing starter.

These tomato and mozzarella skewers with basil pesto are not only healthy, but also full of flavors and textures. They are perfect for a light start to a delicious meal and are also easy to prepare for when guests arrive.

Pumpkin soup

Preparation time: approx. 45 minutes

Servings: 4

Ingredients:

1 medium-sized pumpkin (Hokkaido, butternut or nutmeg pumpkin), approx. 1.5 kg

1 large onion, chopped

2 cloves of garlic, chopped

1 liter vegetable stock

200 ml coconut milk (optional)

2 tablespoons olive oil or coconut oil

1 teaspoon ground ginger

1 teaspoon ground turmeric

1 teaspoon of ground cumin

Salt and pepper to taste

Optional: toasted pumpkin seeds or croutons to garnish

Instructions:

Preparing the pumpkin:

Cut the pumpkin in half and remove the seeds with a spoon.

Cut the pumpkin flesh into cubes, removing the skin if desired.

Fry the onion and garlic:

In a large saucepan, heat the olive oil or coconut oil.

Add the chopped onion and garlic and sauté over a medium heat until translucent.

Add the pumpkin and spices:

Add the diced pumpkin to the pot and sauté with the onions and garlic for about 5 minutes, until lightly browned.

Add the ground ginger, turmeric and cumin and fry for a further 2 minutes, stirring constantly to release the flavors.

Cook the soup:

Add the vegetable stock to cover the pumpkin.

Bring the soup to the boil and then reduce the heat to a gentle simmer.

Simmer for about 20-25 minutes until the pumpkin is soft.

Puree the soup:

Remove the soup from the heat and puree with a hand blender or in a blender until smooth.

Optional: Add the coconut milk and blend again briefly to make the soup creamier.

Season the pumpkin soup to taste with salt and pepper.

Serve:

Serve hot and garnish with roasted pumpkin seeds or croutons if desired.

This delicious pumpkin soup is perfect for fall and winter days and is easy to prepare. It is warm, comforting and full of flavor. Serve the soup as a starter or as a main course with a piece of fresh bread or a salad.

Mozzarella beetroot towers

Preparation time: approx. 25 minutes

Servings: 2

Ingredients:

2 medium-sized beets, cooked and peeled

2 mozzarella balls

2 large tomatoes

1 bunch of fresh basil

2 tablespoons balsamic vinegar

2 tablespoons olive oil

Salt and pepper to taste

Optional: balsamic glaze for garnish

Instructions:

Preparation of the ingredients:

Cut the cooked and peeled beet into slices about 1 cm thick.

Also cut the mozzarella balls into slices.

Wash and slice the tomatoes.

Pluck the basil leaves from the stalks and set aside.

Assemble the towers:

Start on a plate with a slice of beet as the base.

Place a slice of mozzarella on top, followed by a slice of tomato.

Sprinkle with a few basil leaves and season with a pinch of salt and pepper.

Repeat this process until one has 2-3 layers, depending on the size of the ingredients and how high one wants to make the tower.

Finish with a slice of beet.

Making the dressing:

In a small bowl, mix together the balsamic vinegar and olive oil. Season to taste with salt and pepper.

Serve:

Arrange the towers on plates.

Drizzle the dressing over the towers.

Garnish with a little balsamic glaze if desired.

Serve immediately and enjoy!

This mozzarella and beet tower is not only a feast for the eyes, but also a taste sensation with the combination of sweet beet, creamy mozzarella, juicy tomatoes and fresh basil. It is a simple but elegant starter or side dish for special occasions or a light lunch.

Main courses

Fried mackerel fillet with steamed vegetables

Preparation time: approx. 25 minutes

Servings: 2

Ingredients:

2 mackerel fillets (approx. 150-200 g each)

Juice of 1 lemon

Salt and pepper to taste

2 tablespoons of olive oil

2 cloves of garlic, chopped

1 onion, cut into thin rings

1 bell pepper, cut into strips

1 zucchini, sliced

1 carrot, peeled and thinly sliced

1 handful of fresh spinach leaves

Fresh herbs to garnish (optional)

Instructions:

Prepare the mackerel fillets:

Rinse the mackerel fillets under cold water and pat dry with kitchen paper.

Sprinkle the fillets with lemon juice and season with salt and pepper.

Prepare the vegetables:

Peel and finely chop the garlic cloves.

Prepare the onion, bell pepper, zucchini and carrot and cut into the desired shape.

Steam the vegetables:

Heat 1 tablespoon of olive oil in a frying pan.

Add the chopped garlic and fry briefly until fragrant.

Add the onion rings and fry, stirring, until translucent.

Add the peppers, zucchini and carrot and sauté for about 5-7 minutes until the vegetables are soft but still firm to the bite.

Finally, add the fresh spinach leaves and sauté briefly until they collapse. Remove the pan from the heat and keep warm.

Fry the mackerel fillets:

Heat the remaining olive oil in a separate pan.

Place the mackerel fillets skin-side down in the pan and fry for about 3-4 minutes until the skin is crispy and the meat is cooked through.

Carefully turn the fillets over and fry again for 1-2 minutes until the meat on the other side is also cooked through.

Serve:

Arrange the steamed vegetables on plates.

Place the fried mackerel fillets on top.

Garnish with fresh herbs as desired.

Serve immediately and enjoy!

This dish is not only healthy, but also rich in flavor and nutrients. It is perfect for a light dinner or a healthy lunch snack.

Grilled chicken with sweet potato puree

Preparation time: approx. 45 minutes

Servings: 2

Ingredients:

For the grilled chicken:

2 chicken breast fillets

Juice of half a lemon

2 cloves of garlic, chopped

Fresh or dried rosemary and thyme leaves

Salt and pepper to taste

2 tablespoons of olive oil

For the sweet potato puree:

2 large sweet potatoes

2 tablespoons butter

1/4 cup milk or cream (optional)

Salt and pepper to taste

Instructions:

Preparation of the grilled chicken:

Rinse the chicken breasts and pat dry.

In a bowl, mix together the lemon juice, minced garlic, rosemary, thyme, salt, pepper and olive oil.

Turn the chicken breast fillets in the marinade and leave to marinate for at least 15-20 minutes.

Prepare the sweet potato puree:

Peel the sweet potatoes and cut into cubes.

Cover the sweet potato cubes with water in a pan and bring to boil. Cook for approx. 15-20 minutes until the sweet potatoes are soft.

Grill the chicken:

While the sweet potatoes are cooking, preheat the grill.

Place the marinated chicken breasts on the grill and grill for about 6-8 minutes per side, depending on thickness, until cooked through and nicely grill-marked. The exact grilling time may vary depending on the grill.

Preparation of the sweet potato puree:

Drain the cooked sweet potatoes and return them to the pot.

Add the butter to the sweet potatoes and mash to a puree using a potato masher or fork.

If necessary, add milk or cream to achieve the desired consistency. Season to taste with salt and pepper.

Serve:

Serve the grilled chicken with the sweet potato puree on plates.

Garnish with fresh herbs if desired.

Serve immediately and enjoy!

This dish offers a perfect combination of juicy grilled chicken and creamy sweet potato puree, which is a real treat with its flavors.

Vegetable stir-fry with wholegrain pasta

Preparation time: approx. 25 minutes

Servings: 2-3

Ingredients:

200 g wholegrain pasta (e.g. wholegrain spaghetti or wholegrain penne)

2 tablespoons olive oil

2 cloves of garlic, chopped

1 onion, thinly sliced

1 bell pepper, cut into strips

1 zucchini, sliced

1 carrot, thinly sliced

1 handful cherry tomatoes, halved

2 cups baby spinach

Salt and pepper to taste

Optional: fresh herbs such as basil or parsley, chopped

Optional: Parmesan cheese to serve

Instructions:

Preparation of the whole wheat pasta:

Cook the wholegrain pasta in boiling salted water until al dente according to the instructions on the packaging. Drain and set aside.

Preparing the vegetable stir-fry:

Heat the olive oil in a large frying pan over a medium heat.

Add the chopped garlic and onion slices and sauté for 1-2 minutes until fragrant and lightly golden brown.

Add the peppers, zucchinis and carrots to the pan and fry for a further 5-7 minutes until the vegetables are soft but still crunchy.

Add the halved cherry tomatoes and cook for a further 2-3 minutes until softened.

Add the spinach and cook, stirring constantly, until it has collapsed.

Season with salt and pepper and add fresh herbs to taste.

Combining pasta and vegetables:

Add the cooked wholegrain pasta to the vegetable pan and mix well so that the flavors are evenly distributed.

Remove the pan from the heat.

Serve:

Divide the vegetable stir-fry with wholegrain pasta between plates.

Sprinkle with chopped herbs to taste and serve with freshly grated Parmesan cheese.

Serve immediately and enjoy!

This vegetable stir-fry with wholegrain pasta is not only healthy and full of flavor, but also easy to prepare and provides a delicious and balanced meal.

Tofu stir fry with rice

Preparation time: approx. 30 minutes

Servings: 2-3

Ingredients:

For the tofu stir fry:

200 g firm tofu, cut into cubes

2 tablespoons of soy sauce

1 tablespoon sesame oil or neutral vegetable oil

2 cloves of garlic, chopped

1 onion, thinly sliced

1 red bell pepper, cut into strips

1 yellow bell pepper, cut into strips

1 carrot, cut into thin strips

100 g sugar snap peas

2 spring onions, sliced

Optional: ginger, chopped

Optional: hot chilli peppers, chopped (depending on desired level of heat)

Salt and pepper to taste

For the rice:

1 cup jasmine rice (or other rice of choice)

2 cups of water

Instructions:

Preparation of the rice:

Rinse the rice thoroughly in cold water until the water runs clear.

Place the rinsed rice in a saucepan and add 2 cups of water.

Bring the rice to the boil, then reduce the heat, put the lid on and simmer the rice for about 15-20 minutes until it is soft and the water has been absorbed. Remove the pan from the heat and leave the rice to rest with the lid on for about 5 minutes.

Marinate and fry the tofu:

Marinate the tofu cubes in a bowl with soy sauce and leave to stand for a few minutes.

Heat the sesame oil (or neutral oil) in a large frying pan over a medium heat.

Add the marinated tofu cubes to the pan and fry for 5-7 minutes until golden brown and crispy. Stir occasionally to ensure even browning.

Remove the fried tofu from the pan and set aside.

Preparation of the stir fry:

Heat a little more oil in the same pan, if needed.

Add the chopped garlic, onion slices and optionally the chopped ginger to the pan and fry for about 1 minute until fragrant.

Add the peppers, carrots and mangetout and fry for a further 5-7 minutes until the vegetables are soft but still crunchy.

Return the fried tofu to the pan and mix with the vegetables.

Add the spring onions and chopped chilli peppers, if using. Season to taste with salt and pepper.

Serve:

Serve the tofu stir fry with rice on plates.

Garnish with fresh herbs or additional soy sauce as desired.

Serve immediately and enjoy!

This tofu stir fry with rice is a delicious and nutritious meal that is full of flavors and texture. It offers a good balance of protein, carbohydrates and vegetables and is perfect for a quick weeknight dinner.

Vegetable curry with chicken

Preparation time: approx. 40 minutes

Servings: 4

Ingredients:

500 g chicken breast, cut into cubes

2 tablespoons vegetable oil (e.g. sunflower oil)

1 onion, chopped

3 cloves of garlic, chopped

1 tablespoon fresh ginger, chopped

2-3 tablespoons curry paste (depending on taste and spiciness)

1 can (400 ml) unsweetened coconut milk

2 carrots, thinly sliced

1 red bell pepper, cut into strips

1 yellow bell pepper, cut into strips

1 zucchini, cut into cubes

1 cup peas

Salt and pepper to taste

Optional: fresh coriander or parsley to garnish

Optional: lime wedges to serve

Cooked rice or naan bread (Indian flatbread) to serve

Instructions:

Fry the chicken:

Heat the vegetable oil in a large frying pan or wok.

Add the chicken cubes and fry over a medium-high heat for about 5-7 minutes until golden brown and cooked through. Stir occasionally to ensure even browning.

Remove the fried chicken cubes from the pan and set aside.

Prepare the vegetable curry:

In the same pan, sauté the chopped onion, chopped garlic and chopped ginger over a medium heat for about 2-3 minutes until soft and fragrant.

Add the curry paste and fry for a further 1-2 minutes to release the flavors.

Add the carrot, bell pepper and zucchini pieces and fry for about 5 minutes until the vegetables soften slightly.

Add the coconut milk and stir well to distribute the curry paste evenly.

Add the peas and simmer for a further 5 minutes until the vegetables are cooked and the sauce has thickened slightly.

Season to taste with salt and pepper.

Assemble the curry:

Return the sautéed chicken cubes to the pan and mix well with the vegetables and sauce.

Heat again briefly until the chicken is warmed through again.

Serve:

Serve the vegetable curry with the chicken on warmed plates.

Garnish with fresh herbs such as coriander or parsley as desired.

Serve with lime wedges and cooked rice or naan bread.

Serve immediately and enjoy!

Vegetable curry with chicken is rich in flavor and aromas and offers a delicious blend of tender chicken, colorful vegetables and a creamy coconut milk sauce.

Quinoa salad with avocado and black beans

Preparation time: approx. 30 minutes

Servings: 4

Ingredients:

1 cup quinoa

2 cups of water or vegetable stock

1 can (approx. 400 g) black beans, drained and rinsed

2 ripe avocados, pitted and diced

1 large tomato, diced

1/2 red onion, finely chopped

1 red bell pepper, diced

1/2 bunch fresh coriander, chopped

juice of 2 limes

3 tablespoons olive oil

Salt and pepper to taste

Optional: 1 jalapeño (medium hot bell pepper) or green chili, deseeded and finely chopped

Optional: 1 clove of garlic, finely chopped

Optional: Fresh spinach or rocket to serve

Instructions:

Cook the quinoa:

Rinse the quinoa thoroughly in cold water to remove the bitter substances.

Bring the water or vegetable stock to the boil in a pan.

Add the rinsed quinoa and bring to the boil. Reduce the heat, put the lid on and simmer the quinoa for about 15 minutes until it is soft and the water has been completely absorbed.

Remove the pan from the heat and fluff the quinoa with a fork. Leave to cool.

Preparation of the ingredients:

While the quinoa is cooking and cooling, drain and thoroughly rinse the black beans.

Cut the avocados in half, remove the stone and carefully scoop the flesh out of the skin with a spoon. Cut into cubes and set aside.

Prepare the tomato, red onion, red bell pepper and fresh coriander and place in a large bowl.

Prepare the dressing:

In a small bowl, mix together the juice of 2 limes, olive oil, salt and pepper.

If desired, add minced garlic and jalapeño or green chile and mix well.

Assemble the salad:

Add the cooled quinoa to the prepared ingredients in the bowl.

Add the drained black beans.

Pour the dressing over the salad and mix gently until everything is well combined.

Serve:

Place the quinoa salad with avocado and black beans on plates or a serving platter.

Garnish with fresh spinach or rocket as desired.

Serve immediately and enjoy!

This quinoa salad with avocado and black beans is a delicious and nutritious meal that is rich in protein, fiber and healthy fats. It's perfect as a main course for a light lunch or dinner or as a side dish for barbecues.

Roasted vegetable tabbouleh

Preparation time: approx. 40 minutes

Servings: 4

Ingredients:

For the roasted vegetables:

2 cups mixed vegetables of choice, cut into small pieces (e.g. bell pepper, zucchini, eggplant, cherry tomatoes)

2 tablespoons olive oil

Salt and pepper to taste

Optional: garlic powder, paprika powder, cumin for additional flavor

For the tabbouleh:

1 cup bulgur

2 cups boiling water or vegetable stock

1/4 cup olive oil

Juice of 1-2 lemons

1/2 cup fresh parsley, chopped

1/4 cup fresh mint, chopped

2 spring onions, finely chopped

1/2 cucumber, seeded and cut into small pieces

Salt and pepper to taste

Instructions:

Preparation of the roasted vegetables:

Preheat the oven to 200°C (293°F).

Cut the mixed vegetables into small pieces and lay them out on a baking tray.

Drizzle the vegetables with olive oil and season with salt, pepper and optional spices to taste.

Bake the vegetables in the preheated oven for 20-25 minutes until soft and lightly browned. Stir occasionally so that the vegetables brown evenly.

Preparation of the tabbouleh:

In a bowl, pour boiling water or vegetable stock over the bulgur.

Cover the bowl and leave the bulgur to soak for approx. 15-20 minutes until it is soft and has completely absorbed the water.

Fluff up the bulgur with a fork and leave to cool.

Assemble the salad:

In a large bowl, mix the chilled bulgur with the roasted vegetables.

Add the chopped parsley, mint, spring onions and cucumber.

Pour the olive oil and lemon juice over the salad and mix well.

Season to taste with salt and pepper.

Serve:

Serve the roasted vegetable tabbouleh in a bowl.

Garnish with additional fresh herbs as desired.

Serve immediately or enjoy chilled as a side dish or light main course!

This roasted vegetable tabbouleh is a delicious twist on the classic tabbouleh recipe and offers a wealth of flavors and textures. It is a versatile dish that can be served as a side dish or as a light main course and can be enjoyed both hot and cold.

Greek quinoa salad

Preparation time: approx. 25 minutes

Servings: 4

Ingredients:

1 cup quinoa

2 cups water or vegetable stock

1 cucumber, diced

1 red bell pepper, diced

1 yellow bell pepper, diced

1/2 red onion, finely chopped

1 cup cherry tomatoes, halved

1/2 cup pitted Kalamata olives

200 g feta cheese, cut into cubes

1/4 cup fresh parsley, chopped

1/4 cup fresh oregano, chopped

juice of 1-2 lemons

3 tablespoons olive oil

Salt and pepper to taste

Instructions:

Cook the quinoa:

Rinse the quinoa thoroughly under cold water to remove the bitter substances.

Bring the water or vegetable stock to the boil in a pan.

Add the rinsed quinoa, bring to the boil, reduce the heat, put the lid on and simmer for approx. 15 minutes until the liquid has been absorbed and the quinoa is soft.

Remove the pan from the heat and fluff up the quinoa with a fork. Leave to cool.

Preparing the ingredients:

While the quinoa is cooking and cooling, prepare the vegetables and feta cheese.

Place the cucumber, red and yellow peppers, red onion and cherry tomatoes in a large bowl.

Add the kalamata olives.

Cut the feta cheese into cubes and add to the bowl.

Chop the fresh parsley and oregano and set aside.

Assemble the salad:

Add the cooled quinoa to the prepared ingredients in the bowl.

Pour the lemon juice and olive oil over the salad.

Mix everything carefully until all the ingredients are well combined.

Season to taste with salt and pepper.

Serve:

Place the Greek quinoa salad on plates or a serving platter.

Garnish with additional parsley and oregano if desired.

Serve immediately or enjoy chilled!

This Greek quinoa salad is a delicious and nutritious meal that is rich in flavors and textures. It is perfect as a main course for a light lunch or dinner or as a side dish for barbecues.

Eggplant thalers with feta cheese

Preparation time: approx. 30 minutes

Servings: 4

Ingredients:

2 medium-sized eggplants

200 g feta cheese, crumbled

2 tomatoes, thinly sliced

1/4 cup olive oil

2 cloves of garlic, finely chopped

2 tablespoons fresh parsley, chopped

1 tablespoon fresh oregano, chopped (or 1 teaspoon dried oregano)

Salt and pepper to taste

Instructions:

Prepare the eggplants:

Wash the eggplants and cut off the ends.

Cut the eggplants lengthwise into slices about 1 cm thick.

Salt the eggplant slices:

Place the eggplant slices on a baking tray and lightly salt.

Leave to rest for approx. 15 minutes so that the eggplants absorb some water and the bitter taste is reduced.

Grill or roast the eggplant slices:

While the eggplant slices are resting, preheat the grill or heat a grill pan or normal frying pan with a little olive oil.

Dab the eggplant slices to remove any excess water.

Brush both sides of the eggplant slices with olive oil and grill or fry on the grill or in the pan for about 3-4 minutes per side until they are soft and lightly browned. Depending on the size of the pan or grill, the eggplant slices may need to be cooked in several batches.

Set the cooked eggplant slices to one side and leave to cool.

Prepare the filling:

While the eggplant slices are cooling, crumble the feta cheese in a bowl.

Add the chopped garlic cloves, parsley and oregano to the feta cheese.

Season with salt and pepper and mix well.

Assemble the eggplant thalers:

Take one slice of eggplant at a time and place some of the feta mixture in the middle.

Place a slice of tomato on top.

Place another slice of eggplant on top to form a thaler.

Continue with the remaining slices of eggplant and the filling until all the thaler are ready.

Serve:

Arrange the eggplant thalers on a serving platter.

Garnish with additional parsley or basil and a squeeze of lemon juice, if desired.

Serve immediately and enjoy!

These eggplant thalers with feta cheese are a delicious vegetarian dish full of Mediterranean flavors. They make a great starter, side dish or light main course and are a great way to enjoy eggplants.

Spring onions with feta cheese, pasta and walnuts

Preparation time: approx. 25 minutes

Servings: 2-3

Ingredients:

200 g linguine or another type of pasta of one's choice

2 bunches of spring onions, cut into thin slices

100 g feta cheese, crumbled

1/2 cup walnuts, roughly chopped

2 cloves of garlic, finely chopped

2 tablespoons olive oil

juice of 1 lemon

Salt and pepper to taste

Optional: Fresh parsley or basil for garnish

Instructions:

Cook the pasta:

Bring water to the boil in a large pan and cook the pasta according to the instructions on the packet until al dente.

Drain the cooked pasta and set aside. Keep a little of the cooking water to use later for the sauce.

Sauté the spring onions:

In a large frying pan, heat the olive oil over a medium heat.

Add the chopped garlic cloves and sauté for about 1 minute until fragrant.

Add the sliced spring onions and fry for a further 3-4 minutes until softened.

Add the feta cheese and walnuts:

Add the crumbled feta cheese and roughly chopped walnuts to the pan and mix briefly until the feta cheese is slightly melted.

Prepare the sauce:

Pour the lemon juice over the spring onions, feta cheese and walnuts.

If desired, add some of the reserved pasta cooking water to thin and thicken the sauce.

Season to taste with salt and pepper and mix well.

Mix the pasta and sauce together:

Add the cooked pasta to the pan with the sauce and mix gently until the pasta is evenly coated with the sauce.

Serve:

Serve the spring onions with feta cheese, pasta and walnuts on plates or in bowls.

Garnish with fresh parsley or basil as desired.

Serve immediately and enjoy!

This dish of spring onions with feta cheese, pasta and walnuts is a delicious combination of savory flavors and different textures. It is quick and easy to prepare and makes a great main course for a quick dinner or as a side dish to other dishes.

Roast potatoes with sage, cheese and wrapped ham

Preparation time: approx. 30 minutes

Servings: 2-3

Ingredients:

500 g waxy potatoes, peeled and sliced

100 g smoked ham

6-8 fresh sage leaves

100 g spicy cheese (e.g. Gouda, mountain cheese or Emmental), cut into thin slices

2 tablespoons olive oil or butter

Salt and pepper to taste

Instructions:

Prepare the potatoes:

Cut the peeled potatoes into thin slices. They should be about the same thickness so that they cook evenly.

Wrap the ham:

Spread out the smoked ham and place a slice of cheese on top of each and season with pepper.

Place a sage leaf on top of the cheese and wrap the ham around the cheese and sage leaf to form a sort of parcel. Repeat this process with the remaining ham, cheese and sage leaves.

Fry the wrapped ham:

Heat a frying pan over a medium heat and melt the olive oil or butter in it.

Place the coated ham parcels in the pan and fry on both sides for about 3-4 minutes until the ham is crispy and the cheese has melted. Make sure that the cheese does not run out.

Fry the roast potatoes:

While the coated hams are frying, heat some olive oil or butter in another pan.

Add the potato slices to the pan and fry over a medium heat for about 10-15 minutes, turning occasionally, until golden brown and crispy. Make sure they do not stick together during frying.

Serve:

Arrange the fried roast potatoes on a plate.

Place the coated ham next to the fried potatoes.

Garnish with fresh sage if desired.

Serve immediately and enjoy!

These roast potatoes with sage, cheese and wrapped ham are a delicious twist on the classic dish and offer a perfect combination of crispy potatoes, tangy cheese and aromatic sage. It is a hearty dish that is ideal for a delicious lunch or dinner.

Fried eggs and roast potatoes

Preparation time: approx. 30 minutes

Servings: 2-3

Ingredients:

4 medium-sized potatoes, preferably waxy

2 tablespoons of oil or butter

1 onion, finely chopped (optional)

Salt and pepper to taste

4 eggs

Optional: fresh herbs for garnish (e.g. parsley or chives)

Instructions:

Prepare the potatoes:

Wash and peel the potatoes thoroughly. Then cut into even, small cubes.

Fry the roast potatoes:

In a large frying pan, heat the oil or butter over a medium heat.

Add the chopped onions (if using) and sauté for about 2 minutes until translucent.

Add the diced potatoes to the pan and spread evenly.

Fry the potatoes, turning occasionally, until golden brown and crispy, about 15-20 minutes.

Season with salt and pepper.

Fry the fried eggs:

Heat a little oil in a separate frying pan.

Carefully crack the eggs into the pan one at a time, taking care not to break the yolks.

Fry the eggs over a medium heat until the egg whites have set and the edges are crispy. If desired, the yolks can remain slightly runny.

Season with salt and pepper.

Serve:

Arrange the fried potatoes on plates.

Carefully place the fried eggs on top of the fried potatoes.

Garnish with fresh herbs as desired.

Serve immediately and enjoy!

This combination of fried eggs and fried potatoes is a classic and hearty dish that can be served for breakfast or as a delicious dinner. The crispy fried potatoes harmonize perfectly with the juicy fried eggs and provide a delicious and filling meal.

Grilled salmon fillet with asparagus and lemon-dill sauce

Preparation time: approx. 30 minutes

Servings: 2-3

Ingredients:

2 salmon fillets (approx. 150-200 g each)

500 g fresh green asparagus, woody ends removed

2 tablespoons of olive oil

Salt and pepper to taste

For the lemon-dill sauce:

1/2 cup Greek yogurt

Juice and zest of 1 lemon

1 tablespoon fresh dill, chopped

1 clove garlic, finely chopped (optional)

Salt and pepper to taste

Instructions:

Preparing the barbecue:

Preheat the grill to medium-high heat.

Preparing the lemon-dill sauce:

In a small bowl, mix the Greek yogurt with lemon juice, lemon zest, chopped dill and finely chopped garlic (if using).

Season to taste with salt and pepper.

Cover the sauce and refrigerate until ready to use.

Prepare the salmon and asparagus:

Coat the salmon fillets with olive oil and season with salt and pepper.

Drizzle the green asparagus with a little olive oil and season with salt and pepper.

Grill the salmon and asparagus:

Place the salmon fillets and asparagus on the grill.

Grill the salmon for about 4-6 minutes per side until cooked through and lightly browned. The exact cooking time depends on the thickness of the salmon fillets.

Grill the asparagus for about 6-8 minutes, turning occasionally, until tender and lightly browned.

Serve:

Arrange the grilled salmon on plates.

Place the grilled asparagus next to the salmon.

Drizzle the lemon-dill sauce over the salmon and asparagus or serve separately.

Garnish with fresh dill if desired.

Serve immediately and enjoy!

This recipe for grilled salmon fillet with asparagus and lemon-dill sauce is a light and delicious way to enjoy spring. The combination of juicy salmon, tender asparagus and a refreshing lemon-dill sauce is easy to prepare and perfect for a healthy and delicious main course.

Vegetable curry with coconut milk

Preparation time: approx. 30 minutes

Servings: 4

Ingredients:

2 tablespoons vegetable oil (e.g. coconut oil or rapeseed oil)

1 onion, chopped

2 cloves of garlic, chopped

1 tablespoon fresh ginger, finely chopped or grated

2-3 tablespoons curry paste (depending on desired spiciness and taste)

400 ml unsweetened coconut milk

500 g mixed vegetables of one's choice (e.g. carrots, peppers, broccoli, peas, zucchinis), cut into bite-sized pieces

Salt and pepper to taste

Fresh coriander or parsley to garnish (optional)

Cooked rice or naan bread (Indian flatbread) to serve

Instructions:

Prepare the vegetables:

Wash and peel the vegetables and cut into bite-sized pieces.

Fry the onion, garlic and ginger:

Heat the oil in a large frying pan or saucepan.

Add the chopped onion and fry over a medium heat until translucent.

Add the chopped garlic and ginger and stir-fry for a further 1-2 minutes until fragrant.

Add the curry paste:

Add the curry paste to the pan and stir well to combine with the onions, garlic and ginger. Sauté for about 1-2 minutes to release the flavors.

Add the vegetables:

Add the prepared vegetables to the pan and stir well to coat them with the curry paste.

Sauté the vegetables for about 5-7 minutes until they soften slightly.

Add the coconut milk:

Pour the unsweetened coconut milk over the vegetables and stir well to combine everything.

Reduce the heat and allow the curry to simmer gently until the vegetables are cooked and the sauce has thickened, about 10-15 minutes.

Serve:

Season the vegetable curry with salt and pepper to taste.

Optionally, garnish with fresh coriander or parsley.

Serve the vegetable curry hot over cooked rice or enjoy with naan bread.

This vegetable curry with coconut milk is a delicious and nutritious meal that is quick and easy to prepare. It is **vegan, gluten-free** and full of flavors from the spices and coconut milk. Serve it as a main course for a healthy dinner or as a side dish to other Indian dishes.

Stuffed peppers with quinoa and vegetables

Preparation time: approx. 60 minutes

Servings: 4

Ingredients:

4 large peppers (preferably red or yellow for more color)

1 cup quinoa

2 cups vegetable broth or water

1 onion, chopped

2 garlic cloves, chopped

1 carrot, diced

1 zucchini, diced

1 red bell pepper, diced

1 tin of chopped tomatoes (approx. 400 g)

1 teaspoon ground cumin

1 teaspoon paprika powder

salt and pepper to taste

1/2 cup grated cheese (optional)

Fresh parsley or coriander to garnish

Instructions:

Prepare the peppers:

Preheat the oven to 180°C (356°F).

Cut the peppers in half and remove the seeds and white membranes.

Place the bell pepper halves in an oven dish or on a baking tray and set aside.

Cook the quinoa:

Rinse the quinoa thoroughly under cold water to remove the bitter bits.

Bring the vegetable stock or water to the boil in a pan.

Add the rinsed quinoa, bring to the boil, reduce the heat, put the lid on and simmer for approx. 15-20 minutes until the liquid has been absorbed and the quinoa is soft.

Remove the pan from the heat, fluff the quinoa with a fork and set aside.

Prepare the vegetables:

Heat a little oil in a frying pan and fry the chopped onion and garlic until fragrant.

Add the diced carrot, zucchini and red bell pepper and fry for about 5-7 minutes until the vegetables are soft.

Prepare the filling:

Add the cooked quinoa to the pan with the sautéed vegetables.

Add the chopped tomatoes, ground cumin and paprika powder and mix well.

Season to taste with salt and pepper.

Stuffing and baking the peppers:

Stuff the quinoa and vegetable mixture evenly into the prepared bell pepper halves.

Optionally, sprinkle the grated cheese over the stuffed peppers.

Place the stuffed bell pepper halves in the preheated oven and bake for approx. 25-30 minutes until the peppers are soft and the cheese has melted.

Serve:

Arrange the stuffed peppers on a plate.

Garnish with fresh parsley or coriander.

Serve with a dip or sauce to taste.

Serve immediately and enjoy!

These stuffed peppers with quinoa and vegetables are a delicious and nutritious meal that is **vegetarian, gluten-free** and full of flavor. They are perfect as a main course for a healthy dinner or as a side dish to other dishes.

Grilled chicken with vegetables

Preparation time: approx. 40 minutes

Servings: 2-3

Ingredients:

For the chicken:

2 chicken breast fillets

2 tablespoons of olive oil

1 teaspoon paprika powder

1 teaspoon garlic powder

Salt and pepper to taste

For the vegetables:

2 peppers, cut into strips

1 zucchini, cut into slices

1 eggplant, cut into cubes

1 red onion, cut into wedges

2 tablespoons olive oil

1 teaspoon dried oregano

1 teaspoon dried thyme

Salt and pepper to taste

Instructions:

Preparing the grill:

Preheat the grill to medium-high heat.

Preparing the chicken:

Pat the chicken breasts dry with a paper towel.

In a bowl, mix the olive oil, paprika powder, garlic powder, salt and pepper.

Coat the chicken breast fillets with the marinade and set aside to absorb the flavors.

Prepare the vegetables:

Place the sliced vegetables on a baking tray.

Pour the olive oil over the vegetables and mix well to ensure that the vegetables are evenly coated with oil.

Sprinkle the dried oregano, thyme, salt and pepper over the vegetables and mix again to distribute the spices evenly.

Grill the chicken:

Place the marinated chicken breasts on the preheated grill.

Grill the chicken breasts for about 6-8 minutes per side until they are cooked through and have a nice grill mark. The exact cooking time depends on the thickness of the chicken breast fillets.

Roasting the vegetables:

Place the baking tray with the prepared vegetables in an oven pre-heated to 200°C (392°F).

Roast the vegetables for about 20-25 minutes, turning occasionally, until they are soft and lightly browned.

Serve:

Divide the grilled chicken and roasted vegetables between plates.

Garnish with fresh herbs such as parsley or chives as desired.

Serve immediately and enjoy!

This recipe for grilled chicken with roasted vegetables is a delicious and healthy meal that is easy to prepare and can be served as a main course or as a side dish to other dishes. It offers a delicious combination of succulent chicken and aromatic roasted vegetables that is perfect for any occasion.

Baked salmon with steamed spinach

Preparation time: approx. 30 minutes

Servings: 2

Ingredients:

For the baked salmon:

2 salmon fillets (approx. 150-200 g each)

2 tablespoons of olive oil

1 teaspoon of lemon juice

Salt and pepper to taste

Optional: fresh herbs such as dill or parsley to garnish

For the steamed spinach:

500 g fresh spinach, washed and roughly chopped

2 cloves of garlic, finely chopped

1 tablespoon of olive oil

Salt and pepper to taste

Optional: A pinch of nutmeg to season

Instructions:

Preparing the oven:

Preheat the oven to 180°C (356°F).

Preparing the salmon:

Pat the salmon fillets dry with a paper towel and place on a baking tray lined with baking paper.

Drizzle with olive oil and lemon juice and spread evenly over the salmon fillets.

Season with salt and pepper.

Bake the salmon:

Place the salmon fillets in the preheated oven and bake for about 15-20 minutes, until the salmon is cooked and can be easily separated with a fork. The exact cooking time depends on the thickness of the salmon fillets.

Preparation of the steamed spinach:

In a large frying pan, heat the olive oil over a medium heat.

Add the chopped garlic and sauté for about 1 minute until fragrant.

Add the washed and chopped spinach to the pan. Depending on the size of the pan, one may need to add the spinach in batches and wait for it to collapse.

Sauté the spinach, stirring occasionally, until collapsed and slightly wilted.

Season with salt, pepper and a pinch of nutmeg to taste.

Serve:

Divide the baked salmon between plates and arrange the steamed spinach next to it.

Garnish with fresh herbs such as dill or parsley as desired.

Serve immediately and enjoy!

This recipe for baked salmon with steamed spinach is a healthy and delicious meal that is easy to prepare. The tender salmon harmonizes wonderfully with the fresh spinach and the tangy flavours of the garlic. It makes a perfect main course for a light yet satisfying dinner.

Vegatarian vegetable pan with tofu

Preparation time: approx. 30 minutes

Servings: 2-3

Ingredients:

200 g firm tofu, cut into cubes

2 tablespoons soy sauce

2 tablespoons olive oil or sesame oil

1 onion, thinly sliced

2 cloves of garlic, finely chopped

1 bell pepper, cut into strips

1 carrot, thinly sliced

1 small zucchini, sliced

100 g mushrooms, sliced

2 cups spinach or chard, roughly chopped

2 tablespoon soy sauce

1 tablespoon rice vinegar or apple cider vinegar

1 teaspoon honey or maple syrup (optional)

Salt and pepper to taste

Spring onions or fresh coriander to garnish (optional)

Cooked rice or noodles to serve

Instructions:

Marinate the tofu:

Place the tofu cubes in a bowl and marinate with 2 tablespoons of soy sauce. Leave to stand for at least 10 minutes.

Frying the tofu:

Heat 1 tablespoon of oil in a large frying pan.

Add the marinated tofu cubes and fry on all sides until golden brown. Then remove from the pan and set aside.

Fry the vegetables:

Heat 1 tablespoon of oil in the same pan.

Add the onion slices and chopped garlic and fry for about 2 minutes until fragrant.

Add the bell pepper strips, carrot slices, zucchini slices and mushrooms. Fry for about 5-7 minutes, stirring occasionally, until the vegetables are lightly browned and starting to soften.

Add the tofu and spinach:

Return the browned tofu to the pan.

Add the chopped spinach or chard and stir until slightly wilted.

Seasoning the vegetable pan:

Pour the remaining 2 tablespoons of soy sauce and the vinegar over the vegetables.

Optionally, add the honey or maple syrup to sweeten the sauce.

Season to taste with salt and pepper and mix well.

Serve:

Serve the vegetarian vegetable stir-fry with tofu on plates.

Garnish with spring onions or fresh coriander as desired.

Serve with cooked rice or noodles.

Serve immediately and enjoy!

This vegetarian vegetable stir-fry with tofu is a healthy and delicious meal that is packed with flavor and nutrients. It features a variety of vegetables and protein from the tofu, which is perfectly combined with a spicy soy sauce. It's a simple and versatile dish that can be adapted to suit whichever vegetables one prefers or has to hand.

Zucchinis with feta cheese, potatoes and basil in olive oil

Preparation time: approx. 45 minutes

Servings: 2-3

Ingredients:

2 medium zucchinis

2 large potatoes

100 g feta cheese

2 cloves of garlic, finely chopped

Fresh basil leaves, roughly chopped

3 tablespoons olive oil

Salt and pepper to taste

Instructions:

Preparation of the ingredients:

Wash the zucchinis and cut into thin slices.

Peel the potatoes and cut into thin slices.

Cut the feta cheese into small cubes.

Finely chop the garlic.

Roughly chop the basil leaves.

Fry the ingredients:

Heat 2 tablespoons of olive oil in a large frying pan over a medium heat.

Add the chopped garlic and fry briefly until fragrant.

Add the potato slices to the pan and fry for about 10 minutes, stirring occasionally, until golden brown and crispy. If necessary, add more olive oil if the potatoes become dry.

Add the zucchinis:

Add the zucchini slices to the potatoes in the pan and fry for a further 5-7 minutes until soft and lightly browned. Stir occasionally.

Season and taste:

Season the roasted zucchinis and potatoes with salt and pepper.

Sprinkle the chopped basil over the vegetables and mix well.

Adding the feta cheese:

Sprinkle the feta cheese cubes over the roasted vegetables.

Remove the pan from the heat and allow the feta cheese to melt slightly.

Serve:

Portion the zucchinis with feta cheese, potatoes, garlic and basil in olive oil onto plates.

Garnish with additional chopped basil if desired.

Serve immediately and enjoy!

This delicious mixture of zucchinis, potatoes, feta cheese, garlic and basil in olive oil is a wonderful dish that can be served as a main course or side dish. The flavors of the fresh ingredients and the tangy feta cheese combine to create an unforgettable culinary experience.

Pasta in cream sauce with chopped almonds

Preparation time: approx. 20 minutes

Servings: 2-3

Ingredients:

250 g pasta (e.g. linguine, spaghetti, penne)

1 tablespoon olive oil or butter

2 cloves of garlic, finely chopped

200 ml cream

50 g chopped almonds

Salt and pepper to taste

Fresh parsley or basil to garnish (optional)

Grated Parmesan cheese to serve (optional)

Instructions:

Cook the pasta:

Bring water to the boil in a large pan and salt generously.

Cook the pasta according to the packet instructions until al dente. Drain and set aside, reserving some of the cooking water.

Prepare the cream sauce:

In a large frying pan, heat the olive oil or butter over a medium heat.

Add the finely chopped garlic and sauté for about 1 minute until fragrant.

Pour the cream into the pan and bring to the boil. Reduce the heat and allow the cream to simmer for about 2-3 minutes until it thickens slightly.

Add the chopped almonds:

Add the chopped almonds to the cream sauce and mix well.

Season the sauce to taste with salt and pepper.

Combine the pasta with the cream sauce:

Add the cooked pasta to the pan with the cream sauce and mix gently until the pasta is completely coated with the sauce.

If the sauce is too thick, add some of the reserved pasta water to achieve the desired consistency.

Serve:

Portion the pasta in cream sauce with chopped almonds onto plates.

Garnish with fresh parsley or basil as desired.

Sprinkle with grated Parmesan, if desired.

Serve immediately and enjoy!

This creamy yet easy to prepare pasta with cream sauce and chopped almonds is a delicious dish that is both quick and satisfying. The garlic note adds an extra depth of flavor to the sauce, while the chopped almonds add a nice texture and nutty flavor. It's a great option for a quick weeknight dinner or a special occasion.

Jacket potatoes with curd and chives in olive oil

Preparation time: approx. 30 minutes

Servings: 2-3

Ingredients:

500 g small waxy potatoes (e.g. triplets)

200 g curd

2-3 tablespoons olive oil

2-3 tablespoons chopped fresh chives

Salt and pepper to taste

Instructions:

Boil the potatoes:

Wash the potatoes thoroughly and cover with salted water in a saucepan.

Bring the potatoes to the boil and then reduce the heat. Simmer the potatoes until they are soft. The exact cooking time depends on the size of the potatoes, but it usually takes about 20-25 minutes.

Prepare the curd:

While the potatoes are cooking, place the curd in a bowl.

Add the olive oil and mix well until smooth.

Prepare the chives:

Wash the fresh chives, pat dry and chop finely.

Drain the potatoes and serve:

As soon as the potatoes are soft, drain the water and arrange the potatoes on a serving dish.

Serve:

Serve the hot jacket potatoes with the prepared quark.

Sprinkle the chopped chives over the curd.

Drizzle with a little extra olive oil if desired.

Season with salt and pepper to taste.

Serve immediately and enjoy!

These jacket potatoes with curd and chives in olive oil are a delicious and easy meal to prepare, perfect for a light lunch or dinner. The combination of creamy curd, fresh chives and high-quality olive oil gives the potatoes a wonderful depth of flavor. It's a simple dish that's still incredibly satisfying and ideal for a quick midweek meal.

Chinese wok dish

Preparation time: approx. 30 minutes

Servings: 2-3

Ingredients:

250g lean meat (chicken, beef, pork or prawns), thinly sliced or diced

2-3 cups sliced vegetables (e.g. peppers, broccoli, carrots, sugar snap peas, mushrooms, onions)

3 cloves of garlic, finely chopped

1 piece of ginger (approx. 2 cm), peeled and finely chopped

2-3 spring onions, sliced

2-3 tablespoon soy sauce

1 tablespoon oyster sauce (optional)

1 tablespoon sesame oil

2 tablespoons vegetable oil for frying

Salt and pepper to taste

Optional: chili flakes or fresh chilies for extra heat

Cooked rice or noodles to serve

Instructions:

Preparation of the ingredients:

Cut the meat into thin strips or cubes.

Prepare the vegetables by washing, peeling and cutting them into bite-sized pieces.

Finely chop the garlic and ginger.

Slice the spring onions.

Heat the wok:

Heat a wok or large frying pan over a high heat.

Add the vegetable oil and make sure the wok is well heated before one starts cooking.

Browning the meat:

Add the meat to the hot wok and stir-fry quickly until cooked through. This usually only takes 2-3 minutes, depending on the thickness of the meat.

Remove the meat from the wok and set aside.

Fry the vegetables:

If necessary, add a little more oil to the wok and add the chopped garlic and ginger. Fry briefly until fragrant.

Add the chopped vegetables and stir-fry for about 3-5 minutes until crisp-tender.

Combine and season:

Return the sautéed meat to the wok and mix with the vegetables.

Add the soy sauce, oyster sauce (if using) and sesame oil. Season with salt, pepper and optional chili flakes to taste.

Mix everything well and simmer for about 1-2 minutes to allow the flavors to blend and the dish to finish cooking.

Serve:

Serve the Chinese wok dish hot over cooked rice or noodles.

Garnish with additional spring onions or sesame seeds as desired.

Serve immediately and enjoy!

This recipe provides the basics for a Chinese stir-fry that can be adapted as desired, depending on the ingredients that are preferred or on hand. It's a quick, delicious and healthy option for a home-cooked meal full of flavors and fresh ingredients.

Lamb with green beans and potatoes

Preparation time: approx. 60 minutes

Servings: 4

Ingredients:

500 g lamb (e.g. from the shoulder or leg), cut into cubes

500 g green beans, ends cut off and halved

500 g potatoes, peeled and cut into small cubes

1 onion, finely chopped

3 cloves of garlic, finely chopped

2 tomatoes, chopped

2 tablespoon tomato purée

2 tablespoons olive oil

1 teaspoon ground cumin

1 teaspoon ground turmeric

1 teaspoon ground paprika

Instructions:

Preparation of the ingredients:

Season the lamb with salt, pepper, ground cumin, turmeric and paprika and set aside.

Peel the potatoes and cut into small cubes.

Wash the green beans, cut off the ends and cut in half.

Finely chop the onion and garlic.

Chop the tomatoes.

Fry the lamb:

Heat the olive oil in a large saucepan or frying pan.

Add the chopped onion and garlic and sauté until fragrant.

Add the seasoned lamb and fry, stirring constantly, until browned all over.

Add the tomatoes and tomato purée:

Add the chopped tomatoes and tomato puree to the browned lamb. Stir well and simmer for a few minutes until the tomatoes are soft and the flavors have blended.

Add the potatoes and water:

Add the sliced potatoes to the pot and cover with enough water to cover everything. About 1-2 cups of water should be enough.

Cover the pot and simmer over medium heat until the potatoes are semi-cooked, about 15-20 minutes.

Add the green beans:

Add the halved green beans to the pot and continue to simmer until they are tender and the potatoes are cooked through, about 10-15 minutes.

Serve:

Season the dish with salt and pepper to taste.

Serve hot and enjoy!

This lamb dish with green beans and potatoes is hearty, delicious and perfect for a warming dinner. It combines tender lamb with fresh vegetables and aromatic spices to create a tasty dish that will delight family and friends.

South American midnight soup

Preparation time: approx. 45 minutes

Servings: 4

Ingredients:

2 tablespoons olive oil

1 onion, chopped

2 cloves of garlic, finely chopped

1 red bell pepper, diced

1 green bell pepper, diced

2 carrots, sliced

2 potatoes, diced

1 tin (400 g) chopped tomatoes

1 liter vegetable stock

1 tin (400 g) black beans, drained and rinsed

1 tin (400 g) corn, drained

1 teaspoon ground cumin

1 teaspoon ground paprika

Salt and pepper to taste

Juice of one lime

Fresh coriander or parsley to garnish

Optional: Avocado, sliced, sour cream or grated cheese to serve

Instructions:

Preparing the soup:

In a large pot, heat the olive oil over medium heat.

Add the chopped onion and minced garlic and sauté, stirring occasionally, until softened and fragrant, about 3-4 minutes.

Add vegetables:

Add the diced red and green peppers, carrot and potato slices to the pot. Fry for a further 5 minutes, stirring occasionally, until the vegetables are lightly browned.

Add the tomatoes and stock:

Add the chopped tomatoes, including the juice, to the pot and stir to combine with the vegetables.

Add the vegetable stock and bring the soup to the boil.

Add the beans and corn:

Add the drained and rinsed black beans and drained corn to the soup and stir to combine.

Add the ground cumin and paprika and season the soup lightly with salt and pepper.

Cook and season to taste:

Simmer the soup for about 20-25 minutes until the vegetables are soft and the flavors blend.

Taste the soup and season to taste.

Squeeze the juice of a lime over the soup and stir well.

Serve:

Serve the South American midnight soup in soup bowls.

Garnish with fresh coriander or parsley as desired.

Serve hot and enjoy!

South American midnight soup, also known as "Sopa de Medianoche", is a filling and warming dish that is perfect for cold nights.

Königsberger meatballs

Preparation time: approx. 60 minutes

Servings: 4

Ingredients:

For the meatballs:

500 g mixed minced meat (beef and pork)

1 onion, finely chopped

1 egg

3 tablespoons breadcrumbs

Salt and pepper to taste

1/2 teaspoon ground nutmeg

1 tablespoon chopped parsley

1 tablespoon mustard

For the sauce:

1 liter vegetable stock

2 bay leaves

6 peppercorns

2 tablespoons butter

2 tablespoons flour

200 ml cream

juice of half a lemon

Salt and pepper to taste

For the caper sauce:

50 g capers

1 tablespoon butter

1 tablespoon of flour

Instructions:

Prepare the meatballs:

In a bowl, combine the mixed mince with the finely chopped onion, egg, breadcrumbs, salt, pepper, nutmeg, chopped parsley and mustard.

Knead the mixture well until all the ingredients are evenly distributed.

Remove small portions of the mince mixture and shape into meatballs. These should be about the size of a golf ball.

Cook the meatballs:

Bring the vegetable stock to the boil in a large pan.

Add the bay leaves and peppercorns.

Carefully place the meatballs in the boiling stock and simmer slowly over a medium heat for about 15-20 minutes until they are cooked. They are ready when they are firm and cooked through.

Making the sauce:

In a separate saucepan, melt the butter.

Add the flour and sauté for about 2-3 minutes, stirring constantly, until golden brown (this forms the so-called "roux").

Slowly add the vegetable stock, stirring constantly to obtain a smooth sauce.

Stir in the cream and simmer the sauce for about 10 minutes until it has thickened a little.

Season to taste with salt, pepper and lemon juice.

Making the caper sauce (optional):

Drain the capers.

Melt the butter in a small pan and add the flour to form a roux.

Slowly add the vegetable stock, stirring constantly, until one has a smooth sauce.

Add the drained capers and simmer the sauce for about 5 minutes.

Serve:

Arrange the Königsberger meatballs on warmed plates and pour the sauce over them.

Serve with potatoes or mashed potatoes as desired.

Optionally, pour the caper sauce over the meatballs.

Serve hot and enjoy!

Königsberger meatballs are a classic German dish that is perfect for a hearty and satisfying dinner. The combination of tender meatballs and a creamy sauce with a hint of lemon is simply delicious.

Chicken and vegetable soup

Preparation time: approx. 60 minutes

Servings: 4-6

Ingredients:

500 g chicken breast or chicken thighs, skinless

2 liters chicken stock

2 carrots, peeled and sliced

2 stalks of celery, chopped

1 onion, chopped

2 cloves of garlic, finely chopped

1 cup green beans, cut into pieces

1 cup corn kernels (fresh, frozen or canned)

1 cup peas (fresh or frozen)

2 potatoes, peeled and cut into cubes

1 teaspoon dried thyme leaves

1 teaspoon dried oregano

1 bay leaf

Salt and pepper to taste

Fresh parsley or chives to garnish (optional)

Instructions:

Prepare the chicken stock:

Place the chicken breasts or thighs in a large saucepan with the chicken stock.

Bring the pot to a boil and then reduce the heat so the broth comes to a gentle simmer.

Cook for about 30-40 minutes, until the chicken is cooked through and can be easily shredded with a fork.

Shred the chicken meat:

Remove the cooked chicken from the broth and shred on a cutting board with two forks or cut into bite-sized pieces.

Set the shredded chicken aside.

Prepare the vegetables:

In the meantime, prepare the vegetables: Peel and slice the carrots, chop the celery, finely chop the onion and garlic, chop the green beans and dice the potatoes.

Add the vegetables:

Add the prepared vegetables (carrots, celery, onion, garlic, green beans, sweetcorn, peas and potatoes) to the stock.

Add the dried thyme and oregano leaves and the bay leaf.

Season the soup to taste with salt and pepper.

Cook:

Simmer the soup over a medium heat until the vegetables are soft, about 15-20 minutes.

Add the shredded chicken back into the soup and reheat for a few minutes.

Serve:

Remove the bay leaf before serving.

Serve the chicken and vegetable soup in soup bowls.

Garnish with fresh parsley or chives as desired.

Serve hot and enjoy!

This chicken and vegetable soup is not only delicious and warming, but also packed with healthy vegetables and protein-rich chicken. It's a perfect dish for cold days or when one is simply craving something hearty.

Pasta with cream sauce and mushrooms

Preparation time: approx. 30 minutes

Servings: 4

Ingredients:

350 g pasta (e.g. spaghetti, penne or fettuccine)

300 g mushrooms, sliced

2 cloves of garlic, finely chopped

1 onion, finely chopped

2 tablespoons butter or olive oil

250 ml cream

100 ml vegetable stock

50 g grated Parmesan or Pecorino cheese

Salt and pepper to taste

Fresh parsley or chives to garnish (optional)

Instructions:

Cook the pasta:

Bring a large pan of salted water to the boil.

Cook the pasta according to the instructions on the packaging until al dente.

Once the pasta is cooked, drain it, but reserve about a cup of the cooking water.

Prepare the mushrooms:

In a skillet, heat 1 tablespoon of butter or olive oil over medium heat.

Add the chopped onion and minced garlic and sauté for a few minutes until soft and fragrant.

Add the mushroom slices and continue to fry until lightly browned and the liquid has evaporated. This will take about 5-7 minutes.

Set the fried mushrooms aside.

Prepare the cream sauce:

In the same pan, heat the remaining butter or olive oil.

Add the vegetable stock and cream and bring to the boil.

Add the grated Parmesan and stir well until it has melted and the sauce has thickened slightly.

Season to taste with salt and pepper.

Mix the pasta with the sauce:

Add the cooked pasta to the pan with the cream sauce and mix well until the pasta is evenly coated with the sauce.

If necessary, add a little of the reserved pasta water to thin and emulsify the sauce.

Serve:

Serve the pasta with the creamy mushroom sauce on plates.

Arrange the fried mushroom slices over the pasta.

Garnish with fresh parsley or chives as desired.

Serve hot and enjoy!

This pasta with creamy mushroom sauce is a delicious and satisfying dish that is easy to make and sure to please everyone. It's perfect for a quick dinner during the week or for special occasions when one wants to serve something delicious.

Roast potatoes with chanterelles and thyme

Preparation time: approx. 30 minutes

Servings: 2

Ingredients:

500 g waxy potatoes

200 g fresh chanterelles

2 tablespoons olive oil or butter

2 cloves of garlic, finely chopped

A few sprigs of fresh thyme

Salt and pepper to taste

Optional: chopped parsley to garnish

Instructions:

Preparation of the potatoes:

Wash and peel the potatoes thoroughly. Then cut into slices about 1 cm thick.

Roasting the potatoes:

Heat the olive oil or butter in a large frying pan over a medium heat.

Add the potato slices to the pan and spread evenly so that they form a single layer.

Fry the potatoes, turning occasionally, until they are golden brown and crispy, which may take around 15-20 minutes. Make sure they do not get too dark.

Prepare the chanterelles:

In the meantime, clean the chanterelles thoroughly with a kitchen towel. Halve or quarter large specimens.

Add the garlic and chanterelles:

Add the finely chopped garlic to the pan with the fried potatoes and sauté for about 1 minute until fragrant.

Add the prepared chanterelles to the pan and fry for a further 5-7 minutes, stirring occasionally, until they are soft and begin to release liquid.

Season to taste and garnish:

Season the roasted potatoes and chanterelles with salt and pepper.

Pluck the fresh thyme leaves from the stalks and sprinkle over the roast potatoes and chanterelles.

Garnish with chopped parsley if desired.

Serve:

Arrange the roast potatoes with chanterelles and thyme on plates and serve immediately while they are still warm.

These roast potatoes with chanterelles and thyme are a delicious side dish or a light main course that is quick to prepare and offers the full flavor of fresh ingredients. They are perfect for a cozy dinner at home or as a side dish with grilled meat or fish.

Sauerkraut with bacon and potatoes

Preparation time: approx. 45 minutes

Servings: 4

Ingredients:

500 g waxy potatoes

200 g bacon, diced

500 g sauerkraut (from a can or jar)

1 onion, chopped

2 tablespoons butter or lard

Salt and pepper to taste

Optional: caraway seeds, bay leaves, apple pieces to refine

Instructions:

Prepare the potatoes:

Peel the potatoes and cut into slices about 1 cm thick.

Frying the bacon:

In a large frying pan, fry the diced bacon without adding any additional fat over a medium heat until it is crispy and releases fat.

Remove the crispy bacon from the pan and drain on a plate with kitchen paper and set aside.

Fry the onion and add the sauerkraut:

In the same pan, sauté the chopped onion in a little butter or lard until translucent.

Add the sauerkraut and heat over a medium heat for about 10-15 minutes, stirring occasionally. This will soften it and develop its characteristic flavor.

Roast the potatoes:

While the sauerkraut is cooking, heat the remaining butter or lard in a separate pan.

Add the potato slices to the pan and fry, turning occasionally, until golden brown and crispy.

Combine and season:

Once the potatoes are crispy, add the crispy bacon back to the pan and fry briefly with the potatoes to warm the bacon.

Add the fried sauerkraut to the pan with the potatoes and bacon and mix everything well.

Season to taste with salt, pepper and other spices such as caraway seeds and bay leaves. A few pieces of apple can also be added to balance out the acidity of the sauerkraut.

Serve:

Arrange the sauerkraut, potato and bacon mixture on plates and serve hot.

This hearty meal goes well with a glass of beer or a glass of white wine.

Enjoy this rustic dish of sauerkraut, bacon and potatoes, which is perfect for cold days and can envelop one with its hearty flavor and warmth.

Indian-style white cabbage

Preparation time: approx. 30 minutes

Servings: 4

Ingredients:

1 small white cabbage (approx. 600-800 g)

2 tablespoons coconut oil or neutral vegetable oil

2 teaspoons ground curcuma (turmeric)

1 teaspoon ground cumin

1/2 teaspoon ground coriander

1/2 teaspoon ground ginger

1-2 chili peppers, finely chopped (depending on desired spiciness)

50 g grated coconut

Salt to taste

Freshly ground black pepper to taste

Fresh coriander or parsley to garnish (optional)

Lime wedges to serve

Instructions:

Prepare the white cabbage:

Quarter the white cabbage, cut out the stalk and cut or slice the cabbage into fine strips. Wash the cabbage thoroughly and drain.

Sauté the white cabbage:

In a large frying pan or wok, heat the coconut oil over a medium heat.

Add the chopped chili and fry briefly until fragrant.

Add the prepared white cabbage to the pan and fry for about 5-7 minutes, stirring occasionally, until lightly browned and starting to soften.

Add the spices and grated coconut:

Sprinkle the ground turmeric, cumin, coriander and ginger over the white cabbage and mix well to distribute the spices evenly.

Add the coconut flakes and fry for a further 2-3 minutes until lightly toasted and releasing their flavor.

Serve:

Season the white cabbage mixture with salt and freshly ground black pepper to taste.

Garnish with fresh coriander or parsley as desired.

Serve with lime wedges to enhance the flavor.

Serve the white cabbage mixture hot as a side dish with grilled meat, fish or vegetarian dishes.

It can also be served with rice or as a filling for a wrap (rolled in flatbread).

This white cabbage mix with turmeric, grated coconut and chilli peppers is not only delicious, but also healthy and full of flavor. It is perfect as a side dish or main course and is a way to prepare cabbage in a new and appealing way.

Rice with avocado, kidney beans and crème fraîche

Preparation time: approx. 30 minutes

Servings: 4

Ingredients:

1 cup long grain rice

2 avocados, peeled, pitted and sliced

1 tin of kidney beans, drained and rinsed

1/2 cup crème fraîche

1 lemon, juice

2 cloves of garlic, chopped

2 tablespoons olive oil

Salt and pepper to taste

Fresh parsley or coriander for garnish (optional)

Instructions:

Cook the rice:

Cook the long grain rice according to the instructions on the packet until cooked. Set the finished rice to one side.

Prepare the avocados:

Cut the avocados in half, remove the pit and carefully scoop out the flesh with a spoon. Cut into slices and sprinkle with lemon juice to prevent browning.

Preparation of the kidney beans:

Place the drained and rinsed kidney beans in a bowl.

Making the crème fraîche sauce:

In a small bowl, mix the crème fraîche with the juice of half a lemon. Season to taste with salt and pepper.

Frying the garlic:

Heat the olive oil in a frying pan and add the chopped garlic. Sauté over a medium heat until the garlic is fragrant but not brown.

Assembling the dish:

Place the cooked rice, avocado slices and kidney beans in a large serving bowl.

Pour the warm garlic and oil mixture over the rice, avocado and beans and mix gently to coat all the ingredients.

Serve:

Serve the rice with the avocado, kidney beans and crème fraîche on plates.

Garnish with fresh parsley or coriander as desired.

Serve immediately and enjoy!

This rice bowl with avocado, kidney beans and crème fraîche is a delicious and nutritious meal that can be enjoyed hot or cold. It is full of flavors and textures and offers a balanced combination of carbohydrates, proteins and healthy fats.

Romaine lettuce with herring in cream sauce, onions and apples

Preparation time: approx. 20 minutes

Servings: 4

Ingredients:

1 romaine lettuce

200 g herring fillets in cream sauce (from a jar or can)

1 large onion, thinly sliced

2 apples, peeled, cored and thinly sliced

2 tablespoons vinegar (e.g. apple cider vinegar)

2 tablespoons olive oil

Salt and pepper to taste

Optional: fresh herbs for garnish (e.g. parsley or dill)

Instructions:

Preparation of the romaine lettuce:

Wash and dry the romaine lettuce thoroughly. Pluck or cut the leaves into bite-sized pieces and place in a large salad bowl.

Preparing the onions and apples:

Peel the onion and cut into thin slices.

Peel and core the apples and also cut into thin slices.

Preparing the salad dressing:

In a small bowl, mix together the olive oil and vinegar. Season to taste with salt and pepper.

Assembling the salad:

Add the onion and apple slices to the romaine lettuce in the salad bowl.

Roughly chop the herring fillets in cream sauce and add to the salad.

Mix carefully:

Pour the salad dressing over the salad.

Mix everything carefully until the ingredients are evenly coated with the dressing. Be careful not to mash the salad.

Serve:

Arrange the salad on plates.

Garnish with fresh herbs as desired.

Serve immediately and enjoy.

This romaine lettuce with herring in cream sauce, onions and apples is a refreshing yet hearty salad combination. It is perfect as a light meal for warm days or as a side dish to other dishes.

Persian-style rice with chicken, barberries and cashew nuts

Preparation time: approx. 40 minutes

Servings: 4

Ingredients:

300 g basmati rice

500 g chicken breast fillets, cut into bite-sized pieces

1 onion, finely chopped

2 cloves of garlic, finely chopped

100 g dried barberries

50 g cashew nuts

2 tablespoon olive oil or neutral vegetable oil

1 teaspoon ground turmeric

1 teaspoon ground cumin

1 teaspoon paprika powder

Salt and pepper to taste

Fresh parsley or coriander for garnish (optional)

Instructions:

Cook the rice:

Wash the basmati rice thoroughly until the water runs clear. Then cook according to the packet instructions until it is done. The normal ratio is 1 cup of rice to 1.5 cups of water. Set the rice aside and keep warm.

Brown the chicken:

In a large skillet or wok, heat the olive oil.

Add the chopped onion and chopped garlic and fry until translucent.

Add the chicken pieces and fry, stirring occasionally, until golden brown on all sides and cooked through.

Add the spices:

Sprinkle the ground turmeric, cumin and paprika over the chicken and mix well so that the spices are evenly distributed.

Add the barberries and cashews:

Add the dried barberries and cashews to the pan and fry for a further 2-3 minutes until the barberries are slightly swollen and the cashews are toasted.

Serve:

Add the cooked rice to the chicken mixture in the pan and mix gently until everything is well combined.

Season the rice with salt and pepper to taste.

Garnish with fresh parsley or coriander as desired.

Plate up the rice with the chicken, barberries and cashew nuts and serve immediately.

This dish is a delicious combination of tender chicken, aromatic rice and the sour barberries as well as the crunchy crunch of the cashews. It is a wonderful main course that is both delicious and nutritious.

Desserts

Roasted pineapple with honey and cinnamon

Preparation time: approx. 20 minutes

Servings: 4

Ingredients:

1 ripe pineapple

2 tablespoons honey

1 teaspoon of cinnamon

2 tablespoons butter or coconut oil

Optional: vanilla ice cream or yogurt to serve

Instructions:

Preparation of the pineapple:

Cut the pineapple lengthwise into quarters and remove the hard core.

Cut off the outer skin of the pineapple and cut the flesh into thick slices.

Prepare the honey and cinnamon mixture:

In a small bowl, mix the honey and cinnamon until well combined.

Fry the pineapple:

Heat a skillet over medium heat and add butter or the coconut oil.

Place the pineapple slices in the pan and fry for 2-3 minutes on each side until golden brown and slightly caramelized.

Reduce the heat and pour the honey and cinnamon mixture over the pineapple.

Let the pineapple fry for another 2-3 minutes until the honey has caramelized and the pineapple is nicely glazed.

Serve:

Remove the roasted pineapple from the pan and place on a serving platter.

Serve the pineapple warm, either as a dessert on its own or with a scoop of vanilla ice cream or a spoonful of yogurt.

Optionally, the roasted pineapple can also be garnished with a squeeze of lemon juice or a pinch of sea salt to bring out the flavors.

This simple and delicious pineapple dish is a delightful treat that can be served either warm or refreshing. It is perfect as a light dessert or as a sweet touch to a special breakfast or brunch.

Baked banana with chocolate chips

Preparation time: approx. 20 minutes

Servings: 2

Ingredients:

2 ripe bananas

30 g dark chocolate (70% cocoa or more), chopped or coarsely chopped

2 teaspoons honey or maple syrup (optional)

Cinnamon to taste (optional)

Coconut flakes or chopped nuts to garnish (optional)

Instructions:

Preparation of the bananas:

Preheat the oven to 180°C (356°F).

Peel the bananas and cut in half lengthwise. Place the banana halves in a baking dish or on a baking tray lined with baking paper.

Add the chocolate:

Sprinkle the chocolate chips evenly over the banana halves.

Drizzle with honey or maple syrup to taste and season with a pinch of cinnamon, if desired.

Bake:

Place the baked bananas in an oven preheated to 180°C (356°F) and bake for around 10-12 minutes until the chocolate has melted and the bananas are soft.

Serve:

Remove the baked bananas from the oven and serve immediately.

Sprinkle with coconut flakes or chopped nuts as desired.

Serve hot and enjoy!

These baked bananas with chocolate chips are a delicious dessert that is easy to prepare and satisfies the sweet tooth. The bananas can be enjoyed on their own or served with a spoonful of yogurt to complete the taste sensation.

Yoghurt fruit layer dish

Preparation time: approx. 15 minutes

Servings: 4

Ingredients:

500 g Greek yogurt (low-fat or to taste)

2 tablespoons honey or maple syrup

1 teaspoon vanilla extract (optional)

Fresh fruit of one's choice (e.g. berries, mango, pineapple)

Nuts or seeds to garnish (e.g. chopped almonds, walnuts, chia seeds)

Fresh mint leaves to garnish (optional)

Instructions:

Preparation of the yogurt:

Place the Greek yogurt in a medium bowl.

Add the honey or maple syrup and vanilla extract.

Stir everything well until the sweetness is evenly distributed.

Prepare the fruit:

Wash and peel the fresh fruit of one's choice and cut into bite-sized pieces.

Berries can be left whole.

Assembling the layered dish:

Take four dessert glasses or bowls and start with a layer of yogurt at the bottom.

Then place a layer of the prepared fresh fruit on top.

Repeat this process until the glasses are full, finishing with a layer of yogurt.

Garnish:

Sprinkle chopped nuts or seeds over the top layer of yogurt.

Garnish the layered desserts with fresh mint leaves for added freshness, if desired.

The desserts can be served immediately or chilled in the fridge for at least 30 minutes to firm up a little.

Serve:

Serve the healthy yogurt fruit layered desserts in dessert glasses or bowls and enjoy immediately!

This healthy yogurt and fruit layered dessert is a delicious and refreshing option for a dessert or sweet treat that is packed with flavor and nutrients. It is easy to prepare and can be varied depending on one's preferences and the availability of fresh fruit.

Berry smoothie

Preparation time: approx. 5 minutes

Servings: 1-2

Ingredients:

1 banana, peeled and cut into pieces

1 cup mixed berries (e.g. strawberries, raspberries, blueberries)

1/2 cup spinach or kale (optional)

1/2 cup Greek yogurt or almond milk (for a vegan option)

1 tablespoon honey or maple syrup (optional, depending on desired sweetness)

Ice cubes (optional, for a chilled consistency)

Instructions:

Preparation of ingredients:

Peel and cut the banana into chunks.

Prepare the mixed berries by washing them and removing the stems if necessary.

If using spinach or kale, wash thoroughly.

Composition of the smoothie:

In a blender or food processor, add the banana chunks, mixed berries, spinach or kale (if using), Greek yogurt or almond milk and optional honey or maple syrup.

Add a few ice cubes if a chilled smoothie is preferred.

Blend:

Blend all ingredients in a blender or food processor until smooth and evenly mixed. More or less liquid can be added depending on the desired consistency.

Taste and adjust:

Taste the smoothie and adjust the sweetness if needed by adding more honey or maple syrup.

One can also add more berries or spinach to boost the flavor and nutrients.

Serve:

Pour smoothie into glasses and serve immediately.

The smoothie can be garnished with fresh berries or a squeeze of lemon juice if desired.

This berry smoothie is not only delicious, but also rich in antioxidants, vitamins and minerals. It is perfect as a quick breakfast, a snack between meals or as a refreshing drink at any time of day. Experiment with different berries and green leafy vegetables to create one's own favorite smoothie!

Frozen watermelon sorbet slices

Preparation time: approx. 10 minutes (plus freezing time)

Servings: 4

Ingredients:

1 small watermelon

Juice of 1 lime

2 tablespoons honey or maple syrup (optional)

Fresh mint leaves for garnish (optional)

Instructions:

Preparing the watermelon:

Cut the watermelon into slices about 1.5 cm thick.

Remove the rind from the watermelon pieces.

Preparing the watermelon sorbet:

Cut the cored watermelon pieces into small cubes and place them in a blender or food processor.

Add the lime juice and honey or maple syrup.

Blend everything together until a smooth and even consistency is achieved.

Freeze the sorbet layers:

Line a shallow baking dish with baking paper.

Pour the watermelon sorbet mixture into the baking dish and smooth the surface with a spoon.

Place the baking dish in the freezer for at least 4 hours or overnight until the sorbet is firm.

Portioning the sorbet slices:

Remove the frozen watermelon sorbet layer from the freezer and cut it into even rectangles or squares.

Place the cut sorbet slices on dessert plates or in small bowls.

Serve:

Garnish the sorbet slices with fresh mint leaves as desired.

Serve the frozen watermelon sorbet slices immediately as a refreshing and healthy dessert.

These frozen watermelon sorbet slices are a delicious and refreshing dessert, perfect for hot summer days or as a healthy snack between meals. They are easy to prepare and a wonderful way to turn fresh fruit into a tasty treat.

Greek yogurt with honey and roasted figs

Preparation time: approx. 15 minutes

Servings: 4

Ingredients:

500 g Greek yogurt (low-fat or to taste)

4 ripe figs

2 tablespoons honey

1 tablespoon chopped nuts (e.g. walnuts, almonds) or granola (optional)

Fresh mint leaves to garnish (optional)

Instructions:

Preparation of the figs:

Wash the figs, cut in half and remove the stalk.

Roasting the figs:

Heat a frying pan over a medium heat.

Place the figs cut-side down in the pan and roast for about 2-3 minutes until lightly caramelized.

Prepare the Greek yogurt:

Place the Greek yogurt in a serving bowl.

Add honey and nuts:

Drizzle the honey over the yogurt.

Sprinkle the chopped nuts or granola on top.

Serve:

Place the roasted figs on top of the Greek yogurt.

Garnish with fresh mint leaves if desired.

Serve immediately and enjoy!

This healthy dessert is easy to make and offers a delicious combination of creamy Greek yogurt, sweet roasted figs and a hint of honey and nuts. Rich in protein, fiber and healthy fats, it's the perfect sweet ending to any meal.

Chia pudding with fruit and almonds

Preparation time: approx. 10 minutes (plus time for swelling)

Servings: 2

Ingredients:

4 tablespoons chia seeds

1 cup unsweetened almond milk (or another plant-based milk of one's choice)

1 tablespoon maple syrup or honey (optional)

1 teaspoon vanilla extract (optional)

Fresh fruit of one's choice (e.g. berries, mango, pineapple)

Chopped almonds or flaked almonds to garnish

Instructions:

Preparation of the chia pudding:

Place the chia seeds in a bowl.

Pour over the unsweetened almond milk and stir well to ensure that the chia seeds are completely covered with liquid.

If desired, add the maple syrup or honey and vanilla extract and stir again.

Leave to swell:

Refrigerate the chia milk mixture for at least 4 hours or overnight to allow the chia seeds to swell and form a pudding-like consistency. Stir occasionally to avoid lumps forming.

Preparing the fruit:

Wash and peel fresh fruit of one's choice and cut into bite-sized pieces.

Assembling the chia pudding:

Divide the swollen chia pudding evenly between two dessert glasses or bowls.

Top the chia pudding with the prepared fresh fruit.

Garnish:

Sprinkle the desserts with chopped almonds or flaked almonds to add extra texture and flavor.

Serve:

Serve the chia puddings with fruit and almonds immediately and enjoy!

This chia pudding with fruit and almonds is a delicious and nutritious dessert dish that is rich in fiber, protein and healthy fats. It is perfect as a sweet finish to a meal or as a healthy snack between meals.

Coconut chia pudding with fresh berries

Preparation time: approx. 10 minutes (plus time for swelling)

Servings: 2

Ingredients:

4 tablespoons chia seeds

1 cup unsweetened coconut milk

1 tablespoon maple syrup or honey (optional)

1 teaspoon vanilla extract (optional)

Fresh berries of one's choice (e.g. strawberries, raspberries, blueberries)

Grated coconut for garnish (optional)

Fresh mint leaves to garnish (optional)

Instructions:

Preparation of the chia pudding:

Place the chia seeds in a bowl.

Pour over the unsweetened coconut milk and stir well to ensure that the chia seeds are completely covered with liquid.

If desired, add the maple syrup or honey and vanilla extract and stir again.

Leave to swell:

Place the chia and coconut milk mixture in the fridge for at least 4 hours or overnight to allow the chia seeds to swell and form a pudding-like consistency. Stir occasionally to avoid lumps forming.

Preparing the fresh berries:

Wash fresh berries of choice and pat dry.

Assembling the coconut chia pudding:

Divide the swollen chia pudding evenly between two dessert glasses or bowls.

Serve with fresh berries:

Pour the fresh berries over the chia pudding and press in lightly to release some juice.

Garnish:

Sprinkle with shredded coconut as desired.

Garnish with fresh mint leaves to embellish the dessert.

Serve:

Serve the coconut chia pudding with fresh berries immediately and enjoy!

This coconut chia pudding with fresh berries is a delicious and nutritious dessert that is rich in fiber, healthy fats and antioxidants. It is perfect as a sweet finish to a meal or healthy snack between meals.

Avocado chocolate mousse

Preparation time: approx. 15 minutes (plus chilling time)

Servings: 2

Ingredients:

1 ripe avocado

2 tablespoons unsweetened cocoa powder

2-3 tablespoons maple syrup or honey

1 teaspoon vanilla extract

A pinch of salt

Optional: Fresh berries for garnish

Instructions:

Preparation of the avocado:

Slice the ripe avocado lengthwise, remove the pit and scoop out the flesh.

Preparation of the mousse:

Place the avocado flesh in a blender or food processor with the un-sweetened cocoa powder, maple syrup or honey, vanilla extract and a pinch of salt.

Blend everything together until a smooth and creamy consistency is achieved. If necessary, scrape down the sides of the blender with a spatula and blend again to ensure that everything is well mixed.

Chilling time:

Cover the avocado chocolate mousse and place it in the fridge for at least 1 hour so that it can cool slightly and firm up.

Serve:

Divide the chilled avocado chocolate mousse between dessert glasses or bowls.

Optionally, garnish the mousse with fresh berries or other fruit of one's choice.

Serve the avocado chocolate mousse as a delicious and healthy dessert.

This avocado chocolate mousse is a healthy alternative to traditional chocolate mousses. The avocado gives the mousse a creamy texture and provides healthy fats at the same time. Enjoy this desert as a delicious end to a meal or as a sweet snack between meals.

Conclusions

The following CHM rules apply:

- **C**ooking at **H**ome **M**akes one healthier

- **C**ooking at **H**ome **M**akes one save money and time

- **C**ooking at **H**ome **M**akes one happier

Summary

Based on the latest scientific data, the contents of this book show the indisputable benefits of a healthy lifestyle with regular physical activity, necessary rest periods with healthy sleep, a healthy diet, promising lifestyle supplements and noxious substances that can be avoided as far as possible. Cooking at home for oneself is usually healthier, cheaper and less time-consuming and can even be fun.

Even a small dose of exercise has proven to be an effective "medicine pill". Just 10 minutes of exercise a day can help to prevent health problems, manage stress and improve quality of life. With calisthenics, jumping rope and yoga, training can take place practically anywhere and at any time without a gym, equipment or weights. These sports can be practiced regardless of the weather, saving money and time.

Sleep, relaxation and music are underestimated pillars of health maintenance. Medication and dietary supplements to support sleep should be avoided as far as possible due to their not insignificant side effects. Even simple measures can contribute to sleep hygiene. Both listening to music and actively making music are complementary health-promoting measures.

Certain nutritional myths persist despite changes in the study situation. For example, the **bad image of eggs, fat and salt should be partially polished up** and the **danger of sugar should not be ignored**. Aspects of longevity appear to be verifiable and reproducible through keto and low-carb diets with findings at the molecular level. In principle, meat should not be devalued as a bad food.

Lifestyle supplements are promising for a long and healthy life, but not all advertised dietary supplements and exotic plants seem to make sense, as the proven success leaves much to be desired and in the worst case can even be harmful to health. Instead, a balanced diet and regular exercise should be preferred.

In principle, a balanced diet of regional foods with seasonal fruit is a better choice than the regular intake of lifestyle supplements or exotic plant products with the marketing label "superfoods" in order to achieve good health and a possible extension of life.

Vitamins are essential and must therefore be taken in through food, and a balanced diet should provide a sufficient amount of each vitamin. In some cases, such as vitamin D, the body can also produce vitamins by exposing the skin to sunlight. A deficiency of vitamins can lead to various health problems, while an excess of certain vitamins can also be harmful.

If it is desired to take dietary supplements, vitamins and/or superfoods, this should be discussed with a medical doctor or nutritionist, as they could also be harmful to one's health. Medications such as metformin and semaglutide require a prescription and should not be administered without medical supervision.

A dangerous lifestyle, disregard for health risks and regular consumption of noxious substances such as alcohol, drugs and smoking have a negative impact on health and life. If necessary, professional support is required, as those affected are not always able to help themselves. **In addition to physical health, mental health** is also crucial for longevity.

Outlook

In the future, new findings from **empirical medicine** should be investigated further.

TCM

Acupuncture has been used in **Traditional Chinese Medicine (TCM)** for thousands of years and **has been recognized by the World Health Organization (WHO) as an alternative method for 43 diseases since 1979.**[677] The acupuncture points are located on a system of pathways **(meridians)**, some of which can be determined using electrical impedance measurements **(skin resistance points)**.[678] After diagnosis in TCM, either fine, sterile **acupuncture needles** are inserted or **moxibustion**, i.e. the controlled release of heat with burning dried mugwort (Artemisia vulgaris), is applied to the points for a 20-minute treatment.[679] The effect of acupuncture appears to be explained by the body's own release of various messenger substances, which can dilate blood vessels and have pain-inhibiting properties.[679,680]

The following acupuncture points are being researched to **promote health, support the immune system and longevity**:

足三里 Zúsānlǐ (Stomach-36):

This point, located a hand's width below the outside of the kneecap, is also known as the **"longevity point"** and appears to have neuroprotective, anti-cancer and anti-inflammatory effects.[681,682,683] The longevity effect could be due to inhibition of the mTOR signaling pathway.[684]

百会 Bǎihuì (Governor vessel-20):

Stimulation of this point, which is located on the center of the skull, appears to be antioxidant, neuroprotective (especially after a stroke) and longevity (via the mTOR signaling pathway).[684,685,686]

涌泉 Yǒngquán (Kidney-1):

This point, located on the sole of the foot between both bunions, is best treated with moxibustion and can help treat hypertension and prolong life via the mTOR signaling pathway.[684,687]

膻中 Shānzhōng (Conception Vessel-17):

This point, which is located at solar plexus (sternum level), should best be treated with moxibustion, as with Kidney-1, and can have antidepressant and cardioprotective effects.[679,688]

内关 Nèiguān (Pericardium-6):

This acupuncture point, located two thumbs' width from the wrist on the inside of the arm, appears to be cardioprotective in patients with heart disease and improve quality of life in cancer patients.[689,690]

曲池 Qūchí (Large Intestine-11):

Stimulation of this acupuncture point, which is located in the crook of the elbow at the top, is said to have antihypertensive (blood pressure-lowering), neuroprotective and also longevity effects.[682,684,690]

合谷 Hégǔ (Large Intestine-4):

This point is located in the hollow between the thumb and index finger and is also often stimulated for self-treatment with acupressure (acupuncture without needles) and can improve the immune system and have a life-prolonging effect.[691]

TTM

Traditional Tibetan Medicine (TTM), which has been influenced by aspects of **TCM, Ayurvedic medicine** and **ancient Greek or ancient Persian medicine**, offers a further perspective from **empirical medicine** in the field of dietetics (nutritional medicine).[692] An interesting approach that my research group has pursued is that patients with **coronary heart disease** could be helped to achieve a desired **weight reduction** according to the TTM system, even if the investigations to date have not involved a multicenter study design.[693,694] In 2022, a Chinese cross-sectional study confirmed some aspects of our study results in people with **metabolic syndrome**.[695]

Self-healing powers

Despite alcohol-induced liver cirrhosis, a heart attack and depression, **Johann Wolfgang von Goethe** managed to live to a respectable age for the time at 83.[696] "Goethe trusted in **the self-healing powers in man** "Natura sanat, medicus curat" (Nature heals, the doctor heals) "or as he has Mephisto say in Urfaust and Faust I:"The spirit of medicine is easy to grasp, you study the great and small world, to let it go in the end, as God pleases."[696]

Thus, with a sensible lifestyle, a **longevity** can be achieved if simple things are followed in everyday life. **No devil's pact is necessary!** Diet and lifestyle factors have a major influence on health and life expectancy. A balanced diet, regular physical activity, adequate sleep, stress management and avoiding harmful behaviors such as smoking and excessive alcohol consumption are crucial to promoting good health and a longer life. It is recommended to seek the professional advice of a physician, pharmacist, physical therapist and/or licensed fitness trainer before beginning any exercise program, taking supplements or changing dietary plans.

Time phenomenon

The chronological age was discussed in the introduction. "Chronos" (time) is a phenomenon that is difficult to grasp. It is known that time is relative and does not run at the same speed everywhere (principle of **time dilation** in **Albert Einstein**'s special theory of relativity), and there is the newly proposed theory that the **ageing process could contribute to the relativity of time**.[697] In **Salvador Dalí**'s surrealist painting "The Persistence of Memory", the **"melting clocks"** symbolize that **time is transient, subjective** (depending on the viewer's perception) and **non-linear**.[698]

The **linear view** of time in a flow on a timeline from alpha to omega must probably give way to a **cyclical view**, as advanced civilizations such as the **Olmecs** and **Mayas** in Central America or the **Tibetans** had already visualized with the **"wheel of time"**.[699,700]

Thinking processes can also be linear or cyclical, whereas **linear thinking** is considered logical, binary ("yes or no"), fixed and organized, linear thinking lacks "ingenuity, innovation and originality" compared to **cyclical thinking**.[701]

Both in the microcosm **(DNA helix)** and in the macrocosm **(galaxy)**, nature has created cyclical rather than linear forms. In modern physics, there is evidence that **time is an illusion** and that **past, present and future occur simultaneously**.[702]

The deliberately provocative title of the book, **"Eating Immortally"** can be seen as a **motto for life**.

Space, time and age blur into cosmic dimensions:

"Even if we, the gods, are abandoned or forgotten, the stars will never fade. Never. They will burn till the end of time!"[703]

References

1. Johnson AA, English BW, Shokhirev MN, Sinclar DA, Cuellar TL. Human age reversal: Fact or fiction? *Aging Cell*. 2022;21(8):e13664.
2. Inoue K, Tsugawa Y, Mayeda ER, Ritz B. Association of Daily Step Patterns With Mortality in US Adults. *JAMA Netw Open*. 2023;6(3):e235174.
3. Paluch AE, Bajpai S, Bassett DR, Carnethon MR, Ekelund U, Evenson KR, Galuska DA, Jefferis BJ, Kraus WE, Lee IM, Matthews CE, Omura JD, Patel AV, Pieper CF, Rees-Punia E, Dallmeier D, Klenk J, Whincup PH, Dooley EE, Pettee Gabriel K, Palta P, Pompeii LA, Chernofsky A, Larson MG, Vasan RS, Spartano N, Ballin M, Nordström P, Nordström A, Anderssen SA, Hansen BH, Cochrane JA, Dwyer T, Wang J, Ferrucci L, Liu F, Schrack J, Urbanek J, Saint-Maurice PF, Yamamoto N, Yoshitake Y, Newton RL Jr, Yang S, Shiroma EJ, Fulton JE; Steps for Health Collaborative. Daily steps and all-cause mortality: a meta-analysis of 15 international cohorts. *Lancet Public Health*. 2022;7(3):e219-e228.
4. Paluch AE, Bajpai S, Ballin M, Bassett DR, Buford TW, Carnethon MR, Chernofsky A, Dooley EE, Ekelund U, Evenson KR, Galuska DA, Jefferis BJ, Kong L, Kraus WE, Larson MG, Lee IM, Matthews CE, Newton RL Jr, Nordström A, Nordström P, Palta P, Patel AV, Pettee Gabriel K, Pieper CF, Pompeii L, Rees-Punia E, Spartano NL, Vasan RS, Whincup PH, Yang S, Fulton JE; Steps for Health Collaborative. Prospective Association of Daily Steps With Cardiovascular Disease: A Harmonized Meta-Analysis. *Circulation*. 2023;147(2):122-131.
5. Matthews CE, Moore SC, Arem H, Cook MB, Trabert B, Håkansson N, Larsson SC, Wolk A, Gapstur SM, Lynch BM, Milne RL, Freedman ND, Huang WY, Berrington de Gonzalez A, Kitahara CM, Linet MS, Shiroma EJ, Sandin S, Patel AV, Lee IM. Amount and Intensity of Leisure-Time Physical Activity and Lower Cancer Risk. *J Clin Oncol*. 2020;38(7):686-697.
6. Steinberg B. You only need to walk this many steps per week to add 3 years to your life. *New York Post*. 2024;12 March. https://nypost.com/2024/03/12/lifestyle/you-only-need-to-walk-this-many-steps-per-week-to-add-3-years-to-your-life/.
7. Mok A, Khaw KT, Luben R, Wareham N, Brage S. Physical activity trajectories and mortality: population based cohort study. *BMJ*. 2019;365:l2323.
8. Garber CE, Blissmer B, Deschenes MR, Franklin BA, Lamonte MJ, Lee IM, Nieman DC, Swain DP; American College of Sports Medicine. American College of Sports Medicine position stand. Quantity and quality of exercise for developing and maintaining cardiorespiratory, musculoskeletal, and neuromotor fitness in apparently healthy adults: guidance for prescribing exercise. *Med Sci Sports Exerc*. 2011;43(7):1334-59.

9. Li VL, He Y, Contrepois K, Liu H, Kim JT, Wiggenhorn AL, Tanzo JT, Tung AS, Lyu X, Zushin PH, Jansen RS, Michael B, Loh KY, Yang AC, Carl CS, Voldstedlund CT, Wei W, Terrell SM, Moeller BC, Arthur RM, Wallis GA, van de Wetering K, Stahl A, Kiens B, Richter EA, Banik SM, Snyder MP, Xu Y, Long JZ. An exercise-inducible metabolite that suppresses feeding and obesity. *Nature*. 2022;606(7915):785-790.

10. Schumann M, Feuerbacher JF, Sünkeler M, Freitag N, Rønnestad BR, Doma K, Lundberg TR. Compatibility of Concurrent Aerobic and Strength Training for Skeletal Muscle Size and Function: An Updated Systematic Review and Meta-Analysis. *Sports Med*. 2022;52(3):601-612.

11. Guseh JS, Figueroa JF. Evaluating the Health Benefits of Low-Frequency Step-Based Physical Activity-The "Weekend Warrior" Pattern Revisited. *JAMA Netw Open*. 2023;6(3):e235184.

12. Khurshid S, Al-Alusi MA, Churchill TW, Guseh JS, Ellinor PT. Accelerometer-Derived "Weekend Warrior" Physical Activity and Incident Cardiovascular Disease. *JAMA*. 2023;330(3):247-252.

13. Hollingsworth JC, Young KC, Abdullah SF, Wadsworth DD, Abukhader A, Elfenbein B, Holley Z.
Protocol for Minute Calisthenics: a randomized controlled study of a daily, habit-based, bodyweight resistance training program. *BMC Public Health*. 2020;20(1):1242.

14. Baker JA. Comparison of Rope Skipping and Jogging as Methods of Improving Cardiovascular Efficiency of College Men. *Res Q*. 1968;39(2):240-3.

15. Zhang L, Wang D, Liu S, Ren FF, Chi L, Xie C. Effects of Acute High-Intensity Interval Exercise and High-Intensity Continuous Exercise on Inhibitory Function of Overweight and Obese Children. *Int J Environ Res Public Health*. 2022;19(16):10401.

16. Town GP, Sol N, Sinning WE. The effect of rope skipping rate on energy expenditure of males and females. *Med Sci Sports Exerc*. 1980;12(4):295-8.

17. Harrell JS, McMurray RG, Baggett CD, Pennell ML, Pearce PF, Bangdiwala SI. Energy costs of physical activities in children and adolescents. *Med Sci Sports Exerc*. 2005;37(2):329-36.

18. Ajjimaporn A, Rachiwong S, Sikipoknpanich V. Effects of 8 weeks of modified hatha yoga traiing on resting-state brain activity and the p300 ERP in patients with physical disability-related stress. *J Phys Ther Sci*. 2018;30(9):1187-1192.

19. Hofmann SG, Andreoli G, Carpenter JK, Curtiss J. Effect of Hatha Yoga on Anxiety: A Meta-Analysis. *J Evid Based Med*. 2016:9(3):116-124.

20. Cramer H, Sellin C, Schumann D, Dobos G. Yoga in Arterial Hypertension. *Dtsch Arztebl Int*. 2018;115(50):833-9.

21. Vilaval T, Sasinan W, Mayuree C, Chananun P, Somchai S. Effect of acupuncture on blood pressure control in hypertensive patients. *J Tradit Chin Med.* 2019;39(2):246-250.

22. Datta K, Bhutambara A, Narawa Y, Srinath R, Kanitkar M. Improved sleep, cognitive processing and enhanced learning and memory task accuracy with Yoga nidra practice in novices. *PLoS ONE.* 2023;18(12):e0294678.

23. Noetel M, Sanders T, Gallardo-Gómez D, Taylor P, Del Pozo Cruz B, van den Hoek D, Smith JJ, Mahoney J, Spathis J, Moresi M, Pagano R, Pagano L, Vasconcellos R, Arnott H, Varley B, Parker P, Biddle S, Lonsdale C. Effect of exercise for depression: systematic review and network meta-analysis of randomised controlled trials. *BMJ.* 2024;384:e075847.

24. Veerabrahmachar R, Bista S, Bokde R, Jasti N, Bhargav H, Bista S. Immediate Effect of Nada Yoga Meditation on Energy Levels and Alignment of Seven Chakras as Assessed by Electro-photonic Imaging: A Randomized Controlled Crossover Pilot Study. *Adv Mind Body Med.* 2023;37(1):11-16.

25. Kelder P, Salvesen C. In: Die Fünf Tibeter / Der Sechste Tibeter in einem Band. *Fischer Taschenbuch Verlag*; 5. Ed. 2010:1-336.

26. Lobsang T. In: Lu Jong: die älteste tibetische Bewegungslehre zur Heilung von Körper und Geist. *O.W. Barth*; 10. Ed. 2010:1-176.

27. Sahu R. In: Yoga For Beginners: Hatha Yoga: The Complete Guide to Master Hatha Yoga; Benefits, Essentials, Asanas (with Pictures), Hatha Meditation, Common Mistakes, FAQs, and Common Myths. *Independently published.* 2020:1-189.

28. **Dimitrov S**, Lange T, Gouttefangeas C, Jensen ATR, Szczepanski M, Lehnnolz J, Soekadar S, Rammensee HG, Born J, Besedovsky L. Gα_s-coupled receptor signaling and sleep regulate integrin activation of human antigen-specific T cells. *J Exp Med.* 2019;216(3):517-526.

29. Wang C, Bangdiwala SI, Rangarajan S, Lear SA, AlHabib KF, Mohan V, Teo K, Poirier P, Tse LA, Liu Z, Rosengren A, Kumar R, Lopez-Jaramillo P, Yusoff K, Monsef N, Krishnapillai V, Ismail N, Seron P, Dans AL, Kruger L, Yeates K, Leach L, Yusuf R, Orlandini A, Wolyniec M, Bahonar A, Mohan I, Khatib R, Temizhan A, Li W, Yusuf S. Association of estimated sleep duration and naps with mortality and cardiovascular events: a study of 116 632 people from 21 countries. *Eur Heart J.* 2019;40(20):1620-1629.

30. Li J, Cao D, Huang Y, Chen Z, Wang R, Dong Q, Wei Q, Liu L. Sleep duration and health outcomes: an umbrella review. *Sleep Breath.* 2022;26(3):1479-1501.

31. Mitter P, De Crescenzo F, Loo Yong Kee K, Xia J, Roberts S, Chi W, Kurtulmus A, Kyle SD, Geddes JR, Cipriani A. Sleep deprivation as a treatment for major depressive episodes: A systematic review and meta-analysis. *Sleep Med Rev.* 2022;64:101647.

32. Dhand R, Sohal H. Good sleep, bad sleep! The role of daytime naps in healthy adults. *Curr Opin Pulm Med.* 2006;12(6):379-82.

33. Ong JL, Lau TY, Lee XK, van Rijn E, Chee MWL. A daytime nap restores hippocampal function and improves declarative learning. *Sleep.* 2020;43(9):zsaa058.

34. Zheng B, Yu C, Lv J, Guo Y, Bian Z, Zhou M, Yang L, Chen Y, Li X, Zou J, Ning F, Chen J, Chen Z, Li L; China Kadoorie Biobank Collaborative Group. Insomnia symptoms and risk of cardiovascular diseases among 0.5 million adults: A 10-year cohort. *Neurology.* 2019;93(23):e2110-e2120.

35. McAlpine CS, Kiss MG, Rattik S, He S, Vassalli A, Valet C, Anzai A, Chan CT, Mindur JE, Kahles F, Poller WC, Frodermann V, Fenn AM, Gregory AF, Halle L, Iwamoto Y, Hoyer FF, Binder CJ, Libby P, Tafti M, Scammell TE, Nahrendorf M, Swirski FK. Sleep modulates haematopoiesis and protects against atherosclerosis. *Nature.* 2019;566(7744):383-387.

36. Benz F, Meneo D, Baglioni C, Hertenstein E. Insomnia symptoms as risk factor for somatic disorders: An umbrella review of systematic reviews and meta-analyses. *J Sleep Res.* 2023;32(6):e13984.

37. Le Bon O. Relationships between REM and NREM in the NREM-REM sleep cycle: a review on competing concepts. *Sleep Med.* 2020;70:6-16.

38. Ackermann S, Rasch B. Differential effects of non-REM and REM sleep on memory consolidation? *Curr Neurol Neurosci Rep.* 2014;14(2):430.

39. Chinoy ED, Cuellar JA, Huwa KE, Jameson JT, Watson CH, Bessman SC, Hirsch DA, Cooper AD, Drummond SPA, Markwald RR. Performance of seven consumer sleep-tracking devices compared with polysomnography. *Sleep.* 2021;44(5):zsaa291.

40. Hussey KD. Timeless spaces: Field experiments in the physiological study of circadian rhythms, 1938-1963. *Hist Philos Life Sci.* 2023;45(2):17.

41. Boivin DB, Boudreau P, Kosmadopoulos A. Disturbance of the Circadian System in Shift Work and Its Health Impact. *J Biol Rhythms.* 2022;37(1):3-28.

42. Touitou Y, Reinberg A, Touitou D. Association between light at night, melatonin secretion, sleep deprivation, and the internal clock: Health impacts and mechanisms of circadian disruption. *Life Sci.* 2017;173:94-106.

43. Lopresti AL, Smith SJ, Drummond PD. An investigation into an evening intake of a saffron extract (affron®) on sleep quality, cortisol, and melatonin concentrations in adults with poor sleep: a randomised, double-blind, placebo-controlled, multi-dose study. *Sleep Med.* 2021;86:7-18.

44. Shinjyo N, Waddell G, Green J. Valerian Root in Treating Sleep Problems and Associated Disorders-A Systematic Review and Meta-Analysis. *J Evid Based Integr Med.* 2020;25:2515690X20967323.

45. DeKosky ST, Williamson JB. The Long and the Short of Benzodiazepines and Sleep Medications: Short-Term Benefits, Long-Term Harms? *Neurotherapeutics*. 2020;17(1):153-155.

46. Irish LA, Kline CE, Gunn HE, Buysse DJ, Hall MH. The role of sleep hygiene in promoting public health: A review of empirical evidence. *Sleep Med Rev*. 2015;22:23-36.

47. Harvey DL, Milton K, Jones AP, Atkin AJ. International trends in screen-based behaviours from 2012 to 2019. *Prev Med*. 2022;154:106909.

48. Moszeik EN, von Oertzen T, Renner KH. Effectiveness of a short Yoga Nidra meditation on stress, sleep, and well-being in a large and diverse sample. *Curr Psychology*. 2022;41:5272-5286.

49. Song I, Baek K, Kim C, Song C. Effects of nature sounds on the attention and physiological and psychological relaxation. *Urban For Urban Gree*. 2023;86:127987.

50. Precht LM, Mertens F, Brickau DS, Kramm RJ, Margraf J, Stirnberg J, Brailovskaia J. Engaging in physical activity instead of (over)using the smartphone: An experimental investigation of lifestyle interventions to prevent problematic smartphone use and to promote mental health. *Z Gesundh Wiss*. 2023:1-19.

51. Hallam S, Creech A. Can active music making promote health and well-being in older citizens? Findings of the music for life project. *London J Prim Care (Abingdon)*. 2016;8(2):21-25.

52. Daykin N, de Viggiani N, Pilkington P, Moriarty Y. Music making for health, well-being and behaviour change in youth justice settings: a systematic review. *Health Promot Int*. 2013;28(2):197-210.

53. Sutcliffe R, Du K, Ruffman T. Music Making and Neuropsychological Aging: A Review. *Neurosci Biobehav Rev*. 2020;113:479-491.

54. de la Rubia Ortí JE, García-Pardo MP, Iranzo CC, Madrigal JJC, Castillo SS, Rochina MJ, Gascó VJP. Does Music Therapy Improve Anxiety and Depression in Alzheimer's Patients? *J Altern Complement Med*. 2018;24(1):33-36.

55. Pauwels EK, Volterrani D, Mariani G, Kostkiewics M. Mozart, music and medicine. *Med Princ Pract*. 2014;23(5):403-12.

56. Sanfilippo KRM, Stewart L, Glover V. How music may support perinatal mental health: an overview. *Arch Womens Ment Health*. 2021;24(5):831-839.

57. Araújo LS, Wasley D, Redding E, Atkins L, Perkins R, Ginsborg J, Williamon A. Fit to Perform: A Profile of Higher Education Music Students' Physical Fitness. *Front Psychol*. 2020;11:298.

58. Kulinski J, Ofori EK, Visotcky A, Smith A, Sparapani R, Fleg JL. Effects of music on the cardiovascular system. *Trends Cardiovasc Med*. 2022;32(6):390-398.

59. Krucoff MW, Crater SW, Green CL, Maas AC, Seskevich JE, Lane JD, Loeffler KA, Morris K, Bashore TM, Koenig HG. Integrative noetic therapies as adjuncts to percutaneous intervention during unstable coronary syndromes: Monitoring and Actualization of Noetic Training (MANTRA) feasibility pilot. *Am Heart J*. 2001;142(5):760-9.

60. Krucoff MW, Crater SW, Gallup D, Blankenship JC, Cuffe M, Guarneri M, Krieger RA, Kshettry VR, Morris K, Oz M, Pichard A, Sketch MH Jr, Koenig HG, Mark D, Lee KL. Music, imagery, touch, and prayer as adjuncts to interventional cardiac care: the Monitoring and Actualisation of Noetic Trainings (MANTRA) II randomised study. *Lancet*. 2005;366(9481):211-7.

61. Koelsch S, Jäncke L. Music and the heart. *Eur Heart J*. 2015;36(44):3043-9.

62. Bittman B, Croft DT Jr, Brinker J, van Laar R, Vernalis MN, Ellsworth DL. Recreational Music-Making alters gene expression pathways in patients with coronary heart disease. *Med Sci Monit*. 2013;19:139-47.

63. Wong MM, Tahir T, Wong MM, Baron A, Finnerty R. Biomarkers of Stress in Music Interventions: A Systematic Review. *Music Ther*. 2021;58(3):241-277.

64. Linnemann A, Ditzen B, Strahler J, Doerr JM, Nater UM. Music listening as a means of stress reduction in daily life. *Psychoneuroendocrinology*. 2015;60:82-90.

65. Zhao B, Gan L, Graubard BI, Männistö S, Albanes D, Huang J. Associations of Dietary Cholesterol, Serum Cholesterol, and Egg Consumption With Overall and Cause-Specific Mortality: Systematic Review and Updated Meta-Analysis. *Circulation*. 2022;145(20):1506-1520.

66. Zhong VW, Van Horn L, Cornelis MC, Wilkins JT, Ning H, Carnethon MR, Greenland P, Mentz RJ, Tucker KL, Zhao L, Norwood AF, Lloyd-Jones DM, Allen NB. Associations of Dietary Cholesterol or Egg Consumption With Incident Cardiovascular Disease and Mortality. *JAMA*. 2019;321(11):1081-1095.

67. Weggemans RM, Zock PL, Katan MB. Dietary cholesterol from eggs increases the ratio of total cholesterol to high-density lipoprotein cholesterol in humans: a meta-analysis. *Am J Clin Nutr*. 2001;73(5):885-91.

68. Dehghan M, Mente A, Rangarajan S, Mohan V, Lear S, Swaminathan S, Wielgosz A, Seron P, Avezum A, Lopez-Jaramillo P, Turbide G, Chifamba J, AlHabib KF, Mohammadifard N, Szuba A, Khatib R, Altuntas Y, Liu X, Iqbal R, Rosengren A, Yusuf R, Smuts M, Yusufali A, Li N, Diaz R, Yusoff K, Kaur M, Soman B, Ismail N, Gupta R, Dans A, Sheridan P, Teo K, Anand SS, Yusuf S. Association of egg intake with blood lipids, cardiovascular disease, and mortality in 177,000 people in 50 countries. *Am J Clin Nutr*. 2020;111(4):795-803.

69. Carson JAS, Lichtenstein AH, Anderson CAM, Appel LJ, Kris-Etherton PM, Meyer KA, Petersen K, Polonsky T, Van Horn L; American Heart Association Nutrition Committee of the Council on Lifestyle and Cardiometabolic Health; Council on Arteriosclerosis, Thrombosis and Vascular Biology; Council on Cardiovascular and Stroke Nursing; Council on Clinical Cardiology; Council on Peripheral Vascular Disease; and Stroke Council. Dietary Cholesterol and Cardiovascular Risk: A Science Advisory From the American Heart Association. *Circulation*. 2020;141(3):e39-e53.

70. Shin JY, Xun P, Nakamura Y, He K. Egg consumption in relation to risk of cardiovascular disease and diabetes: a systematic review and meta-analysis. *Am J Clin Nutr*. 2013;98(1):146-59.

71. Liu C, Song Z, Li Z, Boon MR, Schönke M, Rensen PCN, Wang Y. Dietary choline increases brown adipose tissue activation markers and improves cholesterol metabolism in female APOE*3-Leiden.CETP mice. *Int J Obes (Lond)*. 2023;47(3):236-243.

72. DiBella M, Thomas MS, Alyousef H, Millar C, Blesso C, Malysheva O, Caudill MA, Fernandez ML. Choline Intake as Supplement or as a Component of Eggs Increases Plasma Choline and Reduces Interleukin-6 without Modifying Plasma Cholesterol in Participants with Metabolic Syndrome. *Nutrients*. 2020;12(10):3120.

73. Tsoupras A, Lordan R, Zabetakis I. Inflammation, not Cholesterol, Is a Cause of Chronic Disease. *Nutrients*. 2018;10(5):604.

74. Grčević M, Kralik Z, Kralik G, Galović O. Effects of dietary marigold extract on lutein content, yolk color and fatty acid profile of omega-3 eggs. *J Sci Food Agric*. 2019;99(5):2292-2299.

75. Mach F, Baigent C, Catapano AL, Koskinas KC, Casula M, Badimon L, Chapman MJ, De Backer GG, Delgado V, Ference BA, Graham IM, Halliday A, Landmesser U, Mihaylova B, Pedersen TR, Riccardi G, Richter DJ, Sabatine MS, Taskinen MR, Tokgozoglu L, Wiklund O; ESC Scientific Document Group. 2019 ESC/EAS Guidelines for the management of dyslipidaemias: lipid modification to reduce cardiovascular risk. *Eur Heart J*. 2020;41(1):111-188.

76. Eckel RH, Jakicic JM, Ard JD, de Jesus JM, Houston Miller N, Hubbard VS, Lee IM, Lichtenstein AH, Loria CM, Millen BE, Nonas CA, Sacks FM, Smith SC Jr, Svetkey LP, Wadden TA, Yanovski SZ, Kendall KA, Morgan LC, Trisolini MG, Velasco G, Wnek J, Anderson JL, Halperin JL, Albert NM, Bozkurt B, Brindis RG, Curtis LH, DeMets D, Hochman JS, Kovacs RJ, Ohman EM, Pressler SJ, Sellke FW, Shen WK, Smith SC Jr, Tomaselli GF; American College of Cardiology/American Heart Association Task Force on Practice Guidelines. 2013 AHA/ACC guideline on lifestyle management to reduce cardiovascular risk: a report of the American College of Cardiology/American Heart Association Task Force on Practice Guidelines. *Circulation*. 2014;129(25 Suppl 2):S76-99.

77. BGH *GesR*. 2008;361.

78. BGH *NJW-RR*. 2014;1053.

79. Peou S, Milliard-Hasting B, Shah SA. Impact of avocado-enriched diets on plasma lipoproteins: A meta-analysis. *J Clin Lipidol.* 2016;10(1):161-71.

80. Estruch R, Ros E, Salas-Salvadó J, Covas MI, Corella D, Arós F, Gómez-Gracia E, Ruiz-Gutiérrez V, Fiol M, Lapetra J, Lamuela-Raventos RM, Serra-Majem L, Pintó X, Basora J, Muñoz MA, Sorlí JV, Martínez JA, Martínez-González MA; PREDIMED Study Investigators. Primary prevention of cardiovascular disease with a Mediterranean diet. *N Engl J Med.* 2013;368(14):1279-90.

81. Del Gobbo LC, Falk MC, Feldman R, Lewis K, Mozaffarian D. Effects of tree nuts on blood lipids, apolipoproteins, and blood pressure: systematic review, meta-analysis, and dose-response of 61 controlled intervention trials. *Am J Clin Nutr.* 2015;102(6):1347-56.

82. O'Neil CE, Fulgoni VL 3rd, Nicklas TA. Tree Nut consumption is associated with better adiposity measures and cardiovascular and metabolic syndrome health risk factors in U.S. Adults: NHANES 2005-2010. *Nutr J.* 2015;14:64.

83. Opie LH, Lecour S. The red wine hypothesis: from concepts to protective signalling molecules. *Eur Heart J.* 2007;28(14):1683-93.

84. Windler E, Beil FU, Berthold HK, Gouni-Berthold I, Kassner U, Klose G, Lorkowski S, März W, Parhofer KG, Plat J, Silbernagel G, Steinhagen-Thiessen E, Weingärtner O, Zyriax BC, Lütjohann D. Phytosterols and Cardiovascular Risk Evaluated against the Background of Phytosterolemia Cases-A German Expert Panel Statement. *Nutrients.* 2023;15(4):828.

85. Kreuzer J. Phytosterols and phytostanols: is it time to rethink that supplemented margarine? *Cardiovasc Res.* 2011;90(3):397-8.

86. Glenn AJ, Guasch-Ferré M, Malik VS, Kendall CWC, Manson JE, Rimm EB, Willett WC, Sun Q, Jenkins DJA, Hu FB, Sievenpiper JL. Portfolio Diet Score and Risk of Cardiovascular Disease: Findings From 3 Prospective Cohort Studies. *Circulation.* 2023;148(22):1750-1763.

87. Makhmudova U, Schulze PC, Lütjohann D, Weingärtner O. Phytosterols and Cardiovascular Disease. *Curr Atheroscler Rep.* 2021;23(11):68.

88. Cheng WW, Liu GQ, Wang LQ, Liu ZS. Glycidyl Fatty Acid Esters in Refined Edible Oils: A Review on Formation, Occurrence, Analysis, and Elimination Methods. *Compr Rev Food Sci Food Saf.* 2017;16(2):263-281.

89. Gavrilova O, Marcus-Samuels B, Graham D, Kim JK, Shulman GI, Castle AL, Vinson C, Eckhaus M, Reitman ML. Surgical implantation of adipose tissue reverses diabetes in lipoatrophic mice. *J Clin Invest.* 2000;105(3):271-8.

90. Shai I, Schwarzfuchs D, Henkin Y, Shahar DR, Witkow S, Greenberg I, Golan R, Fraser D, Bolotin A, Vardi H, Tangi-Rozental O, Zuk-Ramot R, Sarusi B, Brickner D, Schwartz Z, Sheiner E, Marko R, Katorza E, Thiery

J, Fiedler GM, Blüher M, Stumvoll M, Stampfer MJ; Dietary Intervention Randomized Controlled Trial (DIRECT) Group. Weight loss with a low-carbohydrate, Mediterranean, or low-fat diet. *N Engl J Med.* 2008;359(3):229-41.

91. Mozaffarian D, Hao T, Rimm EB, Willett WC, Hu FB. Changes in diet and lifestyle and long-term weight gain in women and men. *N Engl J Med.* 2011;364(25):2392-404.

92. Jensen JD, Smed S. State-of-the-art for food taxes to promote public health. *Proc Nutr Soc.* 2018;77(2):100-105.

93. Sargsyan A, Dubasi HB. Milk Consumption and Prostate Cancer: A Systematic Review. *World J Mens Health.* 2021;39(3):419-428.

94. Savaiano DA, Hutkins RW. Yogurt, cultured fermented milk, and health: a systematic review. *Nutr Rev.* 2021;79(5):599-614.

95. McGandy RB, Hegsted DM, Stare FJ. Dietary fats, carbohydrates and atherosclerotic vascular disease. *N Engl J Med.* 1967;277(5):242-7.

96. Kearns CE, Schmidt LA, Glantz SA. Sugar Industry and Coronary Heart Disease Research: A Historical Analysis of Internal Industry Documents. *JAMA Intern Med.* 2016;176(11):1680-1685.

97. Catapano AL, Graham I, De Backer G, Wiklund O, Chapman MJ, Drexel H, Hoes AW, Jennings CS, Landmesser U, Pedersen TR, Reiner Ž, Riccardi G, Taskinen MR, Tokgozoglu L, Verschuren WMM, Vlachopoulos C, Wood DA, Zamorano JL, Cooney MT; ESC Scientific Document Group. 2016 ESC/EAS Guidelines for the Management of Dyslipidaemias. *Eur Heart J.* 2016;37(39):2999-3058.

98. Sofi F, Dinu M, Pagliai G, Cesari F, Gori AM, Sereni A, Becatti M, Fiorillo C, Marcucci R, Casini A. Low-Calorie Vegetarian Versus Mediterranean Diets for Reducing Body Weight and Improving Cardiovascular Risk Profile: CARDIVEG Study (Cardiovascular Prevention With Vegetarian Diet). *Circulation.* 2018;137(11):1103-1113.

99. Link VM, Subramanian P, Cheung F, Han KL, Stacy A, Chi L, Sellers BA, Koroleva G, Courville AB, Mistry S, Burns A, Apps R, Hall KD, Belkaid Y. Differential peripheral immune signatures elicited by vegan versus ketogenic diets in humans. *Nat Med.* 2024;30(2):560-572.

100. Gohari S, Ghobadi S, Jafari A, Ahangar H, Gohari S, Mahjani M. The effect of dietary approaches to stop hypertension and ketogenic diets intervention on serum uric acid concentration: a systematic review and meta-analysis of randomized controlled trials. *Sci Rep.* 2023;13(1):10492.

101. Shan Z, Guo Y, Hu FB, Liu L, Qi Q. Association of Low-Carbohydrate and Low-Fat Diets With Mortality Among US Adults. *JAMA Intern Med.* 2020;180(4):513-523.

102. McGaugh E, Barthel B. A Review of Ketogenic Diet and Lifestyle. *Mo Med.* 2022;119(1):84-88.

103. Barghouthy Y, Corrales M, Somani B. The Relationship between Modern Fad Diets and Kidney Stone Disease: A Systematic Review of Literature. *Nutrients.* 2021;13(12):4270.

104. Lagiou P, Sandin S, Lof M, Trichopoulos D, Adami HO, Weiderpass E. Low carbohydrate-high protein diet and incidence of cardiovascular diseases in Swedish women: prospective cohort study. *BMJ.* 2012;344:e4026.

105. Lee MB, Hill CM, Bitto A, Kaeberlein M. Antiaging diets: Separating fact from fiction. *Science.* 2021;374(6570):eabe7365.

106. Mao B, Zhang Q, Ma L, Zhao DS, Zhao P, Yan P. Overview of Research into mTOR Inhibitors. *Molecules.* 2022;27(16):5295.

107. Zhang X, Kapoor D, Jeong SJ, Fappi A, Stitham J, Shabrish V, Sergin I, Yousif E, Rodriguez-Velez A, Yeh YS, Park A, Yurdagul Jr A, Rom O, Epelman S, Schilling JD, Sardiello M, Diwan A, Cho J, Stitziel NA, Javaheri A, Lodhi IJ, Mittendorder B, Razani B. Identification of a leucine-mediated threshold effect governing macrophage mTOR signalling and cardiovascular risk. *Nat Metab.* 2024;6:359-377.

108. Zheng Y, Li Y, Satija A, Pan A, Sotos-Prieto M, Rimm E, Willett WC, Hu FB. Association of changes in red meat consumption with total and cause specific mortality among US women and men: two prospective cohort studies. *BMJ.* 2019;365:l2110.

109. Genoni A, Christophersen CT, Lo J, Coghlan M, Boyce MC, Bird AR, Lyons-Wall P, Devine A. Long-term Paleolithic diet is associated with lower resistant starch intake, different gut microbiota composition and increased serum TMAO concentrations. *Eur J Nutr.* 2020;59(5):1845-1858.

110. Zeraatkar D, Han MA, Guyatt GH, Vernooij RWM, El Dib R, Cheung K, Milio K, Zworth M, Bartoszko JJ, Valli C, Rabassa M, Lee Y, Zajac J, Prokop-Dorner A, Lo C, Bala MM, Alonso-Coello P, Hanna SE, Johnston BC. Red and Processed Meat Consumption and Risk for All-Cause Mortality and Cardiometabolic Outcomes: A Systematic Review and Meta-analysis of Cohort Studies. *Ann Intern Med.* 2019;171(10):703-710.

111. Han MA, Zeraatkar D, Guyatt GH, Vernooij RWM, El Dib R, Zhang Y, Algarni A, Leung G, Storman D, Valli C, Rabassa M, Rehman N, Parvizian MK, Zworth M, Bartoszko JJ, Lopes LC, Sit D, Bala MM, Alonso-Coello P, Johnston BC. Reduction of Red and Processed Meat Intake and Cancer Mortality and Incidence: A Systematic Review and Meta-analysis of Cohort Studies. *Ann Intern Med.* 2019;171(10):711-720.

112. Vernooij RWM, Zeraatkar D, Han MA, El Dib R, Zworth M, Milio K, Sit D, Lee Y, Gomaa H, Valli C, Swierz MJ, Chang Y, Hanna SE, Brauer PM, Sievenpiper J, de Souza R, Alonso-Coello P, Bala MM, Guyatt GH, Johnston BC. Patterns of Red and Processed Meat Consumption and Risk for Cardiometabolic and Cancer Outcomes: A Systematic Review and Meta-analysis of Cohort Studies. *Ann Intern Med.* 2019;171(10):732-741.

113. Ramel A, Nwaru BI, Lamberg-Allardt C, Thorisdottir B, Bärebring L, Söderlund F, Arnesen EK, Dierkes J, Åkesson A. White meat consumption and risk of cardiovascular disease and type 2 diabetes: a systematic review and meta-analysis. *Food Nutr Res.* 2023;67:10.29219/fnr.v67.9543.

114. Sebastiani G, Herranz Barbero A, Borrás-Novell C, Alsina Casanova M, Aldecoa-Bilbao V, Andreu-Fernández V, Pascual Tutusaus M, Ferrero Martínez S, Gómez Roig MD, García-Algar O. The Effects of Vegetarian and Vegan Diet during Pregnancy on the Health of Mothers and Offspring. *Nutrients.* 2019;11(3):557.

115. Leung AKC, Lam JM, Wong AHC, Hon KL, Li X. Iron Deficiency Anemia: An Updated Review. *Curr Pediatr Rev.* 2024;20(3):339-356.

116. Coy A, Medina A, Rivera A, Sánchez P. Calcium intake in Colombia: are we still in deficit? *Arch Osteoporos.* 2020;15(1):71.

117. Keefe JA, Moore OM, Ho KS, Wehrens XHT. Role of Ca^{2+} in healthy and pathologic cardiac function: from normal excitation-contraction coupling to mutations that cause inherited arrhythmia. *Arch Toxicol.* 2023;97(1):73-92.

118. Miyajima M. Amino acids: key sources for immunometabolites and immunotransmitters. *Int Immunol.* 2020;32(7):435-446.

119. Che D, Nyingwa PS, Ralinala KM, Maswanganye GMT, Wu G. Amino Acids in the Nutrition, Metabolism, and Health of Domestic Cats. *Adv Exp Med Biol.* 2021;1285:217-231.

120. Soice E, Johnston J. Immortalizing Cells for Human Consumption. *Int J Mol Sci.* 2021;22(21):11660.

121. Mateti T, Laha A, Shenoy P. Artificial Meat Industry: Production Methodology, Challenges, and Future. *JOM.* 2022;74(9):3428-3444.

122. Queiroz LS, Nogueira Silva NF, Jessen F, Mohammadifar MA, Stephani R, Fernandes de Carvalho A, Perrone ÍT, Casanova F. Edible insect as an alternative protein source: a review on the chemistry and functionalities of proteins under different processing methods. *Heliyon.* 2023;9(4):e14831.

123. Bisconsin-Junior A, Feitosa BF, Silva FL, Mariutti LRB. Mycotoxins on edible insects: Should we be worried? *Food Chem Toxicol.* 2023;177:113845.

124. Harris E. WHO: Nations Must Do More to Reduce Salt Consumption by 2025 *JAMA.* 2023;329(14):1143.

125. Mozaffarian D, Fahimi S, Singh GM, Micha R, Khatibzadeh S, Engell RE, Lim S, Danaei G, Ezzati M, Powles J; Global Burden of Diseases Nutrition and Chronic Diseases Expert Group. Global sodium consumption and death from cardiovascular causes. *N Engl J Med.* 2014;371(7):624-34.

126. Wan L, Ogrinz B, Vigo D, Bersenev E, Tuerlinckx F, Van den Bergh O, Aubert AE. Cardiovascular autonomic adaptation to long-term confinement during a 105-day simulated Mars mission. *Aviat Space Environ Med.* 2011;82(7):711-6.

127. He FJ, Tan M, Ma Y, MacGregor GA. Salt Reduction to Prevent Hypertension and Cardiovascular Disease: JACC State-of-the-Art Review. *J Am Coll Cardiol.* 2020;75(6):632-647.

128. DiNicolantonio JJ, Mehta V, Zaman SB, O'Keefe JH. Not Salt But Sugar As Aetiological In Osteoporosis: A Review. *Mo Med.* 2018;115(3):247-252.

129. Wu X, Chen L, Cheng J, Qian J, Fang Z, Wu J. Effect of Dietary Salt Intake on Risk of Gastric Cancer: A Systematic Review and Meta-Analysis of Case-Control Studies. *Nutrients.* 2022;14(20):4260.

130. Braam B, Huang X, Cupples WA, Hamza SM. Understanding the Two Faces of Low-Salt Intake. *Curr Hypertens Rep.* 2017;19(6):49.

131. Yuan Y, Jin A, Neal B, Feng X, Qiao Q, Wang H, Zhang R, Li J, Duan P, Cao L, Zhang H, Hu S, Li H, Gao P, Xie G, Yuan J, Cheng L, Wang S, Zhang H, Niu W, Fang H, Zhao M, Gao R, Chen J, Elliott P, Labarthe D, Wu Y. Salt substitution and salt-supply restriction for lowering blood pressure in elderly care facilities: a cluster-randomized trial. *Nat Med.* 2023;29(4):973-981.

132. de Cabo R, Mattson MP. Effects of Intermittent Fasting on Health, Aging, and Disease. *N Engl J Med.* 2019;381(26):2541-2551.

133. Devrim-Lanpir A, Hill L, Knechtle B. Efficacy of Popular Diets Applied by Endurance Athletes on Sports Performance: Beneficial or Detrimental? A Narrative Review. *Nutrients.* 2021;13(2):491.

134. Song DK, Kim YW. Beneficial effects of intermittent fasting: a narrative review. *J Yeungnam Med Sci.* 2023;40(1):4-11.

135. Pietzner M, Uluvar B, Kolnes KJ, Jeppesen PB, Frivold SV, Skattebo Ø, Johansen EI, Skålhegg BS, Wojtaszewski JFP, Kolnes AJ, Yeo GSH, O'Rahilly S, Jensen J, Langenberg C. Systemic proteome adaptions to 7-day complete caloric restriction in humans. *Nat Metab.* 2024 Mar 1. doi: 10.1038/s42255-024-01008-9. Online ahead of print.

136. Brooks M. Intermittent fasting linked to higher CVD death risk. *Medscape.* 2024;19 March. https://www.medscape.com/viewarticle/intermittent-fasting-linked-higher-cvd-death-risk-2024a1000559.

137. Boccardi V, Pigliautile M, Guazzarini AG, Mecocci P. The Potential of Fasting-Mimicking Diet as a Preventive and Curative Strategy for Alzheimer's Disease. *Biomolecules.* 2023;13(7):1133.

138. Wei M, Brandhorst S, Shelehchi M, Mirzaei H, Cheng CW, Budniak J, Groshen S, Mack WJ, Guen E, Di Biase S, Cohen P, Morgan TE, Dorff T, Hong K, Michalsen A, Laviano A, Longo VD. Fasting-mimicking diet and markers/risk factors for aging, diabetes, cancer, and cardiovascular disease. *Sci Transl Med.* 2017;9(377):eaai8700.

139. Brandhorst S, Levine ME, Wei M, Shelehchi M, Morgan TE, Nayak KS, Dorff T, Hong K, Crimmins EM, Cohen P, Longo VD. Fasting-mimicking diet causes hepatic and blood markers changes indicating reduced biological age and disease risk. *Nat Commun.* 2024;15(1):1309.

140. Bleakley CM, Bieuzen F, Davison GW, Costello JT. Whole-body cryotherapy: empirical evidence and theoretical perspectives. *Open Access J Sports Med.* 2014;5:25-36.

141. Miller KC, Launstein ED, Glovatsky RM. Rectal Temperature Cooling Using 2 Cold-Water Immersion Preparation Strategies. *J Athl Train.* 2023;58(4):355-360.

142. Loap S, Lathe R. Mechanism Underlying Tissue Cryotherapy to Combat Obesity/Overweight: Triggering Thermogenesis. *J Obes.* 2018;2018:5789647.

143. Marlatt KL, Ravussin E. Brown Adipose Tissue: an Update on Recent Findings. *Curr Obes Rep.* 2017;6(4):389-396.

144. Galic S, Loh K, Murray-Segal L, Steinberg GR, Andrews ZB, Kemp BE. AMPK signaling to acetyl-CoA carboxylase is required for fasting- and cold-induced appetite but not thermogenesis. *Elife.* 2018;7:e32656.

145. Bakal K, Danckers M, Denson JL, Sauthoff H. Therapeutic hypothermia after cardiac arrest in a patient with systemic sclerosis and Raynaud phenomenon. *Chest.* 2015;147(2):e27-e30.

146. van den Driessche JJ, Plat J, Mensink RP. Effects of superfoods on risk factors of metabolic syndrome: a systematic review of human intervention trials. *Food Funct.* 2018;9(4):1944-1966.

147. Gulcin İ. Antioxidants and antioxidant methods: an updated overview. *Arch Toxicol.* 2020;94(3):651-715.

148. Price C. The Age of Scurvy. *Distillations Magazine.* 2017;3(2):12-23.

149. Stubbs BJ. Captain Cook's Beer; the anti-scorbutic effects of malt and beer in late 18th century sea voyages. *Asia and Pacific Journal of Clinical Nutrition.* 2003;12(2):129-37.

150. Xu K, Peng R, Zou Y, Jiang X, Sun Q, Song C. Vitamin C intake and multiple health outcomes: an umbrella review of systematic reviews and meta-analyses. *Int J Food Sci Nutr.* 2022;73(5):588-599.

151. Magrì A, Germano G, Lorenzato A, Lamba S, Chilà R, Montone M, Amodio V, Ceruti T, Sassi F, Arena S, Abrignani S, D'Incalci M, Zucchetti M, Di Nicolantonio F, Bardelli A. High-dose vitamin C enhances cancer immunotherapy. *Sci Transl Med.* 2020;12(532):eaay8707.

152. Shaw G, Lee-Barthel A, Ross ML, Wang B, Baar K. Vitamin C-enriched gelatin supplementation before intermittent activity augments collagen synthesis. *Am J Clin Nutr.* 2017;105(1):136-143.

153. Lbban E, Kwon K, Ashor A, Stephan B, Idris I, Tsintzas K, Siervo M. Vitamin C supplementation showed greater effects on systolic blood pressure in hypertensive and diabetic patients: an updated systematic review and meta-analysis of randomised clinical trials. *Int J Food Sci Nutr.* 2023;74(8):814-825.

154. Kook SY, Lee KM, Kim Y, Cha MY, Kang S, Baik SH, Lee H, Park R, Mook-Jung I. High-dose of vitamin C supplementation reduces amyloid plaque burden and ameliorates pathological changes in the brain of 5XFAD mice. *Cell Death Dis.* 2014;5(2):e1083.

155. Santos RD. Vitamin C and primary prevention of cardiovascular disease: the case for Mendelian randomization. *Eur J Prev Cardiol.* 2022;28(16):1838-1839.

156. Kangisser L, Tan E, Bellomo R, Deane AM, Plummer MP. Neuroprotective Properties of Vitamin C: A Scoping Review of Pre-Clinical and Clinical Studies. *J Neurotrauma.* 2021;38(16):2194-2205.

157. Doseděl M, Jirkovský E, Macáková K, Krčmová LK, Javorská L, Pourová J, Mercolini L, Remião F, Nováková L, Mladěnka P, On Behalf Of The Oemonom. Vitamin C-Sources, Physiological Role, Kinetics, Deficiency, Use, Toxicity, and Determination. *Nutrients.* 2021;13(2):615.

158. Olechnowicz J, Tinkov A, Skalny A, Suliburska J. Zinc status is associated with inflammation, oxidative stress, lipid, and glucose metabolism. *J Physiol Sci.* 2018;68(1):19-31.

159. Wessels I, Maywald M, Rink L. Zinc as a Gatekeeper of Immune Function. *Nutrients.* 2017;9(12):1286.

160. Jia S, Wang J, Li S, Wang X, Liu Q, Li Y, Shad M, Ma B, Wang L, Li C, Li X. Genetically encoded zinc-binding collagen-like protein hybrid hydrogels for wound repair. *Int J Biol Macromol.* 2024;254(Pt 1):127592.

161. Baltaci AK, Mogulkoc R, Baltaci SB. Review: The role of zinc in the endocrine system. *Pak J Pharm Sci.* 2019;32(1):231-239.

162. Bolke L, Schlippe G, Gerß J, Voss W. A Collagen Supplement Improves Skin Hydration, Elasticity, Roughness, and Density: Results of a Randomized, Placebo-Controlled, Blind Study. *Nutrients.* 2019;11(10):2494.

163. Sun R, Wang J, Feng J, Cao B. Zinc in Cognitive Impairment and Aging. *Biomolecules.* 2022;12(7):1000.

164. Singh JK, van Attikum H. DNA double-strand break repair: Putting zinc fingers on the sore spot. *Semin Cell Dev Biol.* 2021;113:65-74.

165. Ceballos-Rasgado M, Lowe NM, Mallard S, Clegg A, Moran VH, Harris C, Montez J, Xipsiti M. Adverse Effects of Excessive Zinc Intake in Infants and Children Aged 0-3 Years: A Systematic Review and Meta-Analysis. *Adv Nutr.* 2022;13(6):2488-2518.

166. Nguyen TTU, Yeom JH, Kim W. Beneficial Effects of Vitamin E Supplementation on Endothelial Dysfunction, Inflammation, and Oxidative Stress Biomarkers in Patients Receiving Hemodialysis: A Systematic Review and Meta-Analysis of Randomized Controlled Trials. *Int J Mol Sci.* 2021;22(21):11923.

167. Rychter AM, Hryhorowicz S, Słomski R, Dobrowolska A, Krela-Kaźmierczak I. Antioxidant effects of vitamin E and risk of cardiovascular

disease in women with obesity - A narrative review. *Clin Nutr.* 2022;41(7):1557-1565.

168. Lewis ED, Meydani SN, Wu D. Regulatory role of vitamin E in the immune system and inflammation. *IUBMB Life.* 2019;71(4):487-494.

169. Zainal Z, Khaza'ai H, Kutty Radhakrishnan A, Chang SK. Therapeutic potential of palm oil vitamin E-derived tocotrienols in inflammation and chronic diseases: Evidence from preclinical and clinical studies. *Food Res Int.* 2022;156:111175.

170. Michalak M. Plant-Derived Antioxidants: Significance in Skin Health and the Ageing Process. *Int J Mol Sci.* 2022;23(2):585.

171. US Preventive Services Task Force; Mangione CM, Barry MJ, Nicholson WK, Cabana M, Chelmow D, Coker TR, Davis EM, Donahue KE, Doubeni CA, Jaén CR, Kubik M, Li L, Ogedegbe G, Pbert L, Ruiz JM, Stevermer J, Wong JB. Vitamin, Mineral, and Multivitamin Supplementation to Prevent Cardiovascular Disease and Cancer: US Preventive Services Task Force Recommendation Statement. *JAMA.* 2022;327(23):2326-2333.

172. Zheng WV, Xu W, Li Y, Qin J, Zhou T, Li D, Xu Y, Cheng X, Xiong Y, Chen Z. Anti-aging effect of β-carotene through regulating the KAT7-P15 signaling axis, inflammation and oxidative stress process. *Cell Mol Biol Lett.* 2022;27(1):86.

173. Liu S, Wu Q, Wang S, He Y. Causal associations between circulation β-carotene and cardiovascular disease: A Mendelian randomization study. *Medicine (Baltimore).* 2023;102(48):e36432.

174. Honda M. Z-Isomers of lycopene and β-carotene exhibit greater skin-quality improving action than their all-E-isomers. *Food Chem.* 2023;421:135954.

175. Johra FT, Bepari AK, Bristy AT, Reza HM. A Mechanistic Review of β-Carotene, Lutein, and Zeaxanthin in Eye Health and Disease. *Antioxidants (Basel).* 2020;9(11):1046.

176. Omenn GS. Chemoprevention of lung cancers: lessons from CARET, the beta-carotene and retinol efficacy trial, and prospects for the future. *Eur J Cancer Prev.* 2007;16(3):184-91.

177. Kavalappa YP, Gopal SS, Ponesakki G. Lutein inhibits breast cancer cell growth by suppressing antioxidant and cell survival signals and induces apoptosis. *Cell Physiol.* 2021;236(3):1798-1809.

178. Satia JA, Littman A, Slatore CG, Galanko JA, White E. Long-term use of beta-carotene, retinol, lycopene, and lutein supplements and lung cancer risk: results from the VITamins And Lifestyle (VITAL) study. *Am J Epidemiol.* 2009;169(7):815-28.

179. Li N, Wu X, Zhuang W, Xia L, Chen Y, Wu C, Rao Z, Du L, Zhao R, Yi M, Wan Q, Zhou Y. Tomato and lycopene and multiple health outcomes: Umbrella review. *Food Chem.* 2021;343:128396.

180. Khan UM, Sevindik M, Zarrabi A, Nami M, Ozdemir B, Kaplan DN, Selamoglu Z, Hasan M, Kumar M, Alshehri MM, Sharifi-Rad J. Lycopene: Food Sources, Biological Activities, and Human Health Benefits. *Oxid Med Cell Longev*. 2021;2021:2713511.

181. Kulawik A, Cielecka-Piontek J, Zalewski P. The Importance of Antioxidant Activity for the Health-Promoting Effect of Lycopene. *Nutrients*. 2023;15(17):3821.

182. Razaghi A, Poorebrahim M, Sarhan D, Björnstedt M. Selenium stimulates the antitumour immunity: Insights to future research. *Eur J Cancer*. 2021;155:256-267.

183. Bjørklund G, Shanaida M, Lysiuk R, Antonyak H, Klishch I, Shanaida V, Peana M. Selenium: An Antioxidant with a Critical Role in Anti-Aging. *Molecules*. 2022;27(19):6613.

184. Wang F, Li C, Li S, Cui L, Zhao J, Liao L. Selenium and thyroid diseases. *Front Endocrinol (Lausanne)*. 2023;14:1133000.

185. Xiang S, Dai Z, Man C, Fan Y. Circulating Selenium and Cardiovascular or All-Cause Mortality in the General Population: a Meta-Analysis. *Biol Trace Elem Res*. 2020;195(1):55-62.

186. Zhang F, Li X, Wei Y. Selenium and Selenoproteins in Health. *Biomolecules*. 2023;13(5):799.

187. Hariharan S, Dharmaraj S. Selenium and selenoproteins: it's role in regulation of inflammation. *Inflammopharmacology*. 2020;28(3):667-695.

188. Vinceti M, Filippini T, Del Giovane C, Dennert G, Zwahlen M, Brinkman M, Zeegers MP, Horneber M, D'Amico R, Crespi CM. Selenium for preventing cancer. *Cochrane Database Syst Rev*. 2018;1(1):CD005195.

189. Yuan S, Mason AM, Carter P, Vithayathil M, Kar S, Burgess S, Larsson SC. Selenium and cancer risk: Wide-angled Mendelian randomization analysis. *Int J Cancer*. 2022;150(7):1134-1140.

190. Ferreira RLU, Sena-Evangelista KCM, de Azevedo EP, Pinheiro FI, Cobucci RN, Pedrosa LFC. Selenium in Human Health and Gut Microflora: Bioavailability of Selenocompounds and Relationship With Diseases. *Front Nutr*. 2021;8:685317.

191. Deepika, Maurya PK. Health Benefits of Quercetin in Age-Related Diseases. *Molecules*. 2022;27(8):2498.

192. Qi W, Qi W, Xiong D, Long M. Quercetin: Its Antioxidant Mechanism, Antibacterial Properties and Potential Application in Prevention and Control of Toxipathy. *Molecules*. 2022;27(19):6545.

193. Li Y, Yao J, Han C, Yang J, Chaudhry MT, Wang S, Liu H, Yin Y. Quercetin, Inflammation and Immunity. *Nutrients*. 2016;8(3):167.

194. Hosseini A, Razavi BM, Banach M, Hosseinzadeh H. Quercetin and metabolic syndrome: A review. *Phytother Res*. 2021;35(10):5352-5364.

195. Dabeek WM, Marra MV. Dietary Quercetin and Kaempferol: Bioavailability and Potential Cardiovascular-Related Bioactivity in Humans. *Nutrients*. 2019;11(10):2288.

196. Reyes-Farias M, Carrasco-Pozo C. The Anti-Cancer Effect of Quercetin: Molecular Implications in Cancer Metabolism. *Int J Mol Sci*. 2019;20(13):3177.

197. Zu G, Sun K, Li L, Zu X, Han T, Huang H. Mechanism of quercetin therapeutic targets for Alzheimer disease and type 2 diabetes mellitus. *Sci Rep*. 2021;11(1):22959.

198. Alizadeh SR, Ebrahimzadeh MA. Quercetin derivatives: Drug design, development, and biological activities, a review. *Eur J Med Chem*. 2022;229:114068.

199. Burkina V, Zamaratskaia G, Rasmussen MK. Curcumin and quercetin modify warfarin-induced regulation of porcine CYP1A2 and CYP3A expression and activity *in vitro*. *Xenobiotica*. 2022;52(5):435-441.

200. Diao M, Liang Y, Zhao J, Zhao C, Zhang J, Zhang T. Enhanced cytotoxicity and antioxidant capacity of kaempferol complexed with α-lactalbumin. *Food Chem Toxicol*. 2021;153:112265.

201. Chagas MDSS, Behrens MD, Moragas-Tellis CJ, Penedo GXM, Silva AR, Gonçalves-de-Albuquerque CF. Flavonols and Flavones as Potential anti-Inflammatory, Antioxidant, and Antibacterial Compounds. *Oxid Med Cell Longev*. 2022;2022:9966750.

202. Nejabati HR, Roshangar L. Kaempferol: A potential agent in the prevention of colorectal cancer. *Physiol Rep*. 2022;10(20):e15488.

203. Imran M, Salehi B, Sharifi-Rad J, Aslam Gondal T, Saeed F, Imran A, Shahbaz M, Tsouh Fokou PV, Umair Arshad M, Khan H, Guerreiro SG, Martins N, Estevinho LM. Kaempferol: A Key Emphasis to Its Anticancer Potential. *Molecules*. 2019;24(12):2277.

204. Jin S, Zhang L, Wang L. Kaempferol, a potential neuroprotective agent in neurodegenerative diseases: From chemistry to medicine. *Biomed Pharmacother*. 2023;165:115215.

205. Al-Nour MY, Ibrahim MM, Elsaman T. Ellagic Acid, Kaempferol, and Quercetin from *Acacia nilotica*: Promising Combined Drug With Multiple Mechanisms of Action. *Curr Pharmacol Rep*. 2019;5(4):255-280.

206. Franza L, Carusi V, Nucera E, Pandolfi F. Luteolin, inflammation and cancer: Special emphasis on gut microbiota. *Biofactors*. 2021;47(2):181-189.

207. Huang L, Kim MY, Cho JY. Immunopharmacological Activities of Luteolin in Chronic Diseases *Int J Mol Sci*. 2023;24(3):2136.

208. Imran M, Rauf A, Abu-Izneid T, Nadeem M, Shariati MA, Khan IA, Imran A, Orhan IE, Rizwan M, Atif M, Gondal TA, Mubarak MS. Luteolin, a flavonoid, as an anticancer agent: A review. *Biomed Pharmacother*. 2019;112:108612.

209. Hussain Y, Cui JH, Khan H, Aschner M, Batiha GE, Jeandet P. Luteolin and cancer metastasis suppression: focus on the role of epithelial to mesenchymal transition. *Med Oncol.* 2021;38(6):66.

210. Kempuraj D, Thangavel R, Kempuraj DD, Ahmed ME, Selvakumar GP, Raikwar SP, Zaheer SA, Iyer SS, Govindarajan R, Chandrasekaran PN, Zaheer A. Neuroprotective effects of flavone luteolin in neuroinflammation and neurotrauma. *Biofactors.* 2021;47(2):190-197.

211. Swaminathan A, Basu M, Bekri A, Drapeau P, Kundu TK. The Dietary Flavonoid, Luteolin, Negatively Affects Neuronal Differentiation. *Front Mol Neurosci.* 2019;12:41.

212. Musial C, Kuban-Jankowska A, Gorska-Ponikowska M. Beneficial Properties of Green Tea Catechins. *Int J Mol Sci.* 2020;21(5):1744.

213. Baranwal A, Aggarwal P, Rai A, Kumar N. Pharmacological Actions and Underlying Mechanisms of Catechin: A Review. *Mini Rev Med Chem.* 2022;22(5):821-833.

214. Kerimi A, Williamson G. The cardiovascular benefits of dark chocolate. *Vascul Pharmacol.* 2015;71:11-5.

215. Ohishi T, Miyoshi N, Mori M, Sagara M, Yamori Y. Health Effects of Soy Isoflavones and Green Tea Catechins on Cancer and Cardiovascular Diseases Based on Urinary Biomarker Levels. *Molecules.* 2022;27(24):8899.

216. Sirotkin AV, Kolesárová A. The anti-obesity and health-promoting effects of tea and coffee. *Physiol Res.* 2021;70(2):161-168.

217. Sesso HD, Manson JE, Aragaki AK, Rist PM, Johnson LG, Friedenberg G, Copeland T, Clar A, Mora S, Moorthy MV, Sarkissian A, Carrick WR, Anderson GL; COSMOS Research Group. Effect of cocoa flavanol supplementation for the prevention of cardiovascular disease events: the COcoa Supplement and Multivitamin Outcomes Study (COSMOS) randomized clinical trial. *Am J Clin Nutr.* 2022;115(6):1490-1500.

218. Sesso HD, Rist PM, Aragaki AK, Rautiainen S, Johnson LG, Friedenberg G, Copeland T, Clar A, Mora S, Moorthy MV, Sarkissian A, Wactawski-Wende J, Tinker LF, Carrick WR, Anderson GL, Manson JE; COSMOS Research Group. Multivitamins in the prevention of cancer and cardiovascular disease: the COcoa Supplement and Multivitamin Outcomes Study (COSMOS) randomized clinical trial. *Am J Clin Nutr.* 2022;115(6):1501-1510.

219. Khalatbary AR, Khademi E. The green tea polyphenolic catechin epigallocatechin gallate and neuroprotection. *Nutr Neurosci.* 2020;23(4):281-294.

220. Brickman AM, Yeung LK, Alschuler DM, Ottaviani JI, Kuhnle GGC, Sloan RP, Luttmann-Gibson H, Copeland T, Schroeter H, Sesso HD, Manson JE, Wall M, Small SA. Dietary flavanols restore hippocampal-dependent memory in older adults with lower diet quality and lower habit-

ual flavanol consumption. *Proc Natl Acad Sci U S A.* 2023;120(23):e2216932120.

221. Satoh T, Fujisawa H, Nakamura A, Takahashi N, Watanabe K. Inhibitory Effects of Eight Green Tea Catechins on Cytochrome P450 1A2, 2C9, 2D6, and 3A4 Activities. *J Pharm Pharm Sci.* 2016;19(2):188-97.

222. Mandal B, Das R, Mondal S. Anthocyanin: A Potential Phytochemical Candidate for the Amelioration of Non-Alcoholic Fatty Liver Disease. *Ann Pharm Fr.* 2024:S0003-4509(24)00023-3.

223. Sahoo DK, Heilmann RM, Paital B, Patel A, Yadav VK, Wong D, Jergens AE. Oxidative stress, hormones, and effects of natural antioxidants on intestinal inflammation in inflammatory bowel disease. *Front Endocrinol (Lausanne).* 2023;14:1217165.

224. Kalt W, Cassidy A, Howard LR, Krikorian R, Stull AJ, Tremblay F, Zamora-Ros R. Recent Research on the Health Benefits of Blueberries and Their Anthocyanins. *Adv Nutr.* 2020;11(2):224-236.

225. Krikorian R, Skelton MR, Summer SS, Shidler MD, Sullivan PG. Blueberry Supplementation in Midlife for Dementia Risk Reduction. *Nutrients.* 2022;14(8):1619.

226. Khoo HE, Ng HS, Yap WS, Goh HJH, Yim HS. Nutrients for Prevention of Macular Degeneration and Eye-Related Diseases. *Antioxidants (Basel).* 2019;8(4):85.

227. Gómez-Garduño J, León-Rodríguez R, Alemón-Medina R, Pérez-Guillé BE, Soriano-Rosales RE, González-Ortiz A, Chávez-Pacheco JL, Solorio-López E, Fernandez-Pérez P, Rivera-Espinosa L. Phytochemicals That Interfere With Drug Metabolism and Transport, Modifying Plasma Concentration in Humans and Animals. *Dose Response.* 2022;20(3):15593258221120485.

228. Chung KT, Wong TY, Wei CI, Huang YW, Lin Y. Tannins and human health: a review. *Crit Rev Food Sci Nutr.* 1998;38(6):421-64.

229. Maugeri A, Lombardo GE, Cirmi S, Süntar I, Barreca D, Laganà G, Navarra M. Pharmacology and toxicology of tannins. *Arch Toxicol.* 2022;96(5):1257-1277.

230. Yuan H, Zhou P, Peng Z, Wang C. Antioxidant and Antibacterial Activities of Dodecyl Tannin Derivative Linked with 1,2,3-Triazole. *Chem Biodivers.* 2022;19(1):e202100558.

231. Vendrame S, Adekeye TE, Klimis-Zacas D. The Role of Berry Consumption on Blood Pressure Regulation and Hypertension: An Overview of the Clinical Evidence. *Nutrients.* 2022;14(13):2701.

232. Nishida S, Katsumi N, Matsumoto K. Prevention of the rise in plasma cholesterol and glucose levels by kaki-tannin and characterization of its bile acid binding capacity. *Sci Food Agric.* 2021;101(5):2117-2124.

233. Rajasekar N, Sivanantham A, Ravikumar V, Rajasekaran S. An overview on the role of plant-derived tannins for the treatment of lung cancer. *Phytochemistry*. 2021;188:112799.

234. Fu F, Song C, Wen C, Yang L, Guo Y, Yang X, Shu Z, Li X, Feng Y, Liu B, Sun M, Zhong Y, Chen L, Niu Y, Chen J, Wang G, Yin T, Chen S, Xue L, Cao F. The Metasequoia genome and evolutionary relationships among redwoods. *Plant Commun*. 2023;4(6):100643.

235. Petroski W, Minich DM. Is There Such a Thing as "Anti-Nutrients"? A Narrative Review of Perceived Problematic Plant Compounds. *Nutrients*. 2020;12(10):2929.

236. Abera S, Yohannes W, Chandravanshi BS. Effect of Processing Methods on Antinutritional Factors (Oxalate, Phytate, and Tannin) and Their Interaction with Minerals (Calcium, Iron, and Zinc) in Red, White, and Black Kidney Beans. *Int J Anal Chem*. 2023;2023:6762027.

237. Brito AF, Zang Y. A Review of Lignan Metabolism, Milk Enterolactone Concentration, and Antioxidant Status of Dairy Cows Fed Flaxseed. *Molecules*. 2018;24(1):41.

238. Rattanaburee T, Tanawattanasuntorn T, Thongpanchang T, Tipmanee V, Graidist P. Trans-(-)-Kusunokinin: A Potential Anticancer Lignan Compound against HER2 in Breast Cancer Cell Lines? *Molecules*. 2021;26(15):4537.

239. Jenkins DJA, Kendall CWC, Sievenpiper JL. Plant Polyphenols Lignans and Cardiovascular Disease. *J Am Coll Cardiol*. 2021;78(7):679-682.

240. Parikh M, Maddaford TG, Austria JA, Aliani M, Netticadan T, Pierce GN. Dietary Flaxseed as a Strategy for Improving Human Health. *Nutrients*. 2019;11(5):1171.

241. Ren Y, Xu Z, Qiao Z, Wang X, Yang C. Flaxseed Lignan Alleviates the Paracetamol-Induced Hepatotoxicity Associated with Regulation of Gut Microbiota and Serum Metabolome. *Nutrients*. 2024;16(2):295.

242. Aishwarya V, Solaipriya S, Sivaramakrishnan V. Role of ellagic acid for the prevention and treatment of liver diseases. *Phytother Res*. 2021;35(6):2925-2944.

243. Cota D, Patil D. Antibacterial potential of ellagic acid and gallic acid against IBD bacterial isolates and cytotoxicity against colorectal cancer. *Nat Prod Res*. 2023;37(12):1998-2002.

244. Possamai Rossatto FC, Tharmalingam N, Escobar IE, d'Azevedo PA, Zimmer KR, Mylonakis E. Antifungal Activity of the Phenolic Compounds Ellagic Acid (EA) and Caffeic Acid Phenethyl Ester (CAPE) against Drug-Resistant *Candida auris*. *J Fungi (Basel)*. 2021;7(9):763.

245. Naraki K, Ghasemzadeh Rahbardar M, Ajiboye BO, Hosseinzadeh H. The effect of ellagic acid on the metabolic syndrome: A review article. *Heliyon*. 2023;9(11):e21844.

246. Zhu H, Yan Y, Jiang Y, Meng X. Ellagic Acid and Its Anti-Aging Effects on Central Nervous System. *Int J Mol Sci*. 2022;23(18):10937.

247. Borrelli F, Posadas I, Capasso R, Aviello G, Ascione V, Capasso F. Effect of caffeic acid phenethyl ester on gastric acid secretion in vitro. *Eur J Pharmacol*. 2005;521(1-3):139-43.

248. Purushothaman A, Babu SS, Naroth S, Janardanan D. Antioxidant activity of caffeic acid: thermodynamic and kinetic aspects on the oxidative degradation pathway. *Free Radic Res*. 2022;56(9-10):617-630.

249. Khan F, Bamunuarachchi NI, Tabassum N, Kim YM. Caffeic Acid and Its Derivatives: Antimicrobial Drugs toward Microbial Pathogens. *J Agric Food Chem*. 2021;69(10):2979-3004.

250. Pavlíková N. Caffeic Acid and Diseases-Mechanisms of Action. *Int J Mol Sci*. 2022;24(1):588.

251. Sun R, Wu T, Xing S, Wei S, Bielicki JK, Pan X, Zhou M, Chen J. Caffeic acid protects against atherosclerotic lesions and cognitive decline in ApoE$^{-/-}$ mice. *J Pharmacol Sci*. 2023;151(2):110-118.

252. Muhammad Abdul Kadar NN, Ahmad F, Teoh SL, Yahaya MF. Caffeic Acid on Metabolic Syndrome: A Review. *Molecules*. 2021;26(18):5490.

253. Salau VF, Erukainure OL, Bharuth V, Islam MS. Caffeic acid improves glucose utilization and maintains tissue ultrastructural morphology while modulating metabolic activities implicated in neurodegenerative disorders in isolated rat brains. *J Biochem Mol Toxicol*. 2021;35(1):e22610.

254. Zia A, Farkhondeh T, Pourbagher-Shahri AM, Samarghandian S. The role of curcumin in aging and senescence: Molecular mechanisms. *Biomed Pharmacother*. 2021;134:111119.

255. Dehzad MJ, Ghalandari H, Nouri M, Askarpour M. Antioxidant and anti-inflammatory effects of curcumin/turmeric supplementation in adults: A GRADE-assessed systematic review and dose-response meta-analysis of randomized controlled trials. *Cytokine*. 2023;164:156144.

256. Ming T, Tao Q, Tang S, Zhao H, Yang H, Liu M, Ren S, Xu H. Curcumin: An epigenetic regulator and its application in cancer. *Biomed Pharmacother*. 2022;156:113956.

257. Pourbagher-Shahri AM, Farkhondeh T, Ashrafizadeh M, Talebi M, Samargahndian S. Curcumin and cardiovascular diseases: Focus on cellular targets and cascades. *Biomed Pharmacother*. 2021;136:111214.

258. Askarizadeh A, Barreto GE, Henney NC, Majeed M, Sahebkar A. Neuroprotection by curcumin: A review on brain delivery strategies. *Int J Pharm*. 2020;585:119476.

259. Zhou DD, Luo M, Huang SY, Saimaiti A, Shang A, Gan RY, Li HB. Effects and Mechanisms of Resveratrol on Aging and Age-Related Diseases. *Oxid Med Cell Longev*. 2021;2021:9932218.

260. Rauf A, Imran M, Butt MS, Nadeem M, Peters DG, Mubarak MS. Resveratrol as an anti-cancer agent: A review. *Crit Rev Food Sci Nutr.* 2018;58(9):1428-1447.

261. Chudzińska M, Rogowicz D, Wołowiec Ł, Banach J, Sielski S, Bujak R, Sinkiewicz A, Grześk G. Resveratrol and cardiovascular system-the unfulfilled hopes. *Ir J Med Sci.* 2021;190(3):981-986.

262. Islam F, Nafady MH, Islam MR, Saha S, Rashid S, Akter A, Or-Rashid MH, Akhtar MF, Perveen A, Md Ashraf G, Rahman MH, Hussein Sweilam S. Resveratrol and neuroprotection: an insight into prospective therapeutic approaches against Alzheimer's disease from bench to bedside. *Mol Neurobiol.* 2022;59(7):4384-4404.

263. Galiniak S, Aebisher D, Bartusik-Aebisher D. Health benefits of resveratrol administration. *Acta Biochim Pol.* 2019;66(1):13-21.

264. Jaisamut P, Wanna S, Limsuwan S, Chusri S, Wiwattanawongsa K, Wiwattanapatapee R. Enhanced Oral Bioavailability and Improved Biological Activities of a Quercetin/Resveratrol Combination Using a Liquid Self-Microemulsifying Drug Delivery System. *Planta Med.* 2021;87(4):336-346.

265. Lee SH, Lee JH, Lee HY, Min KJ. Sirtuin signaling in cellular senescence and aging. *BMB Rep.* 2019;52(1):24-34.

266. Juang YP, Liang PH. Biological and Pharmacological Effects of Synthetic Saponins. *Molecules.* 2020;25(21):4974.

267. Diez-Simon C, Eichelsheim C, Mumm R, Hall RD. Chemical and Sensory Characteristics of Soy Sauce: A Review. *J Agric Food Chem.* 2020;68(42):11612-11630.

268. Gorissen SHM, Crombag JJR, Senden JMG, Waterval WAH, Bierau J, Verdijk LB, van Loon LJC. Protein content and amino acid composition of commercially available plant-based protein isolates. *Amino Acids.* 2018;50(12):1685-1695.

269. Ohishi T, Miyoshi N, Mori M, Sagara M, Yamori Y. Health Effects of Soy Isoflavones and Green Tea Catechins on Cancer and Cardiovascular Diseases Based on Urinary Biomarker Levels. *Molecules.* 2022;27(24):8899.

270. Takagi A, Kano M, Kaga C. Possibility of breast cancer prevention: use of soy isoflavones and fermented soy beverage produced using probiotics. *Int J Mol Sci.* 2015;16(5):10907-20.

271. Sahin I, Bilir B, Ali S, Sahin K, Kucuk O. Soy Isoflavones in Integrative Oncology: Increased Efficacy and Decreased Toxicity of Cancer Therapy. *Integr Cancer Ther.* 2019;18:1534735419835310.

272. Ramdath DD, Padhi EM, Sarfaraz S, Renwick S, Duncan AM. Beyond the Cholesterol-Lowering Effect of Soy Protein: A Review of the Effects of Dietary Soy and Its Constituents on Risk Factors for Cardiovascular Disease. *Nutrients.* 2017;9(4):324.

273. Zuo X, Zhao R, Wu M, Wan Q, Li T. Soy Consumption and the Risk of Type 2 Diabetes and Cardiovascular Diseases: A Systematic Review and Meta-Analysis. *Nutrients.* 2023;15(6):1358.

274. Wang X, Yu C, Lv J, Li L, Hu Y, Liu K, Shirai K, Iso H, Dong JY. Consumption of soy products and cardiovascular mortality in people with and without cardiovascular disease: a prospective cohort study of 0.5 million individuals. *Eur J Nutr.* 2021;60(8):4429-4438.

275. George KS, Muñoz J, Akhavan NS, Foley EM, Siebert SC, Tenenbaum G, Khalil DA, Chai SC, Arjmandi BH. Is soy protein effective in reducing cholesterol and improving bone health? *Food Funct.* 2020;11(1):544-551.

276. Chen LR, Chen KH. Utilization of Isoflavones in Soybeans for Women with Menopausal Syndrome: An Overview. *Int J Mol Sci.* 2021;22(6):3212.

277. Seth D, Poowutikul P, Pansare M, Kamat D. Food Allergy: A Review. *Pediatr Ann.* 2020;49(1):e50-e58.

278. López-Cervantes J, Sánchez-Machado D, de la Mora-López DS, Sanches-Silva A. Quinoa (Chenopodium quinoa Willd.): Exploring a Superfood from Andean Indigenous Cultures with Potential to Reduce Cardiovascular Disease (CVD) Risk Markers. *Curr Mol Pharmacol.* 2021;14(6):925-934.

279. Agarwal A, Rizwana, Tripathi AD, Kumar T, Sharma KP, Patel SKS. Nutritional and Functional New Perspectives and Potential Health Benefits of Quinoa and Chia Seeds. *Antioxidants (Basel).* 2023;12(7):1413.

280. Melini V, Melini F. Functional Components and Anti-Nutritional Factors in Gluten-Free Grains: A Focus on Quinoa Seeds. *Foods.* 2021;10(2):351.

281. Jan N, Hussain SZ, Naseer B, Bhat TA. Amaranth and quinoa as potential nutraceuticals: A review of anti-nutritional factors, health benefits and their applications in food, medicinal and cosmetic sectors. *Food Chem X.* 2023;18:100687.

282. Fan X, Guo H, Teng C, Yang X, Qin P, Richel A, Zhang L, Blecker C, Ren G. Supplementation of quinoa peptides alleviates colorectal cancer and restores gut microbiota in AOM/DSS-treated mice. *Food Chem.* 2023;408:135196.

283. Präger L, Simon JC, Treudler R. Food allergy - New risks through vegan diet? Overview of new allergen sources and current data on the potential risk of anaphylaxis. *J Dtsch Dermatol Ges.* 2023;21(11):1308-1313.

284. Hong J, Convers K, Reeves N, Temprano J. Anaphylaxis to quinoa. *Ann Allergy Asthma Immunol.* 2013;110(1):60-1.

285. Riggins CW, Mumm RH. Amaranths. *Curr Biol.* 2021;31(13):R834-R835.

286. Stetter MG, Vidal-Villarejo M, Schmid KJ. Parallel Seed Color Adaptation during Multiple Domestication Attempts of an Ancient New World Grain. *Mol Biol Evol.* 2020;37(5):1407-1419.

287. Niro S, D'Agostino A, Fratianni A, Cinquanta L, Panfili G. Gluten-Free Alternative Grains: Nutritional Evaluation and Bioactive Compounds. *Foods.* 2019;8(6):208.

288. Chmelík Z, Šnejdrlová M, Vrablík M. Amaranth as a potential dietary adjunct of lifestyle modification to improve cardiovascular risk profile. *Nutr Res.* 2019;72:36-45.

289. Nardo AE, Suárez S, Quiroga AV, Añón MC. Amaranth as a Source of Antihypertensive Peptides. *Front Plant Sci.* 2020;11:578631.

290. Gélinas B, Seguin P. Oxalate in grain amaranth. *J Agric Food Chem.* 2007;55(12):4789-94.

291. Mancuso C, Santangelo R. Panax ginseng and Panax quinquefolius: From pharmacology to toxicology. *Food Chem Toxicol.* 2017;107(Pt A):362-372.

292. Valdés-González JA, Sánchez M, Moratilla-Rivera I, Iglesias I, Gómez-Serranillos MP. Immunomodulatory, Anti-Inflammatory, and Anti-Cancer Properties of Ginseng: A Pharmacological Update. *Molecules.* 2023;28(9):3863.

293. Yoon J, Park B, Hong KW, Jung DH. The effects of Korean Red Ginseng on stress-related neurotransmitters and gene expression: A randomized, double-blind, placebo-controlled trial. *J Ginseng Res.* 2023;47(6):766-772.

294. Muñoz-Castellanos B, Martínez-López P, Bailón-Moreno R, Esquius L. Effect of Ginseng Intake on Muscle Damage Induced by Exercise in Healthy Adults. *Nutrients.* 2023;16(1):90.

295. Yang S, Li F, Lu S, Ren L, Bian S, Liu M, Zhao D, Wang S, Wang J. Ginseng root extract attenuates inflammation by inhibiting the MAPK/NF-$\varkappa$B signaling pathway and activating autophagy and p62-Nrf2-Keap1 signaling in vitro and in vivo. *J Ethnopharmacol.* 2022;283:114739.

296. Zhao L, Zhang Y, Li Y, Li C, Shi K, Zhang K, Liu N. Therapeutic effects of ginseng and ginsenosides on colorectal cancer. *Food Funct.* 2022;13(12):6450-6466.

297. Yao W, Guan Y. Ginsenosides in cancer: A focus on the regulation of cell metabolism. *Biomed Pharmacother.* 2022;156:113756.

298. de Oliveira Zanuso B, de Oliveira Dos Santos AR, Miola VFB, Guissoni Campos LM, Spilla CSG, Barbalho SM. Panax ginseng and aging related disorders: A systematic review. *Exp Gerontol.* 2022;161:111731.

299. Chen YY, Liu QP, An P, Jia M, Luan X, Tang JY, Zhang H. Ginsenoside Rd: A promising natural neuroprotective agent. *Phytomedicine.* 2022;95:153883.

300. Malík M, Tlustoš P. Nootropics as Cognitive Enhancers: Types, Dosage and Side Effects of Smart Drugs. *Nutrients.* 2022;14(16):3367.

301. Choi MK, Song IS. Interactions of ginseng with therapeutic drugs. *Arch Pharm Res.* 2019;42(10):862-878.

302. Jin S, Lee S, Jeon JH, Kim H, Choi MK, Song IS. Enhanced Intestinal Permeability and Plasma Concentration of Metformin in Rats by the Repeated Administration of Red Ginseng Extract. *Pharmaceutics.* 2019;11(4):189.

303. Ahmed A, Saleem MA, Saeed F, Afzaal M, Imran A, Nadeem M, Ambreen S, Imran M, Hussain M, Jbawi EA. *Gynostemma pentaphyllum* an immortal herb with promising therapeutic potential: a comprehensive review on its phytochemistry and pharmacological perspective. *International Journal of Food Properties*. 2023;26(1), 808-832.

304. Wang Z, Wang Z, Huang W, Suo J, Chen X, Ding K, Sun Q, Zhang H. Antioxidant and anti-inflammatory activities of an anti-diabetic polysaccharide extracted from Gynostemma pentaphyllum herb. *Int J Biol Macromol*. 2020;145:484-491.

305. Liu H, Li X, Duan Y, Xie JB, Piao XL. Mechanism of gypenosides of Gynostemma pentaphyllum inducing apoptosis of renal cell carcinoma by PI3K/AKT/mTOR pathway. *J Ethnopharmacol*. 2021;271:113907.

306. Su C, Li N, Ren R, Wang Y, Su X, Lu F, Zong R, Yang L, Ma X. Progress in the Medicinal Value, Bioactive Compounds, and Pharmacological Activities of Gynostemma pentaphyllum. *Molecules*. 2021;26(20):6249.

307. Choi EK, Won YH, Kim SY, Noh SO, Park SH, Jung SJ, Lee CK, Hwang BY, Lee MK, Ha KC, Baek HI, Kim HM, Ko MH, Chae SW. Supplementation with extract of Gynostemma pentaphyllum leaves reduces anxiety in healthy subjects with chronic psychological stress: A randomized, double-blind, placebo-controlled clinical trial. *Phytomedicine*. 2019;52:198-205.

308. Dai N, Zhao FF, Fang M, Pu FL, Kong LY, Liu JP. Gynostemma pentaphyllum for dyslipidemia: A systematic review of randomized controlled trials. *Front Pharmacol*. 2022;13:917521.

309. Shaito A, Thuan DTB, Phu HT, Nguyen THD, Hasan H, Halabi S, Abdelhady S, Nasrallah GK, Eid AH, Pintus G. Herbal Medicine for Cardiovascular Diseases: Efficacy, Mechanisms, and Safety. *Front Pharmacol*. 2020;11:422.

310. Phu HT, Thuan DTB, Nguyen THD, Posadino AM, Eid AH, Pintus G. Herbal Medicine for Cardiovascular Diseases: Efficacy, Mechanisms, and Safety. *Curr Vasc Pharmacol*. 2020;18(4):369-393.

311. Lv J, Shen X, Shen X, Zhao S, Xu R, Yan Q, Lu J, Zhu D, Zhao Y, Dong J, Wang J, Shen X. NPLC0393 from Gynostemma pentaphyllum ameliorates Alzheimer's disease-like pathology in mice by targeting protein phosphatase magnesium-dependent 1A phosphatase. *Phytother Res*. 2023;37(10):4771-4790.

312. Tan H, Liu ZL, Liu MJ. Antithrombotic effect of Gynostemma pentaphyllum. *Zhongguo Zhong Xi Yi Jie He Za Zhi*. 1993;13(5):278-80,261.

313. Siwek M, Woroń J, Wrzosek A, Gupało J, Chrobak AA. Harder, better, faster, stronger? Retrospective chart review of adverse events of interactions between adaptogens and antidepressant drugs. *Front Pharmacol*. 2023;14:1271776.

314. VGH Baden-Württemberg *openJur*. 2022,13460.

315. Seng J. Poesie und Leben: Zur Entstehung von Goethes 'Gingo biloba'-Gedicht. In: Bohnenkamp, A: Jahrbuch Freies deutsches Hochstift 2021. *Jahrbuch des Freien Deutschen Hochstifts.* 2022:94-108.

316. Lyman BS. The etymology of 'ginkgo.' *Science.* 1885;6(130):84.

317. Li Y, Zhu X, Wang K, Zhu L, Murray M, Zhou F. The potential of Ginkgo biloba in the treatment of human diseases and the relationship to Nrf2-mediated antioxidant protection. *J Pharm Pharmacol.* 2022;74(12):1689-1699.

318. Xie C, Jiang J, Liu J, Yuan G, Zhao Z. Ginkgolide B attenuates collagen-induced rheumatoid arthritis and regulates fibroblast-like synoviocytes-mediated apoptosis and inflammation. *Ann Transl Med.* 2020;8(22):1497.

319. Yu J, Wang J, Yang J, Ouyang T, Gao H, Kan H, Yang Y. New insight into the mechanisms of Ginkgo biloba leaves in the treatment of cancer. *Phytomedicine.* 2024;122:155088.

320. Kook H, Yu CW, Choi D, Ahn TH, Chang K, Cho JM, Kim SJ, Park CG, Cho DK, Kim SH, Lee HC, Jin HY, Chae IH, Kwon K, Ahn SG, Kim JH, Lee SR, Kim JS, Kim SY, Lim SW. Efficacy and Safety of SID142 in Patients With Peripheral Arterial Disease: A Multicenter, Randomized, Double-Blind, Active-Controlled, Parallel-Group, Phase III Clinical Trial. *Clin Ther.* 2022;44(4):508-528.

321. Ye W, Wang J, Little PJ, Zou J, Zheng Z, Lu J, Yin Y, Liu H, Zhang D, Liu P, Xu S, Ye W, Liu Z. Anti-atherosclerotic effects and molecular targets of ginkgolide B from *Ginkgo biloba. Acta Pharm Sin B.* 2024;14(1):1-19.

322. Silva H, Martins FG. Cardiovascular Activity of Ginkgo biloba-An Insight from Healthy Subjects. *Biology (Basel).* 2022;12(1):15.

323. Xie L, Zhu Q, Lu J. Can We Use *Ginkgo biloba* Extract to Treat Alzheimer's Disease? Lessons from Preclinical and Clinical Studies. *Cells.* 2022;11(3):479.

324. Boateng ID. A critical review of current technologies used to reduce ginkgotoxin, ginkgotoxin-5'-glucoside, ginkgolic acid, allergic glycoprotein, and cyanide in Ginkgo biloba L. seed. *Food Chem.* 2022;382:132408.

325. Diamond BJ, Bailey MR. Ginkgo biloba: indications, mechanisms, and safety. *Psychiatr Clin North Am.* 2013;36(1):73-83.

326. Arenas-Jal M, Suñé-Negre JM, García-Montoya E. Coenzyme Q10 supplementation: Efficacy, safety, and formulation challenges. *Compr Rev Food Sci Food Saf.* 2020;19(2):574-594.

327. Al Saadi T, Assaf Y, Farwati M, Turkmani K, Al-Mouakeh A, Shebli B, Khoja M, Essali A, Madmani ME. Coenzyme Q10 for heart failure. *Cochrane Database Syst Rev.* 2021;(2)(2):CD008684.

328. Tsai IC, Hsu CW, Chang CH, Tseng PT, Chang KV. Effectiveness of Coenzyme Q10 Supplementation for Reducing Fatigue: A Systematic Review and Meta-Analysis of Randomized Controlled Trials. *Front Pharmacol.* 2022;13:883251.

329. Fladerer JP, Grollitsch S. Comparison of Coenzyme Q10 (Ubiquinone) and Reduced Coenzyme Q10 (Ubiquinol) as Supplement to Prevent Cardiovascular Disease and Reduce Cardiovascular Mortality. *Curr Cardiol Rep.* 2023;25(12):1759-1767.

330. Thapa M, Dallmann G. Role of coenzymes in cancer metabolism. *Semin Cell Dev Biol.* 2020;98:44-53.

331. Mantle D, Heaton RA, Hargreaves IP. Coenzyme Q10 and Immune Function: An Overview. *Antioxidants (Basel).* 2021;10(5):759.

332. Wu H, Zhong Z, Lin S, Qiu C, Xie P, Lv S, Cui L, Wu T. Coenzyme Q_{10} Sunscreen Prevents Progression of Ultraviolet-Induced Skin Damage in Mice. *Biomed Res Int.* 2020;2020:9039843.

333. Zhou Q, Zhou S, Chan E. Effect of coenzyme Q10 on warfarin hydroxylation in rat and human liver microsomes. *Curr Drug Metab.* 2005;6(2):67-81.

334. Holick MF. The One-Hundred-Year Anniversary of the Discovery of the Sunshine Vitamin D_3: Historical, Personal Experience and Evidence-Based Perspectives. *Nutrients.* 2023;15(3):593.

335. Miller WL, Imel EA. Rickets, Vitamin D, and Ca/P Metabolism. *Horm Res Paediatr.* 2022;95(6):579-592.

336. LeBoff MS, Greenspan SL, Insogna KL, Lewiecki EM, Saag KG, Singer AJ, Siris ES. The clinician's guide to prevention and treatment of osteoporosis. *Osteoporos Int.* 2022;33(10):2049-2102.

337. Sîrbe C, Rednic S, Grama A, Pop TL. An Update on the Effects of Vitamin D on the Immune System and Autoimmune Diseases. *Int J Mol Sci.* 2022;23(17):9784.

338. Costenbader KH, Cook NR, Lee IM, Hahn J, Walter J, Bubes V, Kotler G, Yang N, Friedman S, Alexander EK, Manson JE. Vitamin D and Marine n-3 Fatty Acids for Autoimmune Disease Prevention: Outcomes at Two Years after VITAL Trial Completion. *Arthritis Rheumatol.* 2024 Jan 25. doi: 10.1002/art.42811. Online ahead of print.

339. Latic N, Erben RG. Vitamin D and Cardiovascular Disease, with Emphasis on Hypertension, Atherosclerosis, and Heart Failure. *Int J Mol Sci.* 2020;21(18):6483.

340. Akpınar Ş, Karadağ MG. Is Vitamin D Important in Anxiety or Depression? What Is the Truth? *Curr Nutr Rep.* 2022;11(4):675-681.

341. Cui X, McGrath JJ, Burne THJ, Eyles DW. Vitamin D and schizophrenia: 20 years on. *Mol Psychiatry.* 2021;26(7):2708-2720.

342. Wan M, Patel J, Rait G, Shroff R. Hypervitaminosis D and nephrocalcinosis: too much of a good thing? *Pediatr Nephrol.* 2022;37(10):2225-2229.

343. Viljoen M, Bipath P, Tosh C. Pellagra in South Africa from 1897 to 2019: a scoping review. *Public Health Nutr.* 2021;24(8):2062-2076.

344. Davidson M, Rashidi N, Nurgali K, Apostolopoulos V. The Role of Tryptophan Metabolites in Neuropsychiatric Disorders. *Int J Mol Sci.* 2022;23(17):9968.

345. Campbell JM. Supplementation with NAD$^+$ and Its Precursors to Prevent Cognitive Decline across Disease Contexts. *Nutrients.* 2022;14(15):3231.

346. Superko HR, Zhao XQ, Hodis HN, Guyton JR. Niacin and heart disease prevention: Engraving its tombstone is a mistake. *J Clin Lipidol.* 2017;11(6):1309-1317.

347. Tuteja S. Activation of HCAR2 by niacin: benefits beyond lipid lowering. *Pharmacogenomics.* 2019;20(16):1143-1150.

348. Ruparelia N, Digby JE, Choudhury RP. Effects of niacin on atherosclerosis and vascular function. *Curr Opin Cardiol.* 2011;26(1):66-70.

349. Mikkelsen K, Apostolopoulos V. B Vitamins and Ageing. *Subcell Biochem.* 2018;90:451-470.

350. Tian S, Wu L, Zheng H, Zhong X, Liu M, Yu X, Wu W. Dietary niacin intake in relation to depression among adults: a population-based study. *BMC Psychiatry.* 2023;23(1):678.

351. Madaan P, Sikka P, Malik DS. Cosmeceutical Aptitudes of Niacinamide: A Review.
Recent Adv Antiinfect Drug Discov. 2021;16(3):196-208.

352. Papaliodis D, Boucher W, Kempuraj D, Michaelian M, Wolfberg A, House M, Theoharides TC. Niacin-induced "flush" involves release of prostaglandin D2 from mast cells and serotonin from platelets: evidence from human cells in vitro and an animal model. *J Pharmacol Exp Ther.* 2008;327(3):665-72.

353. Ferrell M, Wang Z, Anderson JT, Li XS, Witkowski M, DiDonato JA, Hilser JR, Hartiala JA, Haghikia A, Cajka T, Fiehn O, Sangwan N, Demuth I, König M, Steinhagen-Thiessen E, Landmesser U, Tang WHW, Allayee H, Hazen SL. A terminal metabolite of niacin promotes vascular inflammation and contributes to cardiovascular disease risk. *Nat Med.* 2024;30(2):424-434.

354. Calder PC. Omega-3 fatty acids and inflammatory processes: from molecules to man. *Biochem Soc Trans.* 2017;45(5):1105-1115.

355. Williams EJ, Berthon BS, Stoodley I, Williams LM, Wood LG. Nutrition in Asthma. *Semin Respir Crit Care Med.* 2022;43(5):646-661.

356. Schreiner P, Martinho-Grueber M, Studerus D, Vavricka SR, Tilg H, Biedermann L; on behalf of Swiss IBDnet, an official working group of the Swiss Society of Gastroenterology. Nutrition in Inflammatory Bowel Disease. *Digestion.* 2020;101 Suppl 1:120-135.

357. Bhatt DL, Steg PG, Miller M, Brinton EA, Jacobson TA, Ketchum SB, et al.; REDUCE-IT Investigators. Cardiovascular Risk Reduction with Icosapent Ethyl for Hypertriglyceridemia. *N Engl J Med*. 2019;380(1):11-22.

358. Harris WS, Tintle NL, Imamura F, Qian F, Korat AVA, Marklund M, Djoussé L, Bassett JK, Carmichael PH, Chen YY, Hirakawa Y, Küpers LK, Laguzzi F, Lankinen M, Murphy RA, Samieri C, Senn MK, Shi P, Virtanen JK, Brouwer IA, Chien KL, Eiriksdottir G, Forouhi NG, Geleijnse JM, Giles GG, Gudnason V, Helmer C, Hodge A, Jackson R, Khaw KT, Laakso M, Lai H, Laurin D, Leander K, Lindsay J, Micha R, Mursu J, Ninomiya T, Post W, Psaty BM, Risérus U, Robinson JG, Shadyab AH, Snetselaar L, Sala-Vila A, Sun Y, Steffen LM, Tsai MY, Wareham NJ, Wood AC, Wu JHY, Hu F, Sun Q, Siscovick DS, Lemaitre RN, Mozaffarian D; Fatty Acids and Outcomes Research Consortium (FORCE). Blood n-3 fatty acid levels and total and cause-specific mortality from 17 prospective studies. *Nat Commun*. 2021;12(1):2329.

359. Abdelhamid AS, Brown TJ, Brainard JS, Biswas P, Thorpe GC, Moore HJ, Deane KH, AlAbdulghafoor FK, Summerbell CD, Worthington HV, Song F, Hooper L. Omega-3 fatty acids for the primary and secondary prevention of cardiovascular disease. *Cochrane Database Syst Rev*. 2018;7(7):CD003177.

360. Markozannes G, Ntzani EE, Tsapas A, Mantzoros CS, Tsiara S, Xanthos T, Karpettas N, Patrikios I, Rizos EC. Dose-related meta-analysis for Omega-3 fatty acids supplementation on major adverse cardiovascular events. *Clin Nutr*. 2022;41(4):923-30.

361. Appleton KM, Voyias PD, Sallis HM, Dawson S, Ness AR, Churchill R, Perry R. Omega-3 fatty acids for depression in adults. *Cochrane Database Syst Rev*. 2021;11(11):CD004692.

362. Thomsen BJ, Chow EY, Sapijaszko MJ. The Potential Uses of Omega-3 Fatty Acids in Dermatology: A Review. *J Cutan Med Surg*. 2020;24(5):481-494.

363. Jiang H, Shi X, Fan Y, Wang D, Li B, Zhou J, Pei C, Ma L. Dietary omega-3 polyunsaturated fatty acids and fish intake and risk of age-related macular degeneration. *Clin Nutr*. 2021;40(12):5662-5673.

364. Bowen KJ, Harris WS, Kris-Etherton PM. Omega-3 Fatty Acids and Cardiovascular Disease: Are There Benefits? *Curr Treat Options Cardiovasc Med*. 2016;18(11):69.

365. Farag MA, Gad MZ. Omega-9 fatty acids: potential roles in inflammation and cancer management. *J Genet Eng Biotechnol*. 2022;20(1):48.

366. Johnson M, Bradford C. Omega-3, Omega-6 and Omega-9 Fatty Acids: Implications for Cardiovascular and Other Diseases. *J Glycomics Lipidomics*. 2014;4(4):1000123.

367. Wang Y, Jin J, Wu G, Wei W, Jin Q, Wang X. Omega-9 monounsaturated fatty acids: a review of current scientific evidence of sources, metabolism, benefits, recommended intake, and edible safety. *Crit Rev Food Sci Nutr.* 2024 Feb 11:1-21. doi: 10.1080/10408398.2024.2313181. Online ahead of print.

368. Lin CY, Hsu CY, Elzoghby AO, Alalaiwe A, Hwang TL, Fang JY. Oleic acid as the active agent and lipid matrix in cilomilast-loaded nanocarriers to assist PDE4 inhibition of activated neutrophils for mitigating psoriasis-like lesions. *Acta Biomater.* 2019;90:350-361.

369. Delgado GE, Krämer BK, Lorkowski S, März W, von Schacky C, Kleber ME. Individual omega-9 monounsaturated fatty acids and mortality-The Ludwigshafen Risk and Cardiovascular Health Study. *J Clin Lipidol.* 2017;11(1):126-135.e5.

370. Galanty A, Grudzińska M, Paździora W, Paśko P. Erucic Acid-Both Sides of the Story: A Concise Review on Its Beneficial and Toxic Properties. *Molecules.* 2023;28(4):1924.

371. Belz GG, Palm D. Paracelsus: Dosis sola facit venenum. *Dtsch Arztebl.* 1993; 90(22): A-1630.

372. Rajman L, Chwalek K, Sinclair DA. Therapeutic Potential of NAD-Boosting Molecules: The In Vivo Evidence. *Cell Metab.* 2018;27(3):529-547.

373. Lopaschuk GD, Karwi QG, Tian R, Wende AR, Abel ED. Cardiac Energy Metabolism in Heart Failure. *Circ Res.* 2021;128(10):1487-1513.

374. Covarrubias AJ, Perrone R, Grozio A, Verdin E. NAD$^+$ metabolism and its roles in cellular processes during ageing. *Nat Rev Mol Cell Biol.* 2021;22(2):119-141.

375. Kida Y, Goligorsky MS. Sirtuins, Cell Senescence, and Vascular Aging. *Can J Cardiol.* 2016;32(5):634-41.

376. Dai H, Sinclair DA, Ellis JL, Steegborn C. Sirtuin activators and inhibitors: Promises, achievements, and challenges. *Pharmacol Ther.* 2018;188:140-154.

377. Song Q, Zhou X, Xu K, Liu S, Zhu X, Yang J. The Safety and Antiaging Effects of Nicotinamide Mononucleotide in Human Clinical Trials: an Update. *Adv Nutr.* 2023;14(6):1416-1435.

378. Nadeeshani H, Li J, Ying T, Zhang B, Lu J. Nicotinamide mononucleotide (NMN) as an anti-aging health product - Promises and safety concerns. *J Adv Res.* 2021;37:267-278.

379. Herman R, Kravos NA, Jensterle M, Janež A, Dolžan V. Metformin and Insulin Resistance: A Review of the Underlying Mechanisms behind Changes in GLUT4-Mediated Glucose Transport. *Int J Mol Sci.* 2022;23(3):1264.

380. Kristófi R, Eriksson JW. Metformin as an anti-inflammatory agent: a short review. *J Endocrinol.* 2021;251(2):R11-R22.

381. Lv Z, Guo Y. Metformin and Its Benefits for Various Diseases. *Front Endocrinol (Lausanne)*. 2020;11:191.

382. Huang X, Sun T, Wang J, Hong X, Chen H, Yan T, Zhou C, Sun D, Yang C, Yu T, Su W, Du W, Xiong H. Metformin Reprograms Tryptophan Metabolism to Stimulate CD8+ T-cell Function in Colorectal Cancer. *Cancer Res*. 2023;83(14):2358-2371.

383. Cejuela M, Martin-Castillo B, Menendez JA, Pernas S. Metformin and Breast Cancer: Where Are We Now? *Int J Mol Sci*. 2022;23(5):2705.

384. Ma T, Tian X, Zhang B, Li M, Wang Y, Yang C, Wu J, Wei X, Qu Q, Yu Y, Long S, Feng JW, Li C, Zhang C, Xie C, Wu Y, Xu Z, Chen J, Yu Y, Huang X, He Y, Yao L, Zhang L, Zhu M, Wang W, Wang ZC, Zhang M, Bao Y, Jia W, Lin SY, Ye Z, Piao HL, Deng X, Zhang CS, Lin SC. Low-dose metformin targets the lysosomal AMPK pathway through PEN2. *Nature*. 2022;603(7899):159-165.

385. Infante M, Leoni M, Caprio M, Fabbri A. Long-term metformin therapy and vitamin B12 deficiency: An association to bear in mind. *World J Diabetes*. 2021;12(7):916-931.

386. Kushner RF, Calanna S, Davies M, Dicker D, Garvey WT, Goldman B, Lingvay I, Thomsen M, Wadden TA, Wharton S, Wilding JPH, Rubino D. Semaglutide 2.4 mg for the Treatment of Obesity: Key Elements of the STEP Trials 1 to 5. *Obesity (Silver Spring)*. 2020;28(6):1050-1061.

387. Bergmann NC, Davies MJ, Lingvay I, Knop FK. Semaglutide for the treatment of overweight and obesity: A review. *Diabetes Obes Metab*. 2023;25(1):18-35.

388. Lincoff AM, Brown-Frandsen K, Colhoun HM, Deanfield J, Emerson SS, Esbjerg S, Hardt-Lindberg S, Hovingh GK, Kahn SE, Kushner RF, Lingvay I, Oral TK, Michelsen MM, Plutzky J, Tornøe CW, Ryan DH; SELECT Trial Investigators. Semaglutide and Cardiovascular Outcomes in Obesity without Diabetes. *N Engl J Med*. 2023;389(24):2221-2232.

389. Hussein H, Zaccardi F, Khunti K, Davies MJ, Patsko E, Dhalwani NN, Kloecker DE, Ioannidou E, Gray LJ. Efficacy and tolerability of sodium-glucose co-transporter-2 inhibitors and glucagon-like peptide-1 receptor agonists: A systematic review and network meta-analysis. *Diabetes Obes Metab*. 2020;22(7):1035-1046.

390. McIntyre RS, Mansur RB, Rosenblat JD, Kwan ATH. The association between glucagon-like peptide-1 receptor agonists (GLP-1 RAs) and suicidality: reports to the Food and Drug Administration Adverse Event Reporting System (FAERS). *Expert Opin Drug Saf*. 2024;23(1):47-55.

391. Wang W, Volkow ND, Berger NA, Davis PB, Kaelber DC, Xu R. Association of semaglutide with risk of suicidal ideation in a real-world cohort. *Nat Med*. 2024;30(1):168-176.

392. Tobaiqy M, Elkout H. Psychiatric adverse events associated with semaglutide, liraglutide and tirzepatide: a pharmacovigilance analysis of individu-

al case safety reports submitted to the EudraVigilance database. *Int J Clin Pharm.* 2024 Jan 24. doi: 10.1007/s11096-023-01694-7. Online ahead of print.

393. Berkel HJ. Does an 'aspirin-a-day' keep the doctor away? *Br J Cancer.*1999;81(1):1-2.

394. Montinari MR, Minelli S, De Caterina R. The first 3500 years of aspirin history from its roots - A concise summary. *Vascul Pharmacol.* 2019;113:1-8.

395. Ugurlucan M, Caglar IM, Caglar FN, Ziyade S, Karatepe O, Yildiz Y, Zencirci E, Ugurlucan FG, Arslan AH, Korkmaz S, Filizcan U, Cicek S. Aspirin: from a historical perspective. *Recent Pat Cardiovasc Drug Discov.* 2012;7(1):71-6.

396. Gall EP. The safety of treating rheumatoid arthritis with aspirin. *JAMA.* 1982;247(1):63-4.

397. Moore N, Le Parc JM, van Ganse E, Wall R, Schneid H, Cairns R. Tolerability of ibuprofen, aspirin and paracetamol for the treatment of cold and flu symptoms and sore throat pain. *Int J Clin Pract.* 2002;56(10):732-4.

398. Patrono C, Rocca B. Less Thromboxane, Longer Life. *J Am Coll Cardiol.* 2022;80(3):251-255.

399. Soodi D, VanWormer JJ, Rezkalla SH. Aspirin in Primary Prevention of Cardiovascular Events. *Clin Med Res.* 2020;18(2-3):89-94.

400. Zheng SL, Roddick AJ. Association of Aspirin Use for Primary Prevention With Cardiovascular Events and Bleeding Events: A Systematic Review and Meta-analysis. *JAMA.* 2019;321(3):277-287.

401. Bigalke B, Geisler T, Hövelborn T, May AE, Gawaz M. Management of perioperative stent thrombosis in patients undergoing surgery. *Platelets.* 2010;21(7):578-82.

402. Kamada T, Satoh K, Itoh T, Ito M, Iwamoto J, Okimoto T, Kanno T, Sugimoto M, Chiba T, Nomura S, Mieda M, Hiraishi H, Yoshino J, Takagi A, Watanabe S, Koike K. Evidence-based clinical practice guidelines for peptic ulcer disease 2020. *J Gastroenterol.* 2021;56(4):303-322.

403. Szczeklik A. Aspirin-induced asthma: a tribute to John Vane as a source of inspiration. *Pharmacol Rep.* 2010;62(3):526-9.

404. Fitzgerald DA. Aspirin and Reye syndrome. *Paediatr Drugs.* 2007;9(3):205-6.

405. Yu D, Liao JK. Emerging views of statin pleiotropy and cholesterol lowering. *Cardiovasc Res.* 2022;118(2):413-423.

406. Hussain A, Kaler J, Ray SD. The Benefits Outweigh the Risks of Treating Hypercholesterolemia: The Statin Dilemma. *Cureus.* 2023;15(1):e33648.

407. Cholesterol Treatment Trialists' (CTT) Collaboration; Baigent C, Blackwell L, Emberson J, Holland LE, Reith C, Bhala N, Peto R, Barnes EH, Keech A, Simes J, Collins R. Efficacy and safety of more intensive lowering of

LDL cholesterol: a meta-analysis of data from 170,000 participants in 26 randomised trials. *Lancet.* 2010;376(9753):1670-81.

408. Ference BA, Ginsberg HN, Graham I, Ray KK, Packard CJ, Bruckert E, Hegele RA, Krauss RM, Raal FJ, Schunkert H, Watts GF, Borén J, Fazio S, Horton JD, Masana L, Nicholls SJ, Nordestgaard BG, van de Sluis B, Taskinen MR, Tokgözoglu L, Landmesser U, Laufs U, Wiklund O, Stock JK, Chapman MJ, Catapano AL. Low-density lipoproteins cause atherosclerotic cardiovascular disease. 1. Evidence from genetic, epidemiologic, and clinical studies. A consensus statement from the European Atherosclerosis Society Consensus Panel. *Eur Heart J.* 2017;38(32):2459-2472.

409. Ballaz S, Bourin M. High Sensitivity C-reactive Protein (hsCRP) and its Implications in Cardiovascular Outcomes. *Curr Pharm Des.* 2021;27(2):263-275.

410. Zhang Y, Liang M, Sun C, Qu G, Shi T, Min M, Wu Y, Sun Y. Statin Use and Risk of Pancreatic Cancer: An Updated Meta-analysis of 26 Studies. *Pancreas.* 2019;48(2):142-150.

411. Tran KT, McMenamin ÚC, Coleman HG, Cardwell CR, Murchie P, Iversen L, Lee AJ, Thrift AP. Statin use and risk of liver cancer: Evidence from two population-based studies. *Int J Cancer.* 2020;146(5):1250-1260.

412. Vinci P, Panizon E, Tosoni LM, Cerrato C, Pellicori F, Mearelli F, Biasinutto C, Fiotti N, Di Girolamo FG, Biolo G. Statin-Associated Myopathy: Emphasis on Mechanisms and Targeted Therapy. *Int J Mol Sci.* 2021;22(21):11687.

413. Furberg CD, Pitt B. Withdrawal of cerivastatin from the world market. *Curr Control Trials Cardiovasc Med.* 2001;2(5):205-207.

414. Liu A, Wu Q, Guo J, Ares I, Rodríguez JL, Martínez-Larrañaga MR, Yuan Z, Anadón A, Wang X, Martínez MA. Statins: Adverse reactions, oxidative stress and metabolic interactions. *Pharmacol Ther.* 2019;195:54-84.

415. Casula M, Mozzanica F, Scotti L, Tragni E, Pirillo A, Corrao G, Catapano AL. Statin use and risk of new-onset diabetes: A meta-analysis of observational studies. *Nutr Metab Cardiovasc Dis.* 2017;27(5):396-406.

416. Mansi IA, Chansard M, Lingvay I, Zhang S, Halm EA, Alvarez CA. Association of Statin Therapy Initiation With Diabetes Progression: A Retrospective Matched-Cohort Study. *JAMA Intern Med.* 2021;181(12):1562-1574.

417. Adhikari A, Tripathy S, Chuzi S, Peterson J, Stone NJ. Association between statin use and cognitive function: A systematic review of randomized clinical trials and observational studies. *J Clin Lipidol.* 2021;15(1):22-32.e12.

418. Heckman MA, Weil J, Gonzalez de Mejia E. Caffeine (1, 3, 7-trimethylxanthine) in foods: a comprehensive review on consumption, functionality, safety, and regulatory matters. *J Food Sci.* 2010;75(3):R77-87.

419. Nieber K. The Impact of Coffee on Health. *Planta Med.* 2017;83(16):1256-1263.

420. Jeukendrup AE, Randell R. Fat burners: nutrition supplements that increase fat metabolism. *Obes Rev.* 2011;12(10):841-51.

421. Guest NS, VanDusseldorp TA, Nelson MT, Grgic J, Schoenfeld BJ, Jenkins NDM, Arent SM, Antonio J, Stout JR, Trexler ET, Smith-Ryan AE, Goldstein ER, Kalman DS, Campbell BI. International society of sports nutrition position stand: caffeine and exercise performance. *J Int Soc Sports Nutr.* 2021;18(1):1.

422. Zulli A, Smith RM, Kubatka P, Novak J, Uehara Y, Loftus H, Qaradakhi T, Pohanka M, Kobyliak N, Zagatina A, Klimas J, Hayes A, La Rocca G, Soucek M, Kruzliak P. Caffeine and cardiovascular diseases: critical review of current research. *Eur J Nutr.* 2016;55(4):1331-43.

423. Grzegorzewski J, Bartsch F, Köller A, König M. Pharmacokinetics of Caffeine: A Systematic Analysis of Reported Data for Application in Metabolic Phenotyping and Liver Function Testing. *Front Pharmacol.* 2022;12:752826.

424. Smit HJ. Theobromine and the pharmacology of cocoa. *Handb Exp Pharmacol.* 2011;(200):201-34.

425. Judelson DA, Preston AG, Miller DL, Muñoz CX, Kellogg MD, Lieberman HR. Effects of theobromine and caffeine on mood and vigilance. *J Clin Psychopharmacol.* 2013;33(4):499-506.

426. Ried K, Sullivan TR, Fakler P, Frank OR, Stocks NP. Effect of cocoa on blood pressure. *Cochrane Database Syst Rev.* 2012;(8):CD008893.

427. Monteiro J, Alves MG, Oliveira PF, Silva BM. Pharmacological potential of methylxanthines: Retrospective analysis and future expectations. *Crit Rev Food Sci Nutr.* 2019;59(16):2597-2625.

428. Sharifi-Zahabi E, Rezvani N, Hajizadeh-Sharafabad F, Hosseini-Baharanchi FS, Shidfar F, Rahimi M. A comprehensive insight into the molecular effect of theobromine on cardiovascular-related risk factors: A systematic review of in vitro and in vivo studies. *Food Funct.* 2023;14(18):8431-8441.

429. Bhat JA, Kumar M. Neuroprotective Effects of Theobromine in permanent bilateral common carotid artery occlusion rat model of cerebral hypoperfusion. *Metab Brain Dis.* 2022;37(6):1787-1801.

430. Patanè S, Marte F, La Rosa FC, Rocca R. Atrial fibrillation associated with chocolate intake abuse and chronic salbutamol inhalation abuse. *Int J Cardiol.* 2010;145(2):e74-e76.

431. Brosnan JT, Brosnan ME. The sulfur-containing amino acids: an overview. *J Nutr.* 2006;136(6 Suppl):1636S-1640S.

432. Singh P, Gollapalli K, Mangiola S, Schranner D, Yusuf MA, Chamoli M, Shi SL, Lopes Bastos B, Nair T, Riermeier A, Vayndorf EM, Wu JZ, Nilakhe A, Nguyen CQ, Muir M, Kiflezghi MG, Foulger A, Junker A, Devine

J, Sharan K, Chinta SJ, Rajput S, Rane A, Baumert P, Schönfelder M, Iavarone F, di Lorenzo G, Kumari S, Gupta A, Sarkar R, Khyriem C, Chawla AS, Sharma A, Sarper N, Chattopadhyay N, Biswal BK, Settembre C, Nagarajan P, Targoff KL, Picard M, Gupta S, Velagapudi V, Papenfuss AT, Kaya A, Ferreira MG, Kennedy BK, Andersen JK, Lithgow GJ, Ali AM, Mukhopadhyay A, Palotie A, Kastenmüller G, Kaeberlein M, Wackerhage H, Pal B, Yadav VK. Taurine deficiency as a driver of aging. *Science.* 2023;380(6649):eabn9257.

433. Jong CJ, Sandal P, Schaffer SW. The Role of Taurine in Mitochondria Health: More Than Just an Antioxidant. *Molecules.* 2021;26(16):4913.

434. Qaradakhi T, Gadanec LK, McSweeney KR, Abraham JR, Apostolopoulos V, Zulli A. The Anti-Inflammatory Effect of Taurine on Cardiovascular Disease. *Nutrients.* 2020;12(9):2847.

435. Khalaf K, Tornese P, Cocco A, Albanese A. Tauroursodeoxycholic acid: a potential therapeutic tool in neurodegenerative diseases. *Transl Neurodegener.* 2022;11(1):33.

436. Baliou S, Adamaki M, Ioannou P, Pappa A, Panayiotidis MI, Spandidos DA, Christodoulou I, Kyriakopoulos AM, Zoumpourlis V. Protective role of taurine against oxidative stress (Review). *Mol Med Rep.* 2021;24(2):605.

437. Ma N, He F, Kawanokuchi J, Wang G, Yamashita T. Taurine and Its Anticancer Functions: In Vivo and In Vitro Study. *Adv Exp Med Biol.* 2022;1370:121-128.

438. Costantino A, Maiese A, Lazzari J, Casula C, Turillazzi E, Frati P, Fineschi V. The Dark Side of Energy Drinks: A Comprehensive Review of Their Impact on the Human Body. *Nutrients.* 2023;15(18):3922.

439. Curran CP, Marczinski CA. Taurine, caffeine, and energy drinks: Reviewing the risks to the adolescent brain. *Birth Defects Res.* 2017;109(20):1640-1648.

440. Taranukhin AG, Saransaari P, Kiianmaa K, Gunnar T, Oja SS. Comparison of Toxicity of Taurine and GABA in Combination with Alcohol in 7-Day-Old Mice. *Adv Exp Med Biol.* 2017;975 Pt 2:1021-1033.

441. Borlinghaus J, Albrecht F, Gruhlke MC, Nwachukwu ID, Slusarenko AJ. Allicin: chemistry and biological properties. *Molecules.* 2014;19(8):12591-618.

442. Choo S, Chin VK, Wong EH, Madhavan P, Tay ST, Yong PVC, Chong PP. Review: antimicrobial properties of allicin used alone or in combination with other medications. *Folia Microbiol (Praha).* 2020;65(3):451-465.

443. Hu J, Li C, Zhou Y, Ding J, Li X, Li Y. Allicin Inhibits Porcine Reproductive and Respiratory Syndrome Virus Infection In Vitro and Alleviates Inflammatory Responses. *Viruses.* 2023;15(5):1050.

444. Arellano Buendia AS, Juárez Rojas JG, García-Arroyo F, Aparicio Trejo OE, Sánchez-Muñoz F, Argüello-García R, Sánchez-Lozada LG, Bojalil R, Osorio-Alonso H. Antioxidant and anti-inflammatory effects of allicin in

the kidney of an experimental model of metabolic syndrome. *PeerJ.* 2023;11:e16132.

445. Sánchez-Gloria JL, Arellano-Buendía AS, Juárez-Rojas JG, García-Arroyo FE, Argüello-García R, Sánchez-Muñoz F, Sánchez-Lozada LG, Osorio-Alonso H. Cellular Mechanisms Underlying the Cardioprotective Role of Allicin on Cardiovascular Diseases. *Int J Mol Sci.* 2022;23(16):9082.

446. Pereverzev A, Ostroumova OD. Potential drug interactions with garlic. *Medical alphabet.* 2021;1(29):47-51.

447. Thomas PA, Dering M, Giertych MJ, Iszkuło G, Tomaszewski D, Briggs J. Biological Flora of Britain and Ireland: Viscum album. *J Ecol.* 2023;111(3):701-739.

448. Poles J, Karhu E, McGill M, McDaniel HR, Lewis JE. The effects of twenty-four nutrients and phytonutrients on immune system function and inflammation: A narrative review. *J Clin Transl Res.* 2021;7(3):333-376.

449. Nicoletti M. The Anti-Inflammatory Activity of *Viscum album. Plants (Basel).* 2023;12(7):1460.

450. Steigenberger C, Schnell-Inderst P, Flatscher-Thöni M, Plank LM, Siebert U. Patient' and social aspects related to complementary mistletoe therapy in patients with breast cancer: A systematic review commissioned by the German agency for Health Technology Assessment. *Eur J Oncol Nurs.* 2023;65:102338.

451. Ma YH, Cheng WZ, Gong F, Ma AL, Yu QW, Zhang JY, Hu CY, Chen XH, Zhang DQ. Active Chinese mistletoe lectin-55 enhances colon cancer surveillance through regulating innate and adaptive immune responses. *World J Gastroenterol.* 2008;14(34):5274-81.

452. Ma L, Phalke S, Stévigny C, Souard F, Vermijlen D. Mistletoe-Extract Drugs Stimulate Anti-Cancer Vγ9Vδ2 T Cells. *Cells.* 2020;9(6):1560.

453. Suveren E, Baxter GF, Iskit AB, Turker AU. Cardioprotective effects of Viscum album L. subsp. album (European misletoe) leaf extracts in myocardial ischemia and reperfusion. *J Ethnopharmacol.* 2017;209:203-209.

454. Myers SP, Cheras PA. The other side of the coin: safety of complementary and alternative medicine. *Med J Aust.* 2004;181(4):222-5.

455. Steele ML, Axtner J, Happe A, Kröz M, Matthes H, Schad F. Adverse Drug Reactions and Expected Effects to Therapy with Subcutaneous Mistletoe Extracts (Viscum album L.) in Cancer Patients. *Evid Based Complement Alternat Med.* 2014;2014:724258.

456. Rosell S, Samuelsson G. Effect of mistletoe viscotoxin and phoratoxin on blood circulation. *Toxicon.* 1966;4(2):107-10.

457. Von Wolzogen H. Die Motive in Wagner's „Götterdämmerung". *Musikal Wochenbl.* 1879;10(1):261.

458. Wang Y, Wang H, Ma T, Liu G, Feng X, Liu X, Ma X, Liu S, Shi D, Wang B, Kang J, Wang H, Wang Z. Hawthorn extract inhibited the PI3k/Akt

pathway to prolong the lifespan of Drosophila melanogaster. *J Food Biochem.* 2022;46(8):e14169.

459. Kim E, Jang E, Lee JH. Potential Roles and Key Mechanisms of Hawthorn Extract against Various Liver Diseases. *Nutrients.* 2022;14(4):867.

460. Verma T, Sinha M, Bansal N, Yadav SR, Shah K, Chauhan NS. Plants Used as Antihypertensive. *Nat Prod Bioprospect.* 2021;11(2):155-184.

461. Wu M, Liu L, Xing Y, Yang S, Li H, Cao Y. Roles and Mechanisms of Hawthorn and Its Extracts on Atherosclerosis: A Review. *Front Pharmacol.* 2020;11:118.

462. Z Rashid B, Dizaye KF. The Impact of Procyanidin Extracted from Crataegus azarolus on Rats with Induced Heart Failure. *Cell Mol Biol (Noisy-le-grand).* 2022;68(9):179-185.

463. Tauchert M. Efficacy and safety of crataegus extract WS 1442 in comparison with placebo in patients with chronic stable New York Heart Association class-III heart failure. *Am Heart J.* 2002;143(5):910-5.

464. Orhan IE. Phytochemical and Pharmacological Activity Profile of Crataegus oxyacantha L. (Hawthorn) - A Cardiotonic Herb. *Curr Med Chem.* 2018;25(37):4854-4865.

465. Nitzan K, David D, Franko M, Toledano R, Fidelman S, Tenenbaum YS, Blonder M, Armoza-Eilat S, Shamir A, Rehavi M, Ben-Chaim Y, Doron R. Anxiolytic and antidepressants' effect of Crataegus pinnatifida (Shan Zha): biochemical mechanisms. *Transl Psychiatry.* 2022;12(1):208.

466. De Simone M, De Feo R, Choucha A, Ciaglia E, Fezeu F. Enhancing Sleep Quality: Assessing the Efficacy of a Fixed Combination of Linden, Hawthorn, Vitamin B1, and Melatonin. *Med Sci (Basel).* 2023;12(1):2.

467. Daniele C, Mazzanti G, Pittler MH, Ernst E. Adverse-event profile of Crataegus spp.: a systematic review. *Drug Saf.* 2006;29(6):523-35.

468. Sah A, Naseef PP, Kuruniyan MS, Jain GK, Zakir F, Aggarwal G. A Comprehensive Study of Therapeutic Applications of Chamomile. *Pharmaceuticals (Basel).* 2022;15(10):1284.

469. Dai YL, Li Y, Wang Q, Niu FJ, Li KW, Wang YY, Wang J, Zhou CZ, Gao LN. Chamomile: A Review of Its Traditional Uses, Chemical Constituents, Pharmacological Activities and Quality Control Studies. *Molecules.* 2022;28(1):133.

470. De Cicco P, Ercolano G, Sirignano C, Rubino V, Rigano D, Ianaro A, Formisano C. Chamomile essential oils exert anti-inflammatory effects involving human and murine macrophages: Evidence to support a therapeutic action. *J Ethnopharmacol.* 2023;311:116391.

471. Turk MA, Liu Y, Pope JE. Non-pharmacological interventions in the treatment of rheumatoid arthritis: A systematic review and meta-analysis. *Autoimmun Rev.* 2023;22(6):103323.

472. Chaves PFP, Iacomini M, Cordeiro LMC. Chemical characterization of fructooligosaccharides, inulin and structurally diverse polysaccharides from chamomile tea. *Carbohydr Polym*. 2019;214:269-275.

473. Pratas A, Malhão B, Palma R, Mendonça P, Cervantes R, Marques-Ramos A. Effects of apigenin on gastric cancer cells. *Biomed Pharmacother*. 2024;172:116251.

474. Nieman KM, Zhu Y, Tucker M, Koecher K. The Role of Dietary Ingredients in Mental Energy - A Scoping Review of Randomized Controlled Trials. *J Am Nutr Assoc*. 2024;43(2):167-182.

475. Denisow-Pietrzyk M, Pietrzyk Ł, Denisow B. Asteraceae species as potential environmental factors of allergy. *Environ Sci Pollut Res Int*. 2019;26(7):6290-6300.

476. Kimura R, Schwartz JA, Romeiser JL, Senzel L, Galanakis D, Halper D, Bennett-Guerrero E. The Acute Effect of Chamomile Intake on Blood Coagulation Tests in Healthy Volunteers: A Randomized Trial. *J Appl Lab Med*. 2024:jfad120. Online ahead of print.

477. Povolo C, Foschini A, Ribaudo G. Optimization of the extraction of bioactive molecules from *Lycium barbarum* fruits and evaluation of the antioxidant activity: a combined study. *Nat Prod Res*. 2019;33(18):2694-2698.

478. Wetters S, Horn T, Nick P. Goji Who? Morphological and DNA Based Authentication of a "Superfood". *Front Plant Sci*. 2018;9:1859.

479. Vidović BB, Milinčić DD, Marčetić MD, Djuriš JD, Ilić TD, Kostić AŽ, Pešić MB. Health Benefits and Applications of Goji Berries in Functional Food Products Development: A Review. *Antioxidants (Basel)*. 2022;11(2):248.

480. Georgiev KD, Slavov IJ, Iliev IA. Antioxidant Activity and Antiproliferative Effects of Lycium barbarum's (Goji berry) Fractions on Breast Cancer Cell Lines. *Folia Med (Plovdiv)*. 2019;61(1):104-112.

481. Ji H, Ma J, Guo L, Huang Y, Wang W, Sun X, Sun R. Amino acid sequence identification of goji berry cyclic peptides and anticervical carcinoma activity detection. *J Pept Sci*. 2021;27(8):e3326.

482. Kwaśnik P, Lemieszek MK, Rzeski W. Impact of phytochemicals and plant extracts on viability and proliferation of NK cell line NK-92 - a closer look at immunomodulatory properties of goji berries extract in human colon cancer cells. *Ann Agric Environ Med*. 2021;28(2):291-299.

483. Sanghavi A, Srivatsa A, Adiga D, Chopra A, Lobo R, Kabekkodu SP, Gadag S, Nayak U, Sivaraman K, Shah A. Goji berry (Lycium barbarum) inhibits the proliferation, adhesion, and migration of oral cancer cells by inhibiting the ERK, AKT, and CyclinD cell signaling pathways: an in-vitro study. *F1000Res*. 2022;11:1563.

484. Kazybay B, Sun Q, Dukenbayev K, Nurkesh AA, Xu N, Kutzhanova A, Razbekova M, Kabylda A, Yang Q, Wang Q, Ma C, Xie Y. Network Pharmacology with Experimental Investigation of the Mechanisms

of *Rhizoma Polygonati* against Prostate Cancer with Additional Herbzymatic Activity. *ACS Omega*. 2022;7(17):14465-14477.

485. Patsilinakos A, Ragno R, Carradori S, Petralito S, Cesa S. Carotenoid content of Goji berries: CIELAB, HPLC-DAD analyses and quantitative correlation. *Food Chem*. 2018;268:49-56.

486. Yoo JH, Lee JS, Jang JH, Jung JI, Kim EJ, Choi SY. AGEs Blocker™ (Goji Berry, Fig, and Korean Mint Mixed Extract) Inhibits Skin Aging Caused by Streptozotocin-Induced Glycation in Hairless Mice. *Prev Nutr Food Sci*. 2023;28(2):134-140.

487. Ma ZF, Zhang H, Teh SS, Wang CW, Zhang Y, Hayford F, Wang L, Ma T, Dong Z, Zhang Y, Zhu Y. Goji Berries as a Potential Natural Antioxidant Medicine: An Insight into Their Molecular Mechanisms of Action. *Oxid Med Cell Longev*. 2019;2019:2437397.

488. Uchibayashi M. Etymology of ginger. *Yakushigaku Zasshi*. 2001;36(1):58-60.

489. Ling W, Huang Y, Xu JH, Li Y, Huang YM, Ling HB, Sui Y, Zhao HL. Consistent Efficacy of Wendan Decoction for the Treatment of Digestive Reflux Disorders. *Am J Chin Med*. 2015;43(5):893-913.

490. Santos Braga S. Ginger: Panacea or Consumer's Hype? *Applied Sciences*. 2019; 9(8):1570.

491. Chen L, Wang H, Chen Z, Zhuo W, Xu R, Zeng X, He Q, Guan Y, Li H, Liu H. Ginger from ancient times to the new outlook. *Chem Biodivers*. 2022;19(11):e202200757.

492. Bischoff-Kont I, Primke T, Niebergall LS, Zech T, Fürst R. Ginger Constituent 6-Shogaol Inhibits Inflammation- and Angiogenesis-Related Cell Functions in Primary Human Endothelial Cells. *Front Pharmacol*. 2022;13:844767.

493. Haniadka R, Saldanha E, Sunita V, Palatty PL, Fayad R, Baliga MS. A review of the gastroprotective effects of ginger (Zingiber officinale Roscoe). *Food Funct*. 2013;4(6):845-55.

494. Chen L, Wang H, Chen Z, Zhuo W, Xu R, Zeng X, He Q, Guan Y, Li H, Liu H. The Effect of Dried Ginger (Gan Jiang) on Stomach Energy Metabolism and the Related Mechanism in Rats Based on Metabonomics. *Chem Biodivers*. 2022;19(11):e202200757.

495. Hu Y, Amoah AN, Zhang H, Fu R, Qiu Y, Cao Y, Sun Y, Chen H, Liu Y, Lyu Q. Effect of ginger in the treatment of nausea and vomiting compared with vitamin B6 and placebo during pregnancy: a meta-analysis. *J Matern Fetal Neonatal Med*. 2022;35(1):187-196.

496. Choi J, Lee J, Kim K, Choi HK, Lee SA, Lee HJ. Effects of Ginger Intake on Chemotherapy-Induced Nausea and Vomiting: A Systematic Review of Randomized Clinical Trials. *Nutrients*. 2022;14(23):4982.

497. Araya-Quintanilla F, Gutierrez-Espinoza H, Munoz-Yanez MJ, Sanchez-Montoya U, Lopez-Jeldes J. Effectiveness of Ginger on Pain and Function

in Knee Osteoarthritis: A PRISMA Systematic Review and Meta-Analysis. *Pain Physician.* 2020;23(2):E151-E161.

498. Shirvani MA, Motahari-Tabari N, Alipour A. The effect of mefenamic acid and ginger on pain relief in primary dysmenorrhea: a randomized clinical trial. *Arch Gynecol Obstet.* 2015;291(6):1277-81.

499. Fakhri S, Patra JK, Das SK, Das G, Majnooni MB, Farzaei MH. Ginger and Heart Health: From Mechanisms to Therapeutics. *Curr Mol Pharmacol.* 2021;14(6):943-959.

500. Ali BH, Blunden G, Tanira MO, Nemmar A. Some phytochemical, pharmacological and toxicological properties of ginger (Zingiber officinale Roscoe): a review of recent research. *Food Chem Toxicol.* 2008;46(2):409-20.

501. Usman AN, Manju B, Ilhamuddin I, Ahmad M, Ab T, Ariyandy A, Budiaman B, Eragradini AR, Hasan II, Hashim S, Sartini S, Sinrang AW. Ginger potency on the prevention and treatment of breast cancer. *Breast Dis.* 2023;42(1):207-212.

502. Okuhira H, Nakatani Y, Furukawa F, Kanazawa N. Anaphylaxis to ginger induced by herbal medicine. *Allergol Int.* 2020;69(1):159-160.

503. Birt DF, Boylston T, Hendrich S, Jane JL, Hollis J, Li L, McClelland J, Moore S, Phillips GJ, Rowling M, Schalinske K, Scott MP, Whitley EM. Resistant Starch: Promise for Improving Human Health. *Adv Nutr.* 2013;4(6):587-601.

504. Li H, Zhang L, Li J, Wu Q, Qian L, He J, Ni Y, Kovatcheva-Datchary P, Yuan R, Liu S, Shen L, Zhang M, Sheng B, Li P, Kang K, Wu L, Fang Q, Long X, Wang X, Li Y, Ye Y, Ye J, Bao Y, Zhao Y, Xu G, Liu X, Panagiotou G, Xu A, Jia W. Resistant starch intake facilitates weight loss in humans by reshaping the gut microbiota. *Nat Metab.* 2024 Feb 26. doi: 10.1038/s42255-024-00988-y. Online ahead of print.

505. Sanders LM, Dicklin MR, Palacios OM, Maki CE, Wilcox ML, Maki KC. Effects of potato resistant starch intake on insulin sensitivity, related metabolic markers and appetite ratings in men and women at risk for type 2 diabetes: a pilot cross-over randomised controlled trial. *J Hum Nutr Diet.* 2021;34(1):94-105.

506. Wang Z, Wang S, Xu Q, Kong Q, Li F, Lu L, Xu Y, Wei Y. Synthesis and Functions of Resistant Starch. *Adv Nutr.* 2023;14(5):1131-1144.

507. Klosterbuer AS, Hullar MA, Li F, Traylor E, Lampe JW, Thomas W, Slavin JL. Gastrointestinal effects of resistant starch, soluble maize fibre and pullulan in healthy adults. *Br J Nutr.* 2013;110(6):1068-74.

508. Vijayalakshmi S, Xavier D, Srivastava C, Arun A. Vanilla-Natural Vs Artificial: A Review. *Research Journal of Pharmacy and Technology.* 2019;12(6):3068.

509. Liu YN, Kang JW, Zhang Y, Song SS, Xu QX, Zhang H, Lu L, Wei SW, Liang C, Su RW. Vanillin prevents the growth of endometriotic lesions through anti-inflammatory and antioxidant pathways in a mouse model. *Food Funct.* 2023;14(14):6730-6744.

510. Iannuzzi C, Liccardo M, Sirangelo I. Overview of the Role of Vanillin in Neurodegenerative Diseases and Neuropathophysiological Conditions. *Int J Mol Sci.* 2023;24(3):1817.

511. El Hamd MA, El-Maghrabey M, Almawash S, Radwan AS, El-Shaheny R, Magdy G. Citrus/urea nitrogen-doped carbon quantum dots as nanosensors for vanillin determination in infant formula and food products via factorial experimental design fluorimetry and smartphone. *Luminescence.* 2023 Dec 13. doi: 10.1002/bio.4643. Online ahead of print.

512. Szallasi A. Dietary Capsaicin: A Spicy Way to Improve Cardio-Metabolic Health? *Biomolecules.* 2022;12(12):1783.

513. Wang X, Yu L, Li F, Zhang G, Zhou W, Jiang X. Synthesis of amide derivatives containing capsaicin and their antioxidant and antibacterial activities. *J Food Biochem.* 2019;43(12):e13061.

514. Silva JL, Santos EA, Alvarez-Leite JI. Are We Ready to Recommend Capsaicin for Disorders Other Than Neuropathic Pain? *Nutrients.* 2023;15(20):4469.

515. Abdel-Salam OME, Mózsik G. Capsaicin, The Vanilloid Receptor TRPV1 Agonist in Neuroprotection: Mechanisms Involved and Significance. *Neurochem Res.* 2023;48(11):3296-3315.

516. Al Masaoud FS, Alharbi A, Behir MM, Siddiqui AF, Al-Murayeh LM, Al Dail A, Siddiqui R. A challenging case of suspected solanine toxicity in an eleven-year-old Saudi boy. *J Family Med Prim Care.* 2022;11(7):4039-4041.

517. Rauf A, Joshi PB, Ahmad Z, Hemeg HA, Olatunde A, Naz S, Hafeez N, Simal-Gandara J. Edible mushrooms as potential functional foods in amelioration of hypertension. *Phytother Res.* 2023;37(6):2644-2660.

518. Wennig R, Eyer F, Schaper A, Zilker T, Andresen-Streichert H. Mushroom Poisoning. *Dtsch Arztebl Int.* 2020;117(42):701-708.

519. Hoenigl M, Salmanton-García J, Walsh TJ, Nucci M, Neoh CF, Jenks JD, Lackner M, Sprute R, Al-Hatmi AMS, Bassetti M, Carlesse F, Freiberger T, Koehler P, Lehrnbecher T, Kumar A, Prattes J, Richardson M, Revankar S, Slavin MA, Stemler J, Spiess B, Taj-Aldeen SJ, Warris A, Woo PCY, Young JH, Albus K, Arenz D, Arsic-Arsenijevic V, Bouchara JP, Chinniah TR, Chowdhary A, de Hoog GS, Dimopoulos G, Duarte RF, Hamal P, Meis JF, Mfinanga S, Queiroz-Telles F, Patterson TF, Rahav G, Rogers TR, Rotstein C, Wahyuningsih R, Seidel D, Cornely OA. Global guideline for the diagnosis and management of rare mould infections: an initiative of the European Confederation of Medical Mycology in cooperation with the International Society for Human and Animal Mycology and the American Society for Microbiology. *Lancet Infect Dis.* 2021;21(8):e246-e257.

520. van Amsterdam J, Opperhuizen A, van den Brink W. Harm potential of magic mushroom use: a review. *Regul Toxicol Pharmacol.* 2011;59(3):423-9.

521. Crocq MA. History of cannabis and the endocannabinoid system. *Dialogues Clin Neurosci.* 2020;22(3):223-228.

522. Hill KP, Palastro MD. Medical cannabis for the treatment of chronic pain and other disorders: misconceptions and facts. *Pol Arch Intern Med.* 2017;127(11):785-789.

523. Solmi M, De Toffol M, Kim JY, Choi MJ, Stubbs B, Thompson T, Firth J, Miola A, Croatto G, Baggio F, Michelon S, Ballan L, Gerdle B, Monaco F, Simonato P, Scocco P, Ricca V, Castellini G, Fornaro M, Murru A, Vieta E, Fusar-Poli P, Barbui C, Ioannidis JPA, Carvalho AF, Radua J, Correll CU, Cortese S, Murray RM, Castle D, Shin JI, Dragioti E. Balancing risks and benefits of cannabis use: umbrella review of meta-analyses of randomised controlled trials and observational studies. *BMJ.* 2023;382:e072348.

524. Petrilli K, Ofori S, Hines L, Taylor G, Adams S, Freeman TP. Association of cannabis potency with mental ill health and addiction: a systematic review. *Lancet Psychiatry.* 2022;9(9):736-750.

525. Holt A, Nouhravesh N, Strange JE, Kinnberg Nielsen S, Schjerning AM, Vibe Rasmussen P, Torp-Pedersen C, Gislason GH, Schou M, McGettigan P, Lamberts M. Cannabis for chronic pain: cardiovascular safety in a nationwide Danish study. *Eur Heart J.* 2024;45(6):475-484.

526. Jeffers AM, Glantz S, Byers AL, Keyhani S. Association of Cannabis Use With Cardiovascular Outcomes Among US Adults. *J Am Heart Assoc.* 2024;13(5):e030178.

527. Labadie M, Nardon A, Castaing N, Bragança C, Daveluy A, Gaulier JM, El Balkhi S, Grenouillet M; French Poison Centre Research Group; Christine Tournoud. Hexahydrocannabinol poisoning reported to French poison centres. *Clin Toxicol (Phila).* 2024 Mar 1:1-8. doi: 10.1080/15563650.2024.2318409. Online ahead of print.

528. Rigg KK, Kusiak ES. Perceptions of fentanyl among African Americans who misuse opioids: implications for risk reduction. *Harm Reduct J.* 2023;20(1):179.

529. Miyoshi H, Nakamura R, Kido H, Narasaki S, Watanabe T, Yokota M, Ishii T, Kato T, Saeki N, Tsutsumi YM. Impact of fentanyl on acute and chronic pain and its side effects when used with epidural analgesia after thoracic surgery in multimodal analgesia: a retrospective cohort study. *Ann Palliat Med.* 2021;10(5):5119-5127.

530. Judd D, King CR, Galke C. The Opioid Epidemic: A Review of the Contributing Factors, Negative Consequences, and Best Practices. *Cureus.* 2023;15(7):e41621.

531. Tay Wee Teck J, Oteo A, Baldacchino A. Rapid opioid overdose response system technologies. *Curr Opin Psychiatry.* 2023;36(4):308-315.

532. Vallee BL. Alcohol in human history. *EXS.* 1994;71:1-8.

533. Iranpour A, Nakhaee N. A Review of Alcohol-Related Harms: A Recent Update. *Addict Health.* 2019;11(2):129-137.

534. Varghese J, Dakhode S. Effects of Alcohol Consumption on Various Systems of the Human Body: A Systematic Review. *Cureus.* 2022;14(10):e30057.

535. Wu X, Fan X, Miyata T, Kim A, Cajigas-Du Ross CK, Ray S, Huang E, Taiwo M, Arya R, Wu J, Nagy LE. Recent Advances in Understanding of Pathogenesis of Alcohol-Associated Liver Disease. *Annu Rev Pathol.* 2023;18:411-438.

536. Rumgay H, Murphy N, Ferrari P, Soerjomataram I. Alcohol and Cancer: Epidemiology and Biological Mechanisms. *Nutrients.* 2021;13(9):3173.

537. Goodwin ME, Sayette MA. A social contextual review of the effects of alcohol on emotion. *Pharmacol Biochem Behav.* 2022;221:173486.

538. Freisthler B, Wolf JP, Hodge AI, Cao Y. Alcohol Use and Harm to Children by Parents and Other Adults. *Child Maltreat.* 2020;25(3):277-288.

539. Caputo C, Wood E, Jabbour L. Impact of fetal alcohol exposure on body systems: A systematic review. *Birth Defects Res C Embryo Today.* 2016;108(2):174-80.

540. Olson ML, Rossheim ME, Sanders SB, Yurasek AM. Alcohol demand and supersized alcopop consumption among undergraduate college students. *Exp Clin Psychopharmacol.* 2022;30(1):120-125.

541. Mishra S, Mishra MB. Tobacco: Its historical, cultural, oral, and periodontal health association. *J Int Soc Prev Community Dent.* 2013;3(1):12-8.

542. Gardner MN, Brandt AM. "The doctors' choice is America's choice": the physician in US cigarette advertisements, 1930-1953. *Am J Public Health.* 2006;96(2):222-32.

543. Vitória P, Pereira SE, Muinos G, Vries H, Lima ML. Parents modelling, peer influence and peer selection impact on adolescent smoking behavior: A longitudinal study in two age cohorts. *Addict Behav.* 2020;100:106131.

544. Scales MB, Monahan JL, Rhodes N, Roskos-Ewoldsen D, Johnson-Turbes A. Adolescents' perceptions of smoking and stress reduction. *Health Educ Behav.* 2009;36(4):746-58.

545. Kopetz C, Woerner JI. People Downplay Health Risks to Fulfill Their Goals: A Motivational Framework for Guiding Behavioral Policy. *Policy Insights from the Behavioral and Brain Sciences.* 2021;8(1): 92-100.

546. Saha SP, Bhalla DK, Whayne TF Jr, Gairola C. Cigarette smoke and adverse health effects: An overview of research trends and future needs. *Int J Angiol.* 2007;16(3):77-83.

547. Cao S, Yang C, Gan Y, Lu Z. The Health Effects of Passive Smoking: An Overview of Systematic Reviews Based on Observational Epidemiological Evidence. *PLoS One.* 2015;10(10):e0139907.

548. Goodchild M, Nargis N, Tursan d'Espaignet E. Global economic cost of smoking-attributable diseases. *Tob Control.* 2018;27(1):58-64.

549. Sridharan V, Shoda Y, Heffner JL, Bricker J. Addiction Mindsets and Psychological Processes of Quitting Smoking. *Subst Use Misuse.* 2019;54(7):1086-1095.

550. Park E, Kang HY, Lim MK, Kim B, Oh JK. Cancer Risk Following Smoking Cessation in Korea. *JAMA Netw Open.* 2024;7(2):e2354958.

551. Saint-André V, Charbit B, Biton A, Rouilly V, Possémé C, Bertrand A, Rotival M, Bergstedt J, Patin E, Albert ML, Quintana-Murci L, Duffy D; Milieu Intérieur Consortium. Smoking changes adaptive immunity with persistent effects. *Nature.* 2024;626(8000):827-835.

552. Cho ER, Brill IK, Gram IT, Brown PE, Jha P. Smoking Cessation and Short- and Longer-Term Mortality. *NEJM Evid.* 2024;3(3):EVIDoa2300272.

553. Hamadneh S, Hamadneh J. Active and Passive Maternal Smoking During Pregnancy and Birth Outcomes: A Study From a Developing Country. *Ann Glob Health.* 2021;87(1):122.

554. Banderali G, Martelli A, Landi M, Moretti F, Betti F, Radaelli G, Lassandro C, Verduci E.Short and long term health effects of parental tobacco smoking during pregnancy and lactation: a descriptive review. *J Transl Med.* 2015;13:327.

555. Glantz SA, Nguyen N, Oliveira da Silva AL. Population-Based Disease Odds for E-Cigarettes and Dual Use versus Cigarettes. *NEJM Evid.* 2024;3(3):EVIDoa2300229.

556. Pisinger C, Godtfredsen N, Bender AM. A conflict of interest is strongly associated with tobacco industry-favourable results, indicating no harm of e-cigarettes. *Prev Med.* 2019;119:124-131.

557. Kurihara K. Glutamate: from discovery as a food flavor to role as a basic taste (umami). *Am J Clin Nutr.* 2009;90(3):719S-722S.

558. Celestino M, Balmaceda Valdez V, Brun P, Castagliuolo I, Mucignat-Caretta C. Differential effects of sodium chloride and monosodium glutamate on kidney of adult and aging mice. *Sci Rep.* 2021;11(1):481.

559. EFSA Panel on Food Additives and Nutrient Sources added to Food (ANS); Mortensen A, Aguilar F, Crebelli R, Di Domenico A, Dusemund B, Frutos MJ, Galtier P, Gott D, Gundert-Remy U, Leblanc JC, Lindtner O, Moldeus P, Mosesso P, Parent-Massin D, Oskarsson A, Stankovic I, Waalkens-Berendsen I, Woutersen RA, Wright M, Younes M, Boon P, Chrysafidis D, Gürtler R, Tobback P, Altieri A, Rincon AM, Lambré C. Re-evaluation of glutamic acid (E 620), sodium glutamate (E 621), potassium glutamate (E 622), calcium glutamate (E 623), ammonium glutamate (E 624) and magnesium glutamate (E 625) as food additives. *EFSA J.* 2017;15(7):e04910.

560. Boyko M, Gruenbaum BF, Oleshko A, Merzlikin I, Zlotnik A. Diet's Impact on Post-Traumatic Brain Injury Depression: Exploring Neurodegen-

eration, Chronic Blood-Brain Barrier Destruction, and Glutamate Neurotoxicity Mechanisms. *Nutrients.* 2023;15(21):4681.

561. Kraal AZ, Arvanitis NR, Jaeger AP, Ellingrod VL. Could Dietary Glutamate Play a Role in Psychiatric Distress? *Neuropsychobiology.* 2020;79:13-19.

562. Bawaskar HS, Bawaskar PH, Bawaskar PH. Chinese Restaurant Syndrome. *Indian J Crit Care Med.* 2017;21(1):49-50.

563. Loï C, Cynober L. Glutamate: A Safe Nutrient, Not Just a Simple Additive. *Ann Nutr Metab.* 2022;78(3):133-146.

564. Newby DE, Mannucci PM, Tell GS, Baccarelli AA, Brook RD, Donaldson K, Forastiere F, Franchini M, Franco OH, Graham I, Hoek G, Hoffmann B, Hoylaerts MF, Künzli N, Mills N, Pekkanen J, Peters A, Piepoli MF, Rajagopalan S, Storey RF; ESC Working Group on Thrombosis, European Association for Cardiovascular Prevention and Rehabilitation; ESC Heart Failure Association. Expert position paper on air pollution and cardiovascular disease. *Eur Heart J.* 2015;36(2):83-93b.

565. Liu C, Chen R, Sera F, Vicedo-Cabrera AM, Guo Y, Tong S, Coelho MSZS, Saldiva PHN, Lavigne E, Matus P, Valdes Ortega N, Osorio Garcia S, Pascal M, Stafoggia M, Scortichini M, Hashizume M, Honda Y, Hurtado-Díaz M, Cruz J, Nunes B, Teixeira JP, Kim H, Tobias A, Íñiguez C, Forsberg B, Åström C, Ragettli MS, Guo YL, Chen BY, Bell ML, Wright CY, Scovronick N, Garland RM, Milojevic A, Kyselý J, Urban A, Orru H, Indermitte E, Jaakkola JJK, Ryti NRI, Katsouyanni K, Analitis A, Zanobetti A, Schwartz J, Chen J, Wu T, Cohen A, Gasparrini A, Kan H. Ambient Particulate Air Pollution and Daily Mortality in 652 Cities. *N Engl J Med.* 2019;381(8):705-715.

566. Kish R. Are electric vehicles really green? *Econ Aff.* 2023;43(2):275-286.

567. Boogaard PJ. Human biomonitoring of low-level benzene exposures. *Crit Rev Toxicol.* 2022;52(10):799-810.

568. Chiavarini M, Rosignoli P, Sorbara B, Giacchetta I, Fabiani R. Benzene Exposure and Lung Cancer Risk: A Systematic Review and Meta-Analysis of Human Studies. *Int J Environ Res Public Health.* 2024;21(2):205.

569. Shala NK, Stenehjem JS, Babigumira R, Liu FC, Berge LAM, Silverman DT, Friesen MC, Rothman N, Lan Q, Hosgood HD, Samuelsen SO, Bråtveit M, Kirkeleit J, Andreassen BK, Veierød MB, Grimsrud TK. Exposure to benzene and other hydrocarbons and risk of bladder cancer among male offshore petroleum workers. *Br J Cancer.* 2023;129(5):838-851.

570. McFarland MJ, Hauer ME, Reuben A. Half of US population exposed to adverse lead levels in early childhood. *Proc Natl Acad Sci U S A.* 2022;119(11):e2118631119.

571. Münzel T, Gori T, Babisch W, Basner M. Cardiovascular effects of environmental noise exposure. *Eur Heart J.* 2014;35(13):829-36.

572. Alberghini L, Truant A, Santonicola S, Colavita G, Giaccone V. Microplastics in Fish and Fishery Products and Risks for Human Health: A Review. *Int J Environ Res Public Health*. 2022;20(1):789.

573. Yee MS, Hii LW, Looi CK, Lim WM, Wong SF, Kok YY, Tan BK, Wong CY, Leong CO. Impact of Microplastics and Nanoplastics on Human Health. *Nanomaterials (Basel)*. 2021;11(2):496.

574. Tarazona JV, Court-Marques D, Tiramani M, Reich H, Pfeil R, Istace F, Crivellente F. Glyphosate toxicity and carcinogenicity: a review of the scientific basis of the European Union assessment and its differences with IARC. *Arch Toxicol*. 2017;91(8):2723-2743.

575. Costas-Ferreira C, Durán R, Faro LRF. Toxic Effects of Glyphosate on the Nervous System: A Systematic Review. *Int J Mol Sci*. 2022;23(9):4605.

576. Wang PW, Hung YC, Lin TY, Fang JY, Yang PM, Chen MH, Pan TL. Comparison of the Biological Impact of UVA and UVB upon the Skin with Functional Proteomics and Immunohistochemistry. *Antioxidants (Basel)*. 2019;8(12):569.

577. Ferguson KK, Colacino JA, Lewis RC, Meeker JD. Personal care product use among adults in NHANES: associations between urinary phthalate metabolites and phenols and use of mouthwash and sunscreen. *J Expo Sci Environ Epidemiol*. 2017;27(3):326-332.

578. Wolff MS, Buckley JP, Engel SM, McConnell RS, Barr DB. Emerging exposures of developmental toxicants. *Curr Opin Pediatr*. 2017;29(2):218-224.

579. Guarnotta V, Amodei R, Frasca F, Aversa A, Giordano C. Impact of Chemical Endocrine Disruptors and Hormone Modulators on the Endocrine System. *Int J Mol Sci*. 2022;23(10):5710.

580. Tang ZR, Xu XL, Deng SL, Lian ZX, Yu K. Oestrogenic Endocrine Disruptors in the Placenta and the Fetus. *Int J Mol Sci*. 2020;21(4):1519.

581. Sree CG, Buddolla V, Lakshmi BA, Kim YJ. Phthalate toxicity mechanisms: An update. *Comp Biochem Physiol C Toxicol Pharmacol*. 2023;263:109498.

582. Li MC, Chen CH, Guo YL. *Phthalate esters and childhood asthma: A systematic review and congener-specific meta-analysis. Environ Pollut*. 2017;229:655-660.

583. Brassea-Pérez E, Hernández-Camacho CJ, Labrada-Martagón V, Vázquez-Medina JP, Gaxiola-Robles R, Zenteno-Savín T. Oxidative stress induced by phthalates in mammals: State of the art and potential biomarkers. *Environ Res*. 2022;206:112636.

584. Calvo MS, Dunford EK, Uribarri J. Industrial Use of Phosphate Food Additives: A Mechanism Linking Ultra-Processed Food Intake to Cardiorenal Disease Risk? *Nutrients*. 2023;15(16):3510.

585. Ritz E, Hahn K, Ketteler M, Kuhlmann MK, Mann J. Phosphate Additives in Food—a Health Risk. *Dtsch Arztebl Int*. 2012;109(4):49-55.

586. Achinger SG, Ayus JC. Left *ventricular hypertrophy: is hyperphosphatemia among dialysis patients a risk factor? J Am Soc Nephrol*. 2006;17(12 Suppl 3):S255-61.

587. Kotopoulou S, Zampelas A, Magriplis E. Dietary nitrate and nitrite and human health: a narrative review by intake source. *Nutr Rev.* 2022;80(4):762-773.

588. Flores M, Toldrá F. Chemistry, safety, and regulatory considerations in the use of nitrite and nitrate from natural origin in meat products - Invited review. *Meat Sci.* 2021;171:108272.

589. Valent P, Groner B, Schumacher U, Superti-Furga G, Busslinger M, Kralovics R, Zielinski C, Penninger JM, Kerjaschki D, Stingl G, Smolen JS, Valenta R, Lassmann H, Kovar H, Jäger U, Kornek G, Müller M, Sörgel F. Paul Ehrlich (1854-1915) and His Contributions to the Foundation and Birth of Translational Medicine. *J Innate Immun.* 2016;8(2):111-20.

590. Xue H, Thaivalappil A, Cao K. The Potentials of Methylene Blue as an Anti-Aging Drug. *Cells.* 2021;10(12):3379.

591. Saha BK, Burns SL. The Story of Nitric Oxide, Sepsis and Methylene Blue: A Comprehensive Pathophysiologic Review. *Am J Med Sci.* 2020;360(4):329-337.

592. Koszucka A, Nowak A, Nowak I, Motyl I. Acrylamide in human diet, its metabolism, toxicity, inactivation and the associated European Union legal regulations in food industry. *Crit Rev Food Sci Nutr.* 2020;60(10):1677-1692.

593. Rifai L, Saleh FA. A Review on Acrylamide in Food: Occurrence, Toxicity, and Mitigation Strategies. *Int J Toxicol.* 2020;39(2):93-102.

594. Bušová M, Bencko V, Veszelits Laktičová K, Holcátová I, Vargová M. Risk of exposure to acrylamide. *Cent Eur J Public Health.* 2020;28 Suppl:S43-S46.

595. Bukowska B, Mokra K, Michałowicz J. Benzo[a]pyrene-Environmental Occurrence, Human Exposure, and Mechanisms of Toxicity. *Int J Mol Sci.* 2022;23(11):6348.

596. Walker RS, Sattenspiel L, Hill KR. Mortality from contact-related epidemics among indigenous populations in Greater Amazonia. *Sci Rep.* 2015;5:14032.

597. Marr JS, Cathey JT. New hypothesis for cause of epidemic among native Americans, New England, 1616-1619. *Emerg Infect Dis.* 2010;16(2):281-6.

598. Glatter KA, Finkelman P. History of the Plague: An Ancient Pandemic for the Age of COVID-19. *Am J Med.* 2021;134(2):176-181.

599. Barbieri R, Signoli M, Chevé D, Costedoat C, Tzortzis S, Aboudharam G, Raoult D, Drancourt M. Yersinia pestis: the Natural History of Plague. *Clin Microbiol Rev.* 2020;34(1):e00044-19.

600. Viegas C, Moreira R, Faria T, Caetano LA, Carolino E, Gomes AQ, Viegas S. Aspergillus prevalence in air conditioning filters from vehicles: Taxis for patient transportation, forklifts, and personal vehicles. *Arch Environ Occup Health.* 2019;74(6):341-349.

601. Cadena J, Thompson GR 3rd, Patterson TF. Aspergillosis: Epidemiology, Diagnosis, and Treatment. *Infect Dis Clin North Am.* 2021;35(2):415-434.

602. Wilson AM, Canter K, Abney SE, Gerba CP, Myers ER, Hanlin J, Reynolds KA. An application for relating Legionella shower water monitoring results to estimated health outcomes. *Water Res.* 2022;221:118812.

603. Kao AS, Myer S, Wickrama M, Ismail R, Hettiarachchi M. Multidisciplinary Management of Legionella Disease in Immunocompromised Patients. *Cureus.* 2021;13(11):e19214.

604. Oder M, Koklič T, Umek P, Podlipec R, Štrancar J, Dobeic M. Photocatalytic biocidal effect of copper doped TiO2 nanotube coated surfaces under laminar flow, illuminated with UVA light on Legionella pneumophila. *PLoS One.* 2020;15(1):e0227574.

605. Falla AM, Hofstraat SHI, Duffell E, Hahné SJM, Tavoschi L, Veldhuijzen IK. Hepatitis B/C in the countries of the EU/EEA: a systematic review of the prevalence among at-risk groups. *BMC Infect Dis.* 2018;18(1):79.

606. Saseetharran A, Hiebert L, Gupta N, Nyirahabihirwe F, Kamali I, Ward JW. Prevention, testing, and treatment interventions for hepatitis B and C in refugee populations: results of a scoping review. *BMC Infect Dis.* 2023;23(1):866.

607. Showa SP, Nyabadza F, Hove-Musekwa SD. On the efficiency of HIV transmission: Insights through discrete time HIV models. *PLoS One.* 2019;14(9):e0222574.

608. Phanuphak N, Gulick RM. HIV treatment and prevention 2019: current standards of care. *Curr Opin HIV AIDS.* 2020;15(1):4-12.

609. Javanian M, Barary M, Ghebrehewet S, Koppolu V, Vasigala V, Ebrahimpour S.
A brief review of influenza virus infection. *J Med Virol.* 2021;93(8):4638-4646.

610. Sekiya T, Ohno M, Nomura N, Handabile C, Shingai M, Jackson DC, Brown LE, Kida H. Selecting and Using the Appropriate Influenza Vaccine for Each Individual. *Viruses.* 2021;13(6):971.

611. Holmes EC, Goldstein SA, Rasmussen AL, Robertson DL, Crits-Christoph A, Wertheim JO, Anthony SJ, Barclay WS, Boni MF, Doherty PC, Farrar J, Geoghegan JL, Jiang X, Leibowitz JL, Neil SJD, Skern T, Weiss SR, Worobey M, Andersen KG, Garry RF, Rambaut A. The origins of SARS-CoV-2: A critical review. *Cell.* 2021;184(19):4848-4856.

612. Zhang JJ, Dong X, Liu GH, Gao YD. Risk and Protective Factors for COVID-19 Morbidity, Severity, and Mortality. *Clin Rev Allergy Immunol.* 2023;64(1):90-107.

613. GBD 2021 Demographics Collaborators. Global age-sex-specific mortality, life expectancy, and population estimates in 204 countries and territories and 811 subnational locations, 1950-2021, and the impact of the COVID-19 pandemic: a comprehensive demographic analysis for the Global Burden of Disease Study 2021. *Lancet.* 2024;S0140-6735(24)00476-8. Online ahead of print.

614. Narayanan SA, Jamison DA Jr, Guarnieri JW, Zaksas V, Topper M, Koutnik AP, Park J, Clark KB, Enguita FJ, Leitão AL, Das S, Moraes-Vieira PM, Galeano D, Mason CE, Trovão NS, Schwartz RE, Schisler JC, Coelho-Dos-Reis JGA, Wurtele ES, Beheshti A. A comprehensive SARS-CoV-2 and COVID-19 review, Part 2: host extracellular to systemic effects of SARS-CoV-2 infection. *Eur J Hum Genet.* 2024;32(1):10-20.
615. Davis HE, McCorkell L, Vogel JM, Topol EJ. Long COVID: major findings, mechanisms and recommendations. *Nat Rev Microbiol.* 2023;21(3):133-146.
616. Sykes JE. Tick-Borne Diseases. *Vet Clin North Am Small Anim Pract.* 2023;53(1):141-154.
617. Gilbert L. The Impacts of Climate Change on Ticks and Tick-Borne Disease Risk. *Annu Rev Entomol.* 2021;66:373-388.
618. Cavallo I. Ticks survive for 27 years in entomologist's lab. *Binghamton News.* 2022;18 February. https://www.binghamton.edu/news/story/3485/ticks-survive-for-27-years-in-entomologists-lab.
619. Poczai P, Karvalics LZ. The little-known history of cleanliness and the forgotten pioneers of handwashing. *Frontiers in Public Health.* 2022;10:979464.
620. Obeng B, Potts CM, West BE, Burnell JE, Fleming PJ, Shim JK, Kinney MS, Ledue EL, Sangroula S, Baez Vazquez AY, Gosse JA. Pharmaceutical agent cetylpyridinium chloride inhibits immune mast cell function by in terfering with calcium mobilization. *Food Chem Toxicol.* 2023;179:113980.
621. Cohn EF, Clayton BLL, Madhavan M, Lee KA, Yacoub S, Fedorov Y, Scavuzzo MA, Paul Friedman K, Shafer TJ, Tesar PJ. Pervasive environmental chemicals impair oligodendrocyte development. *Nat Neurosci.* 2024 Mar 25. doi: 10.1038/s41593-024-01599-2. Online ahead of print.
622. Ahuja V, Macho M, Ewe D, Singh M, Saha S, Saurav K. Biological and Pharmacological Potential of Xylitol: A Molecular Insight of Unique Metabolism. *Foods.* 2020;9(11):1592.
623. Lowe C, Anthony J. Pilot study of the effectiveness of a xylitol-based drinking water additive to reduce plaque and calculus accumulation in dogs. *The Canadian Veterinary Journal = La Revue Veterinaire Canadienne.* 2020;61(1):63-68.
624. Wilk K, Korytek W, Pelczyńska M, Moszak M, Bogdański P. The Effect of Artificial Sweeteners Use on Sweet Taste Perception and Weight Loss Efficacy: A Review. *Nutrients.* 2022;14(6):1261.
625. Debras C, Chazelas E, Srour B, Druesne-Pecollo N, Esseddik Y, Szabo de Edelenyi F, Agaësse C, De Sa A, Lutchia R, Gigandet S, Huybrechts I, Julia C, Kesse-Guyot E, Allès B, Andreeva VA, Galan P, Hercberg S, Deschasaux-Tanguy M, Touvier M.

Artificial sweeteners and cancer risk: Results from the NutriNet-Sante population-based cohort study. *PLoS Med.* 2022;19(3):e1003950.

626. Naddaf M. Aspartame is a possible carcinogen: the science behind the decision. *Nature.* 2023 Jul 14. doi: 10.1038/d41586-023-02306-0.

627. Witkowski M, Nemet I, Alamri H, Wilcox J, Gupta N, Nimer N, Haghikia A, Li XS, Wu Y, Saha PP, Demuth I, König M, Steinhagen-Thiessen E, Cajka T, Fiehn O, Landmesser U, Tang WHW, Hazen SL. The artificial sweetener erythritol and cardiovascular event risk. *Nat Med.* 2023;29(3):710-718.

628. Peteliuk V, Rybchuk L, Bayliak M, Storey KB, Lushchak O. Natural sweetener *Stevia rebaudiana*: Functionalities, health benefits and potential risks. *EXCLI J.* 2021;20:1412-1430.

629. Du M, Stitzinger SH, Spille JH, Cho WK, Lee C, Hijaz M, Quintana A, Cissé II. Direct observation of a condensate effect on super-enhancer controlled gene bursting. *Cell.* 2024:S0092-8674(24)00362-3.

630. Chkhaberidze N, Axobadze K, Kereselidz M, Pitskhelauri N, Jorbenadze M, Chikhladze N. Study of Epidemiological Characteristics of Fatal Injuries Using Death Registry Data in Georgia. *Bull Emerg Trauma.* 2023;11(2):75-82.

631. Gaissmaier W, Gigerenzer G. 9/11, Act II: a fine-grained analysis of regional variations in traffic fatalities in the aftermath of the terrorist attacks. *Psychol Sci.* 2012;23(12):1449-54.

632. Passmore J, Yon Y, Mikkelsen B. Progress in reducing road-traffic injuries in the WHO European region. *Lancet Public Health.* 2019;4(6):e272-e273.

633. Laver L, Pengas IP, Mei-Dan O. Injuries in extreme sports. *J Orthop Surg Res.* 2017;12(1):59.

634. Emery CA, Pasanen K. Current trends in sport injury prevention. *Best Pract Res Clin Rheumatol.* 2019;33(1):3-15.

635. Read C, Beaumont C, Isbell J, Dombrowsky A, Brabston E, Ponce B, Hale H, Mccollough K, Estes R, Momaya AM. Spectator injuries in sports. *J Sports Med Phys Fitness.* 2019;59(3):520-523.

636. Jiang D. Risk Management of Sports Venues and Olympic Sports Cooperation Spirit under Complex Environment. *J Environ Public Health.* 2022;2022:9127539.

637. Kumar S, Joseph S, Abraham A. Prevalence of depression amongst the Elderly population in old age homes of Mangalore city. *J Family Med Prim Care.* 2021;10(5):1868-1872.

638. Ribeiro JD, Huang X, Fox KR, Franklin JC. Depression and hopelessness as risk factors for suicide ideation, attempts and death: meta-analysis of longitudinal studies. *Br J Psychiatry.* 2018;212(5):279-286.

639. Zhang Y, Chen Y, Ma L. Depression and cardiovascular disease in elderly: Current understanding. *J Clin Neurosci.* 2018;47:1-5.

640. Gómez Penedo JM, Schwartz B, Deisenhofer AK, Rubel J, Babl AM, Lutz W. Interpersonal clarification effects in Cognitive-Behavioral Therapy for depression and how they are moderated by the therapeutic alliance. *J Affect Disord.* 2021;279:662-670.

641. Alrasheed M, Hincapie AL, Guo JJ. Drug Expenditure, Price, and Utilization in the U.S. Medicaid: A Trend Analysis for SSRI and SNRI Antidepressants from 1991 to 2018. *J Ment Health Policy Econ.* 2021;24(1):3-11.

642. Kosanovic Rajacic B, Sagud M, Pivac N, Begic D. Illuminating the way: the role of bright light therapy in the treatment of depression. *Expert Rev Neurother.* 2023;23(12):1157-1171.

643. Kandola A, Ashdown-Franks G, Hendrikse J, Sabiston CM, Stubbs B. Physical activity and depression: Towards understanding the antidepressant mechanisms of physical activity. *Neurosci Biobehav Rev.* 2019;107:525-539.

644. Pop LM, Iorga M, Iurcov R. Body-Esteem, Self-Esteem and Loneliness among Social Media Young Users. *Int J Environ Res Public Health.* 2022;19(9):5064.

645. Benedyk A, Reichert M, Giurgiu M, Timm I, Reinhard I, Nigg C, Berthe O, Moldavski A, von der Goltz C, Braun U, Ebner-Priemer U, Meyer-Lindenberg A, Trost H. Real-life behavioral and neural circuit markers of physical activity as a compensatory mechanism for social isolation. *Nat Mental Health.* 2024;2:337-342.

646. Hirano Y, Tamura S. Recent findings on neurofeedback training for auditory hallucinations in schizophrenia. *Curr Opin Psychiatry.* 2021;34(3):245-252.

647. García-Cabeza I, Díaz-Caneja CM, Ovejero M, de Portugal E. Adherence, insight and disability in paranoid schizophrenia. *Psychiatry Res.* 2018;270:274-280.

648. Guaiana G, Abbatecola M, Aali G, Tarantino F, Ebuenyi ID, Lucarini V, Li W, Zhang C, Pinto A. Cognitive behavioural therapy (group) for schizophrenia. *Cochrane Database Syst Rev.* 2022;7(7):CD009608.

649. Faghel-Soubeyrand S, Lecomte T, Bravo MA, Lepage M, Potvin S, Abdel-Baki A, Villeneuve M, Gosselin F. Abnormal visual representations associated with confusion of perceived facial expression in schizophrenia with social anxiety disorder. *NPJ Schizophr.* 2020;6(1):28.

650. Nielssen OB, Malhi GS, McGorry PD, Large MM. Overview of violence to self and others during the first episode of psychosis. *J Clin Psychiatry.* 2012;73(5):e580-7.

651. Leucht S, Bauer S, Siafis S, Hamza T, Wu H, Schneider-Thoma J, Salanti G, Davis JM. Examination of Dosing of Antipsychotic Drugs for Relapse Prevention in Patients With Stable Schizophrenia: A Meta-analysis. *JAMA Psychiatry.* 2021;78(11):1238-1248.

652. Budiono W, Kantono K, Kristianto FC, Avanti C, Herawati F. Psychoeducation Improved Illness Perception and Expressed Emotion of Family

Caregivers of Patients with Schizophrenia. *Int J Environ Res Public Health*. 2021;18(14):7522.

653. Gaebel W, Zielasek J. Schizophrenia in 2020: Trends in diagnosis and therapy. *Psychiatry Clin Neurosci*. 2015;69(11):661-73.

654. Gassner L, Geretsegger M, Mayer-Ferbas J. Effectiveness of music therapy for autism spectrum disorder, dementia, depression, insomnia and schizophrenia: update of systematic reviews. *Eur J Public Health*. 2022;32(1):27-34.

655. Thibaut F. Anxiety disorders: a review of current literature. *Dialogues Clin Neurosci*. 2017;19(2):87-88.

656. Choi KW, Kim YK, Jeon HJ. Comorbid Anxiety and Depression: Clinical and Conceptual Consideration and Transdiagnostic Treatment. *Adv Exp Med Biol*. 2020;1191:219-235.

657. Bauer A, Knapp M, Matijasevich A, Osório A, de Paula CS. The lifetime costs of perinatal depression and anxiety in Brazil. *J Affect Disord*. 2022;319:361-369.

658. Aydemir O, Akkaya C. Association of social anxiety with stigmatisation and low self-esteem in remitted bipolar patients. Acta Neuropsychiatr. 2011;23(5):224-8.

659. Penninx BW, Pine DS, Holmes EA, Reif A. Anxiety disorders. *Lancet*. 2021;397(10277):914-927.

660. Ströhle A, Gensichen J, Domschke K. The Diagnosis and Treatment of Anxiety Disorders. *Dtsch Arztebl Int*. 2018;155(37):611-620.

661. Gong W, Geertshuis SA. Distress and eustress: an analysis of the stress experiences of offshore international students. *Front Psychol*. 2023;14:1144767.

662. Korabelnikova EA, Danilov AB, Danilov AB, Vorobyeva YD, Latysheva NV, Artemenko AR. Sleep Disorders and Headache: A Review of Correlation and Mutual Influence. *Pain Ther*. 2020;9(2):411-425.

663. Song EM, Jung HK, Jung JM. The association between reflux esophagitis and psychosocial stress. *Dig Dis Sci*. 2013;58(2):471-7.

664. Pimple P, Hammadah M, Wilmot K, Ramadan R, Al Mheid I, Levantsevych O, Sullivan S, Lima BB, Kim JH, Garcia EV, Nye J, Shah AJ, Ward L, Raggi P, Bremner JD, Hanfelt J, Lewis TT, Quyyumi AA, Vaccarino V. The Relation of Psychosocial Distress With Myocardial Perfusion and Stress-Induced Myocardial Ischemia. *Psychosom Med*. 2019;81(4):363-371.

665. McLachlan KJJ, Gale CR. The effects of psychological distress and its interaction with socioeconomic position on risk of developing four chronic diseases. *J Psychosom Res*. 2018;109:79-85.

666. Wong AMF. Beyond burnout: looking deeply into physician distress. *Can J Ophthalmol*. 2020;55(3 Suppl 1):7-16.

667. Serpa-Barrientos A, Calvet MLM, Acosta AGD, Fernández ACP, Rivas Díaz LH, Albites FMA, Saintila J. The relationship between positive and

negative stress and posttraumatic growth in university students: the mediating role of resilience. *BMC Psychol.* 2023;11(1):348.

668. Liu T, Li J, Li Q, Liang Y, Gao J, Meng Z, Li P, Yao M, Gu J, Tu H, Gan Y. Environmental eustress promotes liver regeneration through the sympathetic regulation of type 1 innate lymphoid cells to increase IL-22 in mice. *Hepatology.* 2023;78(1):136-149.

669. Bienertova-Vasku J, Lenart P, Scheringer M. Eustress and Distress: Neither Good Nor Bad, but Rather the Same? *Bioessays.* 2020;42(7):e1900238.

670. Wilbert-Lampen U, Leistner D, Greven S, Pohl T, Sper S, Völker C, Güthlin D, Plasse A, Knez A, Küchenhoff H, Steinbeck G. Cardiovascular events during World Cup soccer. *N Engl J Med.* 2008;358(5):475-83.

671. Jawad M, Hone T, Vamos EP, Roderick P, Sullivan R, Millett C. Estimating indirect mortality impacts of armed conflict in civilian populations: panel regression analyses of 193 countries, 1990–2017. *BMC Med.* 2020;18(1):266.

672. Singh B, Singh S, Kaur J, Singh K, Popalzay AW. Conflict and social determinants of health: would global health diplomacy resolve the Afghanistan healthcare conundrum? *Global Security: Health, Science and Policy.* 2023;8:1.

673. Messman BA, Slavish DC, Briggs M, Ruggero CJ, Luft BJ, Kotov R. Daily Sleep-Stress Reactivity and Functional Impairment in World Trade Center Responders. *Ann Behav Med.* 2023;57(7):582-592.

674. Malmros RA. Prevention of terrorism, extremism and radicalisation in Sweden: a sociological institutional perspective on development and change. *European Security.* 2022;31(2):289-312.

675. Singh SB, Zondi LM. Human Beings and Safety: The Role of Community Safety Structures in the Fight Against Crime, Msinga Local Municipality, Dundee, South Africa. *Oriental Anthropologist.* 2020;20(1):10–32.

676. Dornquast C, Kroll LE, Neuhauser HK, Willich SN, Reinhold T, Busch MA. Regional Differences in the Prevalence of Cardiovascular Disease. *Dtsch Arztebl Int.* 2016;113(42):704-711.

677. Lin JG, Kotha P, Chen YH. Understandings of acupuncture application and mechanisms. *Am J Transl Res.* 2022;14(3):1469-1481.

678. Ahn AC, Wu J, Badger GJ, Hammerschlag R, Langevin HM. Electrical impedance along connective tissue planes associated with acupuncture meridians. *BMC Complement Altern Med.* 2005;5:10.

679. Iravani S, Cai L, Ha L, Zhou S, Shi C, Ma Y, Yao Q, Xu K, Zhao B. Moxibustion at 'Danzhong' (RN17) and 'Guanyuan' (RN4) for fatigue symptom in patients with depression: Study protocol clinical trial (SPIRIT Compliant). *Medicine (Baltimore).* 2020;99(7):e19197.

680. Goldman N, Chen M, Fujita T, Xu Q, Peng W, Liu W, Jensen TK, Pei Y, Wang F, Han X, Chen JF, Schnermann J, Takano T, Bekar L, Tieu K,

Nedergaard M. Adenosine A1 receptors mediate local anti-nociceptive effects of acupuncture. *Nat Neurosci.* 2010;13(7):883-8.

681. Lin SS, Zhou B, Chen BJ, Jiang RT, Li B, Illes P, Semyanov A, Tang Y, Verkhratsky A. Electroacupuncture prevents astrocyte atrophy to alleviate depression. *Cell Death Dis.* 2023;14(5):343.

682. Tao J, Zheng Y, Liu W, Yang S, Huang J, Xue X, Shang G, Wang X, Lin R, Chen L. Electro-acupuncture at LI11 and ST36 acupoints exerts neuro-protective effects via reactive astrocyte proliferation after ischemia and reperfusion injury in rats. *Brain Res Bull.* 2016;120:14-24.

683. Oh JE, Kim SN. Anti-Inflammatory Effects of Acupuncture at ST36 Point: A Literature Review in Animal Studies. *Front Immunol.* 2022;12:813748.

684. Wu T, Kou J, Li X, Diwu Y, Li Y, Cao DY, Wang R. Electroacupuncture alleviates traumatic brain injury by inhibiting autophagy via increasing IL-10 production and blocking the AMPK/mTOR signaling pathway in rats. *Metab Brain Dis.* 2023;38(3):921-932.

685. Wang W, Chen C, Wang Q, Ma JG, Li YS, Guan Z, Wang R, Chen X. Electroacupuncture pretreatment preserves telomerase reverse transcrip-tase function and alleviates postoperative cognitive dysfunction by sup-pressing oxidative stress and neuroinflammation in aged mice. *CNS Neuro-sci Ther.* 2024;30(2):e14373.

686. Yang Y, Deng P, Si Y, Xu H, Zhang J, Sun H. Acupuncture at GV20 and ST36 Improves the Recovery of Behavioral Activity in Rats Subjected to Cerebral Ischemia/Reperfusion Injury. *Front Behav Neurosci.* 2022;16:909512.

687. Yang X, Xiong X, Yang G, Wang J. Effectiveness of Stimulation of Acu-point KI 1 by Artemisia vulgaris (Moxa) for the Treatment of Essential Hypertension: A Systematic Review of Randomized Controlled Trials. *Evid Based Complement Alternat Med.* 2014;2014:187484.

688. Yu J, Jiang Y, Tu M, Liao B, Fang J. Investigating Prescriptions and Mech-anisms of Acupuncture for Chronic Stable Angina Pectoris: An Associa-tion Rule Mining and Network Analysis Study. *Evid Based Complement Alter-nat Med.* 2020;2020:1931839.

689. Zhang X, Qiu H, Li C, Cai P, Qi F. The positive role of traditional Chi-nese medicine as an adjunctive therapy for cancer. *Biosci Trends.* 2021;15(5):283-298.

690. Verma N, Rastogi S, Chia YC, Siddique S, Turana Y, Cheng HM, Sogunuru GP, Tay JC, Teo BW, Wang TD, Tsoi KKF, Kario K. Non-

pharmacological management of hypertension. *J Clin Hypertens (Greenwich)*. 2021;23(7):1275-1283.

691. Pavão TS, Vianna P, Pillat MM, Machado AB, Bauer ME. Acupuncture is effective to attenuate stress and stimulate lymphocyte proliferation in the elderly. *Neurosci Lett*. 2010;484(1):47-50.

692. Loizzo JJ, Blackhall LJ, Rapgay L. *Ann NY Acad Sci*. 2009;1172(1):218-30.

693. von Haehling S, Qusar N, Gawaz M, Bigalke B. *Clin Res Cardiol*. 2012;101:Suppl 1,P1695.

694. von Haehling S, Stellos K, Qusar N, Gawaz M, Bigalke B. *Int J Cardiol*. 2013;168(2):1509-15.

695. Li K, Zhang Q, Cai H, He R, Nima Q, Li Y, Suolang D, Cidan Z, Wangqing P, Zhao X, Li J, Liu Q. *Front Nutr*. 2022;9:888317.

696. Göring HD. Patient Goethe – A Pathography. *Akt Dermatol*. 2012;38:183-186.

697. Ajdžanović VZ, Šošić-Jurjević BT, Ranin JT, Filipović BR. Biologia Futura: does the aging process contribute to the relativity of time? *Biol Futur*. 2023;74(1-2):137-143.

698. Andrade FR, Antunes JLF. Time and memory in time series analysis. *Epidemiol Serv Saude*. 2023;32(1):e2022867.

699. Kokalj Ž, Džeroski S, Šprajc I, Štajdohar J, Draksler A, Somrak M. Origins of Mesoamerican astronomy and calendar: Evidence from the Olmec and Maya regions. *Sci Data*. 2023;10(1):558.

700. Hatchell C. In: Naked Seeing: The Great Perfection, the Wheel of Time, and Visionary Buddhism in Renaissance Tibet. *Oxford: Oxford University Press*. 2014:1-496.

701. Castillo M. Thinking in different directions. *AJNR Am J Neuroradiol*. 2014;35(4):615-6.

702. Jaffe A. The illusion of time. *Nature*. 2018;556(7701):304-305.

703. Davis D. Kampf der Titanen ("Clash of the Titans"). [Film] *Metro-Goldwyn-Mayer Studios, Inc. Beverly Hills, CA, USA*. 1981;01h:50m:13s-01h:50m:28s

Glossary

Resveratrol	68,116
Retinal eye disease	106
Reverse grip	21
Reye's syndrome	148
Rheumatoid arthritis	129,138,147,161,165
Rhomboids	21,22,24
Rice	73.89,167,241,309,313
Rickets	133
Right and left lateral movement	34
Right and left single-leg stand	35
Risk assessment	208
Risk management	208
Risk score card	64
Road traffic	206
Roast potatoes	258,260,301
Rodents	196
Romaine lettuce	311
Roman	157,178
Rope skipping	28,29
Roux	194,295
Safflower oil	138
Saffron	45
Sage	258
Sailors' disease	87
Salmon	137,139,261,271
Salt in food	75,77
Salt substitute	78
Sanskrit	31,164
Saponins	118
Sardinia	59
Sauerkraut	87,89,304
Sausage products	70,192,193
Schizophrenia	134,208,210
Screen time	45,47,51
Scurvy	87
Secondary prophylaxis	139,148
Sedentary	17,49
Selective serotonin reuptake inhibitors (SSRI)	209
Selenium	97
Selenosis	98
Self-healing powers	338
Semaglutide	145

T-killer cells (CD8+)   144,158
Tobacco industry   180,183
Tobacco prevention programs   182
Tofu   72,73,119,241,274
Tofu stir fry   241
Tomato mozzarella skewers   229
Tomatoes   72,95,100,172,220,226,229,233,266,288,291
Tongue brushing   202
Tooth brushing   202
Tooth loss   87,94
Traditional Chinese Medicine (TCM) 101,124,126,129,162,164,336,337
Traditional Tibetan medicine (TTM) 337
Traffic fatalities   206
Trans fats   58,171
Trapezius muscle   21,22,25
Triceps brachii   24
Tricyclic antidepressants   209
Trivialization   181
Tryptophan   135
TTM (Traditional Tibetan Medicine) 337
Tuber leaf mushroom poisoning   173
Tuberculosis   196
Twilight of the gods   159
Typhoid fever   195
Ubiquinone-10   130
Ulcerative colitis   105,137
Underhand grip   21
US Preventive Services Task Force 92,94
UV rays   86,92,93,108,132,189,141
Vaccination campaign   200
Vaccines   198,199,201
Valerian   45
Valeriana officinalis   45
Vaporizer   183
Vascular Calcification   42,69,76,133,160
Vegan   69,71,119,121,137,265.321
Vegetable pan   267,274
Vegetable tabbouleh   249
Vegetarian   69,71,119,121,137,255,268,274,308
Vegetarian vegetable pan   274
Viscotoxin   158
VITAL extension trial   133,138
VITAL cohort study   95,96